Hyper-growth in Asian Economies

A Comparative Study of Hong Kong, Japan, Korea, Singapore and Taiwan

EDWARD K. Y. CHEN
University of Hong Kong

D1295727

HM HOLMES & MEIER PUBLISHERS, INC.
New York

First published in the United States of America 1979
by Holmes & Meier Publishers, Inc.
30 Irving Place
New York, N.Y. 10003

Library of Congress Cataloging in Publication Data

Chen, Edward K Y
    Hyper-growth in Asian economies.

    Bibliography: p.
    Includes index.
    1. East Asia—Economic conditions.   2. Economic
development.   I. Title.
HC412.C4218   330.9'5'042   79-13399
ISBN 0-8419-0527-4

Printed in Great Britain

FOR MY WIFE ROSIE FONG-LAM

HYPER-GROWTH IN ASIAN ECONOMIES

Contents

List of Tables

Preface

This book, an outgrowth of a D.Phil. thesis submitted to the University of Oxford, is an empirical analysis of the growth experience of five fast-growing Asian economies; namely, Hong Kong, Japan, Korea, Singapore, and Taiwan. Inspired by the existence of an important gap between theories and facts in development economics, this book is very much concerned with the testing of growth and development theories in the light of the experience of the selected economies.

The rapid growth of Hong Kong, Korea, Singapore and Taiwan in the sixties and early seventies has been the envy of most of the other developing economies. Concomitantly, the rapid recovery of Japan after the Second World War has not been paralleled in the developed world with perhaps the exception of Germany. In many aspects, the growth of Japan in the post-war years bears close resemblances to and also interesting contrasts with the other economies named above. It is for this reason that these five fast-growing Asian economies are grouped together and form the subject matter of a comparative study on the causes and effects of rapid growth.

I wish to make my major acknowledgment to Mr. Walter Eltis, my thesis supervisor at Oxford, who has given me not only advice but more importantly encouragement ever since I came up to him in 1973. I must also thank Mr. Bob Bacon, Mr. Maurice Scott, and Professor Nicholas Stern for their comments on the earlier versions of many chapters in this book. The errors that remain are of course entirely mine. I am also grateful to Professor Ronald Hsia who has kindled my interest in the study of technical progress and economic growth, and Professors Alan Brown and Robin Matthews who have given me help in various ways. Lastly, I must admit that without the research-inducive environment of Oxford and the understanding of my wife Rosie, this book could never have been completed.

Hong Kong   E. K. Y. Chen
Spring 1978

Explanatory Notes

1. The country, Korea, in this book refers to the Republic of Korea, commonly known as South Korea.

2. Unless stated otherwise, post-war refers to post-World War II.

3. A Sector = Agricultural Sector
   M Sector = Manufacturing Sector
   S Sector = Service Sector
   N Sector = Non-Farm Sector

4. Figures in parentheses immediately below the regression coefficients, unless stated otherwise, are their standard errors.

5. In the tables reporting statistical results:
   $D-W$ = Durbin-Watson Statistic
   R^2 = Coefficient of Determination
   $\bar{R}^2$ = R^2 corrected for the degrees of freedom
   F = F-Statistic

1 Introduction: The Purpose and Scope of Study

Considerable work has been done in the past two decades to analyse the growth experience of many developed countries. For instance, attempts have been made to analyse the pattern of long-term economic growth of the now developed nations,[1] and there are other studies which deal with fewer countries or a single country in greater depth on certain specific issues and within a shorter time span.[2] These studies, different from the work on economic history, are not devoted to a pure description of facts but mainly to the explanation of propositions concerning the process of growth and development.

Studies on the growth of developed nations are however not paralleled by similar studies on developing economies.[3] This may not be a surprise to us, considering that the lack of data makes statistical testing impossible and the institutional peculiarities of developing countries which may make the existing tools of analysis (primarily for developed economies) inappropriate. However, empirical analysis of the growth of developing economies should be an interesting and worthwhile endeavour. This is because an understanding of the growth experience of developing economies should not only be of great academic interest but also of importance from the point of view of policy formulation. With some qualifications and modifications, the tools of growth analysis could be made applicable to the study of developing economies. In fact, the modification of growth theory for analysing problems in the less developed countries has emerged as a separate branch of economics known as development theory. Unfortunately, such theoretical analyses in the past two decades have largely grown independently of the accumulation of empirical findings. As a result of the work of international organisations and the increasing emphasis on development planning, large bodies of data concerning developing countries have been made available, but at the same time these data need to be

1

explained within some analytical framework. It is the purpose of the present study to bridge this gap in theories and facts by focusing on the testing of empirical hypotheses in development theory with reference to five Asian economies, viz. Hong Kong, Japan, Korea (the Republic of Korea or South Korea), Singapore and Taiwan. Specifically, the present book examines the patterns, the causes, and the consequences of the economic growth of these five Asian economies. All these economies are successful cases of rapid growth in the post-World War II period. While many other economies were suffering from stagnation and/or hyper-inflation, these countries enjoyed hyper-growth of real income. It is therefore of great interest and importance to analyse their growth experience in greater depth. Moreover, these five Asian economies share many common characteristics such as the Chinese cultural tradition they inherited, the free-enterprise environment they choose, the outward-looking policies they adopt, and the dualistic nature of their economies during the period under consideration. By outward-looking, we mean the emphasis on export promotion rather than import substitution, and by dualistic we mean the existence of both modern and traditional sectors as important elements of the economy. These common features very often enable us to treat the five economies as a homogeneous group in performing empirical tests.

It is debatable whether Japan should be included in our study which is primarily a study of developing economies. It is true that from the point of view of per capita income level attained and the fact that it had completed its major economic transformations long before the Second World War, Japan is in no way a developing economy. However, in the post-war period Japan still possesses many characteristics of a developing economy. For example, the primary sector is still relatively large and there are still wide discrepancies in the average and marginal product per worker in the different sectors of the economy. For instance, the economy still has many features of dual structure in the sense that it includes a large sector of pre-capitalistic production of the traditional type side by side with the large-scale, capitalistic production of the modern type, thus embodying a wide range of differentials in productivity, wage rates, etc. As we shall see in later chapters, there has been a rapid structural change in Japan's post-war growth, in very much the same way as in other fast growing developing countries. Thus, in many ways, the growth experience of Japan in the post-war period is comparable to that in the four other economies under study.

It is important to note that the present study is not a contemporary economic history of the five Asian economies under study in the sense that effort is entirely or mainly devoted to a pure description of the facts of economic growth. Nor is the present study devoted to a single theme such as sources of growth, foreign trade, or income distribution. This book attempts to analyse the facts and to provide explanation for the phenomena observed. In doing so, quantitative and econometric analyses will be used. Although the present study does not cover all aspects of economic growth, it does look into a number of important issues rather than analyse only one central theme. For the detailed statistical estimations and empirical testing of various development hypotheses, the period of analysis is generally 1955–70. The year 1955 has been chosen as the beginning of our analysis as the rapid economic growth in Hong Kong, Japan, Korea, Singapore, and Taiwan can largely be traced back to the mid-1950s.[4] Our detailed statistical estimations end with 1970 despite the fact that data are available for a few years beyond that. This is because the period 1971–5 was a period of considerable ups and downs in the level of economic activity in the economies under study as well as in most other economies. We witness slowing downs in economic growth in 1971–2 and a sudden upsurge of extremely high growth in 1972–3, and then two years of severe recession in 1974 and 1975. These considerable fluctuations during the period 1971–5 mark to a great extent a breakaway from the series of data for the period 1955–70. At any rate, the experience of these economies during the recession and the aftermath certainly deserves a separate study. Nonetheless, in analysing many phenomena of economic growth, such as the trends and patterns of the growth itself and income distribution, the period of analysis covers up to 1974 or 1975.

A comparative study of these economies should produce two kinds of results. First, we shall be able to observe some general features of growth in all these five economies. For instance, there must be some common factors which account for the remarkable growth in these economies. Secondly, we shall be able to observe some specific characteristics associated with the growth experience of individual economies. This is inevitable owing to the existence of certain economic, social, geo-graphical, and historical peculiarities in individual economies. These special characteristics would not, however, disrupt the general pattern of growth but just serve to act as qualifications to the general pattern.

The present study is divided into four parts. In Part I, we shall describe the basic facts of the growth experience in the five economies under study. In Chapter 2, the trend and magnitude of growth in GDP and GDP per capita, labour force, and capital will be discussed. In

Chapter 3, attention is directed to the growth in sectoral output and employment. The structural change taking place in individual econ-omies is then examined, and this is followed by the derivation of some general patterns of growth from the given facts of structural change in all five economies. Part II is mainly concerned with the identification of various causes of economic growth. We shall not attempt to attribute the rapid growth of these five Asian economies to one single factor, but shall discuss a number of partial explanations that complement one another. The importance of scale economies, technical progress, and capital-labour substitution in the economic growth of our group of economies is thus discussed in Chapter 4. For this task, the aggregate production function approach is used and various econometric estimations of the relevant growth parameters are performed. The role of factor inputs and resource reallocation relative to total factor productivity is also examined in this chapter. The contributions of factor inputs and resources reallocation to growth are measured by the national income accounting method with the implicit assumption of an aggregate production function. The findings on total factor productivity supple-ment the results on technical progress obtained from the econometric estimations. Chapter 5 examines some further aspects of technical progress, which is now assumed to be at least partially endogenously determined. In this chapter, the various endogenous technical progress hypotheses relating the rate of technical progress to an index of learning, investment activities, and import of technology are tested against the experience of the five economies. In Chapter 6, the role of foreign trade in economic development is examined. This is a very important aspect of economic development in our group of economies as all of them are highly export-oriented. Moreover, unlike many other developing econ-omies, they are not exporting primary products but manufactured goods. In this chapter, the role of foreign trade in growth is examined by a simultaneous-equation model which traces the intermediate links through which export expansion affects the growth of income.

While Part II is concerned with the major factors contributing to the fast growth observed in these economies, Part III looks at certain possible feedbacks of the growth process to the economy. Specifically, we investigate the relationships between growth and saving in Chapter 7, and the relationships between growth and income distribution in Chapter 8. There is of course no clear-cut one-way relationship between growth on the one hand, and saving and income distribution on the other. There are interactions among these economic phenomena, and as a result we have to examine such relationships as far as possible on a mutually dependent basis. Finally, in Part IV we summarise our findings, and this is followed by some concluding remarks on economic development. Data and their sources and some technical notes related to specific topics in this study are given in the Appendixes.

PART I

The Morphology of Growth

2 The Contours of Economic Growth

All the five economies under study, Hong Kong, Japan, Korea, Singapore, and Taiwan, have experienced very high growth rates in the post-war period, especially since the late 1950s. Their growth rates are not only high by Asian standard, but also in respect of other developed and developing countries. This chapter aims at presenting the various dimensions of growth in the five economies, viz. the growth of GDP and GDP per capita, the growth of the labour force and population, and the growth in capital and its related aspects. The data presented in this chapter will on the one hand give a general idea of the contours of economic growth in these five economies, and on the other hand form the basis on which we can formulate and test hypotheses of growth and development to explain the causes and effects of economic growth in these hyper-growing Asian economies.

GROWTH IN GDP AND GDP PER CAPITA

Table 2.1 sets out the annual growth rates of real GDP and real GDP per capita in the five economies under study. The growth rates are undeniably high. The average annual growth rates of GDP during the period 1955–74 are all above 7 per cent and those of GDP per capita above 5 per cent. This compares very favourably with the corresponding figures of 4.7 per cent and 3.7 per cent for developed market economies; and 5.7 per cent and 3.1 per cent for developing market economies for the period 1960–74.[1] For the period 1955–74 as a whole, Japan had the fastest average growth rates of GDP and GDP per capita (9.5 per cent and 8.3 per cent respectively). For the other four economies, the performance was very similar; the average GDP growth rates ranged from Hong Kong's 8.6 per cent to Korea's 7.8 per cent, and the average GDP per capita growth rates from Singapore's 5.7 per cent to Korea's 5.3 per cent.

Hyper-growth in Asian Economies

TABLE 2.1 Growth of GDP and GDP per capita, 1955–74
(percentages)

	Hong Kong		Japan		Korea		Singapore		Taiwan	
	g	g–n	g	g–n	g	g–n	g	g–n	g	g–n
1955–60 average	9.5	3.9	9.2	8.2	3.9	1.0	1.9[a]	−2.1[a]	6.1	2.5
1961–5 average	12.2	8.6	9.7	8.6	6.3	3.4	7.2	4.4	10.0	6.6
1966–70 average	5.7	4.2	12.2	10.8	11.2	8.7	11.0	8.7	10.0	6.8
1971–4 average	6.7	4.9	6.3	4.7	10.4	8.8	11.0	9.3	7.5	5.6
1955–70 average	9.1	5.6	10.4	9.2	7.1	4.4	7.5[b]	4.5[b]	8.7	5.3
1955–74 average	8.6	5.4	9.5	8.3	7.8	5.3	8.3[c]	5.7[c]	8.4	5.4

g–annual growth rate of GDP at constant market prices.
n–annual growth rate of population.
g–n annual growth rate of GDP per capita at constant market prices.
[a]1957–60 average;   [b]1957–70 average;   [c]1957–74 average.

Sources: Appendix A, Tables A.1–A.5.

If we divide the whole period 1955–74 into sub-periods, then in the early sub-period 1955–60 Japan was the fastest growing nation in GDP per capita, but Hong Kong had the fastest growth rate in GDP. This indicates that the benefits of growth in income in Hong Kong during that sub-period were very much offset by the rapid growth of population resulting from the huge influx of population from mainland China.[2] The rate of growth in both Singapore and Korea was rather slow during this early sub-period. In the second sub-period, 1961–5, Hong Kong remained the most fast-growing economy with respect to the growth in GDP. Indeed, in this sub-period which coincided with the housing boom in Hong Kong, there was a remarkable annual growth rate of 12.2 per cent. In this sub-period, Taiwan's growth rate had also gained momentum; it had an annual average growth rate of 10 per cent which was higher than the 9.7 per cent achieved by Japan during the same period. Owing to its more mature economy and lower rate of population growth, Japan still, side by side with Hong Kong, had the highest rate of growth in GDP per capita. Both economies achieved the high growth rate of 8.6 per cent in per capita income during this sub-period. In the third sub-period 1966–70, each of the economies with the exception of

Hong Kong grew at an average annual rate of over 10 per cent. The relatively sluggish growth of Hong Kong in this sub-period is largely due to the slow growth rates in 1966 and 1967, during which Hong Kong suffered from the banking crises and some political disturbances.[3] As a matter of fact, towards the end of the sixties, Hong Kong began to encounter a number of difficulties which had the effect of limiting its rapid growth. In part such difficulties arose from the tariff and quantitative restrictions imposed on Hong Kong's manufacturing exports by many developed countries. At the same time, the rapid industrialisation and subsequent economic growth in Korea, Taiwan, and Singapore meant that Hong Kong had to face keen competitors in its established markets. In this sense, the growth rates of the economies under study are to some extent interdependent, inasmuch as all these economies owe their growth, to a greater or lesser extent, to the growth in the export of similar types of manufactured products to the almost identical markets.[4] In the late sixties, it seems that the rapid growth of Korea and Singapore has impeded to some extent the growth of Hong Kong. Japan, like Hong Kong, had started its growth momentum earlier than the three other economies under study, and yet Japan has been able to keep up its rapid rate of growth even in the late sixties. This is because, on the one hand, Japan has a large home market for its manufactured products, and on the other hand, though Japan's export products in many cases are similar to those of Hong Kong, Korea, and Taiwan, they are not in direct competition with them because they are in general more sophisticated and therefore sold to customers in higher income brackets. In the most recent sub-period 1971–4, both Singapore and Korea achieved very high growth rates in GDP and GDP per capita while the growth rates of Hong Kong and Japan were much lower. Hong Kong had a relatively sluggish year in 1971 and was quite badly hit by the recession in 1974. The Japanese economy continued to grow up to 1973 until the outbreak of the oil crisis. Japan was so badly hit by the increase in oil prices that its growth rate in 1974 was − 1.2 per cent. The experience of Taiwan was similar to Japan; it achieved a high growth rate of 12.2 per cent in 1973 but almost zero growth in 1974. The outstanding performance of Korea and Singapore during 1971–4 is largely the result of their ability in surviving the oil crisis. In 1974, the growth rates of Korea and Singapore were 8.6 per cent and 6. 4 per cent respectively.

While in general economists agree that the most useful way of measuring a country's economic welfare is in terms of GDP per capita,[5] there is still the problem of making comparisons in GDP per capita across countries arising from the fact that countries have their own currencies. The simplest method of making cross-country comparisons is to convert the GDP per capita into US dollars at official exchange rates. However, income differences among countries as revealed by the above method are misleading; this is because conversion into US dollars at official exchange rates does not make adequate allowance for price differences between countries. The exchange rate reflects the purchasing power of the currency in terms of items entering international trade only, and what we need for our purpose is a purchasing power parity which will correct for the average difference in price level for all goods and services produced in the economy. Several attempts have been made to correct official exchange rates for differences in purchasing power by taking the price structures of commodities into account.[6] These studies show that the income gap between the rich and poor countries on the basis of corrected exchange rates is much narrower than that based on conversion at official exchange rates. This is the result of the fact that the relationship between the purchasing power of the currency and the official exchange rate tends to vary inversely with the level of income per head, because in rich countries the cost of non-traded services is high, and in poor countries the cost is low relative to goods entering international trade. Despite the limitation just discussed, the level of real GDP per capita given in Table 2.2 is based on conversion at official exchange rates. Besides the fact that it is meant to give only a very general picture of the relative standard of living achieved in the five economies, the use of Table 2.2 can be further justified by the fact that the price structures in these five economies should not differ from each

TABLE 2.2 Level of real GDP per capita, 1955–74
(in 1970 US dollars)

	Hong Kong	Japan	Korea	Singapore	Taiwan
1955	408	513	138	–	179
1960	488	758	145	487	203
1965	736	1143	171	601	279
1970	855	1911	259	907	387
1974	1151	2712	362[a]	1716	542

[a] As the Korean won depreciated sharply during the period 1970–4, this figure is based on the 1970 official exchange rate so that comparison can be made with previous years.

Sources: Appendix A, Tables A.1 – A.5.

other significantly inasmuch as all five have very similar institutional backgrounds and, with the exception of Japan, have reached similar stages in the course of economic development.

Table 2.2 shows that Japan has by far the highest level of GDP per head of population, and in fact the gap between Japan and the other four economies has been growing over time. Hong Kong and Singapore had very similar levels of GDP per capita over the period 1960–70. The relatively slower growth of Singapore in the early sixties (i.e. the few years before independence) accounts for its lower level of GDP per capita than Hong Kong in 1965. However, the rapid growth of the Singapore economy after independence enabled it to overtake Hong Kong towards the end of the sixties. By 1974, the level of per capita income in Singapore is considerably higher than Hong Kong. As far as the absolute level of GDP per capita is concerned, Korea and Taiwan lag far behind the other three economies. As Table 2.2 is based on conversion of domestic currency into US dollars at the official exchange rates, the discrepancy in the level of income per head between Korea and Taiwan on the one hand and the other economies on the other must to some extent be overstated. Nonetheless, Table 2.2 should not have distorted the order in the standard of living enjoyed by the five economies under study.

GROWTH IN LABOUR FORCE

The growth rates of population and labour force are shown in Table 2.3. Labour force consists of those who are currently employed, those who are currently unemployed but had jobs previously, and those who are seeking jobs for the first time. Except in the case of Japan, the rate of population increase was high at first but has been declining over time. Hong Kong had the highest rate of population growth for the period 1955–74 as a whole, and for the first two sub-periods, 1955–60 and 1961–5. This high rate of population growth in Hong Kong is the result of both high rates of natural increase (high birth rates together with rapidly declining death rates, especially the infant mortality rates) and immigration. The birth rate started to decline only in the early sixties, and periodically there were still influxes of people from China, especially whenever there was economic and political turmoil there. Nevertheless, the rate of population growth has been very much reduced since the mid-sixties. The huge influx of people from China has by and large stopped, and the birth rate has now been maintained at a constant low level of

18–20 per 1000 of population. Taiwan also had a relatively high rate of population growth until very recently. The birth rate was high but the death rate was rapidly declining. Taiwan has therefore a relatively young population and a high dependence ratio. However, there has been a rather drastic reduction in population growth rates since the late sixties. Throughout the entire period of 1955–74 Taiwan's average annual rate of population growth has been 3 per cent; it had the highest rate of population growth among the five economies under study in the third sub-period 1966–70, and the second highest in the first two sub-periods, 1955–60 and 1961–5. Singapore started with a high rate of population growth (4.6 per cent) during the first sub-period 1955–60, but the rate has declined to below 2 per cent during the most recent period 1971–4. Korea had a moderate rate of population growth in the post-war years, and the trend has been a slight decline from 2.8 per cent in 1955–60 to 2.3 per cent in 1966–70, and then a more rapid decline in the most recent period. Japan had a stable growth of population around 1 per cent per annum throughout the period 1955–70, though the rate has increased to 1.6 per cent more recently. This is typical of many developed economies in North America and Western Europe.

TABLE 2.3 Growth of Population and Labour Force, 1955–74
(percentages)

	Hong Kong		Japan		Korea		Singapore		Taiwan	
	n	L	n	L	n	L	n	L	n	L
1955–60 average	5.6	3.0	0.9	1.5	2.8	2.5	4.6	–	3.5	1.9
1961–5 average	3.3	3.7	1.0	1.2	2.5	4.1	2.7	2.1[a]	3.2	3.5
1966–70 average	1.9	2.6	1.1	1.5	2.3	2.4	2.1	6.0	3.1	4.6
1971–4 average	1.8	3.4	1.6	0.5	1.6	4.5	1.7	3.7	1.9	4.5
1955–70 average	3.6	3.1	1.0	1.4	2.5	3.0	2.8	3.2[b]	3.3	3.3
1955–74 average	3.2	3.2	1.1	1.1	2.3	3.3	2.6	3.9[c]	3.0	3.5

n–annual growth rate of the population.
L–annual growth rate of the labour force.
[a]1957–65 average;   [b]1957–70 average;   [c]1957–74 average

Sources: Appendix A, Tables A.1 – A.5.

In many developing countries, the labour force grows more slowly than population. This is usually the result of two factors: first, the fall in death rates is greatest among children and the birth rates remain high; second, there are great increases in school enrolment with the process of development. Both factors reduce the proportion of population available for work. This pattern is however not fully exhibited by the economies under study. To a great extent, such a pattern was found in Hong Kong, Korea, Singapore and Taiwan in the first sub-period 1955–60. Such a pattern was however not followed after 1960. As can be seen from Table 2.3 labour force grew faster than population in all cases after 1960 with the exception of Singapore during 1961–5 and Japan during 1971–4. In the case of Hong Kong during the period 1955–60, the argument of high birth rates and rapid decline of children's death rates is largely applicable, and we observe that population grew much faster than the labour force. In the second sub-period, the birth rate declined while the rate of population growth was still considerable because of the influx of people from China as a result of the collapse of the Great Leap Forward and the natural disasters in 1961–2. Most of the refugees who came were people of working age, and so they constituted an important source of labour supply. In the third and fourth sub-periods, there was a decline in birth rates and those born during the decade of 'baby boom' after the Second World War were ready to enter the labour force. This can be clearly seen from the labour participation rates shown in Table 2.4. When one compares the labour participation rates of Hong Kong in 1971 with earlier years one finds that the rates of labour participation of the whole population increase while the rates of participation of those who are 15 or above remain more or less unchanged. Throughout the entire period 1955–70 Japan's labour force grew faster than its population. This was due to the fact that the birth rate declined sharply after the short-lived 'baby boom' in the early post-war years. Gradually, more and more of these post-war babies reached working age in the sixties. In Table 2.4 it can be seen that from 1955 down to 1970, labour participation rates for the whole population gradually increased while the participation rates for the working-age population remained more or less constant. This means that the growth of the labour force was not due to increased labour participation of the working-age population, but largely to the increasing proportion of working-age people in the total population. It is of interest to note that the female labour participation rate was already very high in Japan in 1955, and as a result there is not much room for increases in the labour supply supported by increases in the female labour participation rates. Very often a rise in the

TABLE 2.4 Labour Participation Rates, 1955–71

		1961	1966	1971
Hong Kong	M	90.4	87.8	85.6
		(53.8)	(51.9)	(54.8)
	F	36.8	43.2	44.7
		(22.8)	(26.2)	(28.8)
	T	64.1	65.5	65.4
		(38.7)	(40.1)	(42.0)
		1955	1960	1965	1970
Japan	M	85.2	85.0	83.2	84.3
		(55.7)	(58.5)	(61.1)	(63.3)
	F	50.6	50.9	49.9	50.9
		(34.3)	(36.2)	(37.5)	(39.2)
	T	67.3	67.4	66.0	67.1
		(44.8)	(42.9)	(49.1)	(51.0)
		1955	1960	1965	1970
Korea	M	87.4	78.9	–	75.6
		(52.4)	(42.9)	(41.8)	(42.8)
	F	73.0	28.0	–	39.1
		(45.8)	(17.3)	(22.4)	(23.2)
	T	80.0	52.0	55.4	57.0
		(49.1)	(30.2)	(32.1)	(33.0)
		1957			1969
Singapore	M	87.7			54.3
		(51.6)			(32.5)
	F	21.6			21.1
		(12.7)			(12.4)
	T	57.9			38.4
		(33.2)			(22.8)
		1956		1966	1970
Taiwan	M	86.1		92.3	84.8
		(50.6)		(50.0)	(51.6)
	F	19.3		29.6	32.7
		(12.6)		(16.1)	(19.3)
	T	53.1		62.7	60.6
		(32.0)		(34.0)	(36.3)

M–Male, F–Female, T–Total
The figures without parentheses are percentages of those over 15 years old; figures in parentheses are percentages of the total population.

Sources: International Labour Office, *Yearbook of Labour Statistics*, Geneva, various years.

female participation rate is an important factor in accounting for the increases in the labour supply in developing countries.[7] While this stage of development is relevant to the other four economies, it cannot be found in post-war Japan. Furthermore, the slow population growth in the fifties and early sixties has resulted in a slow growth of the labour force in the first half of the seventies. On the other hand, there is a tendency for the rate of population growth in Japan to rise during 1971–4.

Table 2.3 shows that Korea had a relatively high growth rate (2.5 per cent) of the labour force during the period 1955–60. This was largely due to the fact that the few years after the Korean War (1950–4) constituted the period of reconstruction and demobilisation during which there was a great demand for labour. The unusually high labour participation rates for Korea in 1955 shown in Table 2.4 can be explained by the intensive mobilisation of human resources for reconstruction immediately after the war. A very high rate of labour force growth is witnessed in the period 1961–5. This was largely brought about by the creation of employment opportunities as a result of the beginning of industrialisation and rapid growth after the period of stagnation and political unrest in 1959–62. The labour participation rates, particularly the female participation rates, increased considerably. Labour force growth rates slowed down during the period 1966–70, but began to pick up again in 1971–4 when the babies born during the post-Korean war years became ready to join the labour force.

The growth of the labour force in Taiwan during the first sub-period is rather slow. This is explained by the fact that the population was very young because of high birth rates in the early fifties, and that the female labour participation rates were relatively low. The rapid growth of the labour force in the subsequent periods are explained by two factors. First, there was a general increase in labour participation rates because the babies born in the late forties and early fifties have gradually joined the working population. Second, there has been a great increase in female labour participation rates, especially those of young females. It can be seen from Table 2.4 that the female participation rate of the population of working age increased from 19.3 per cent in 1956 to 32.7 per cent in 1970.

Let us now turn very briefly to the changes in labour productivity as measured by output per person employed in the five economies under study during the period 1955–74. The growth rates of labour productivity are reported in Table 2.5. For the period 1957–70, Singapore only achieved a relatively moderate rate of 4.3 per cent per annum. This was the result of the rather stagnant growth in Singapore in the second half of the fifties and the early sixties. The much higher labour productivity growth of Singapore in the seventies is to a considerable

TABLE 2.5 Growth of Labour Productivity, 1955–74
(percentages)

	Hong Kong	Japan	Korea	Singapore	Taiwan
1955–60 average	6.5	7.7	1.4	–	4.2
1961–5 average	8.5	8.5	2.2	5.1	6.5
1966–70 average	3.1	10.7	8.8	5.0	5.4
1971–4 average	3.3	5.8	5.9	7.3	3.0
1955–70 average	6.0	9.0	4.1	4.3[a]	5.4
1955–74 average	5.4	8.3	4.5	5.2[b]	4.9

[a]1957–70 average   [b]1957–74 average

Sources: Appendix A, Tables A.1 – A.5.

extent the result of an increasing proportion of resources directed to the modern sectors of commerce and services which tend to have higher average product per worker than that of the agricultural and industrial sectors. Of course, the rapid increase in productivity in the manufacturing sector cannot be ignored. For the period 1955–74 as a whole, Japan has the highest growth of 8.3 per cent per annum in labour productivity. Hong Kong came second but its rate was only slightly higher than that of Singapore and Taiwan. Japan experienced the highest growth of labour productivity for the first and third sub-periods, and shared the first place with Hong Kong in the second sub-period, during which Taiwan also achieved a high rate of 6.5 per cent per annum. While the performance of Hong Kong and Taiwan was much less satisfactory in the more recent periods 1966–70 and 1971–4, that of Korea and Singapore was quite outstanding. In 1971–4 Singapore had among the economies under-study the highest labour productivity growth rate of 7.3 per cent. Japan achieved a high labour productivity growth rate of over 10 per cent in 1966–70 but attained only 5.8 per cent a rate in 1971–4. Evidently, labour productivity is an important factor in the process of growth and development. In the ensuing chapters, attention will be directed to the relationships between labour productivity and the other variables in our models of growth and development.

GROWTH IN CAPITAL

The growth rates of gross capital stock (measured at constant prices)[8] are shown in Table 2.6. As can be readily seen from the Table, the growth rates of capital during the period under study varied over a wide range both among countries and in individual countries over time. There is a general tendency for the growth rates of capital to increase over the sub-periods under study in Singapore and Taiwan; in both cases, there is a mild increase in average growth rates of capital during the period 1955–65 and a more drastic increase over the more recent two sub-periods. In Korea the average growth rate of capital for the period 1955–60 was at a relatively low level of 2 per cent, and the rate in fact became even lower for the period 1961–5 during which set-backs to economic progress were inevitable owing to political instability.

TABLE 2.6 Growth of Capital Stock, 1955–74
(percentages per annum)

	Hong Kong	Japan	Korea	Singapore	Taiwan
1955–60 average	5.4	7.1	2.0	0.9	3.1
1961–5 average	11.5	11.3	1.4	2.7	4.8
1966–70 average	3.9	9.6	8.4	8.6	8.6
1971–4 average	6.8	8.3	7.5	15.8	12.0
1955–70 average	7.8	9.3	5.3	3.6	5.0
1955–74 average	7.6	9.1	5.8	6.2	6.5

Sources: Appendix A, Tables A.1 – A.5.

However, during the most recent sub-periods, Korea has achieved a relatively high rate of growth in capital of around 8 per cent. In both Hong Kong and Japan, the highest average growth rate of capital occurred in the second sub-period 1961–5 during which both economies attained a relatively high rate of over 11 per cent. In the sub-period 1966–70, while Japan still maintained a relatively high rate of capital growth of 9.6 per cent, the average growth rate of capital in Hong Kong dropped to only 3.9 per cent. This was largely the result of the deterrent effect of the political disturbances in 1966–7 on investment behaviour. The rate of capital accumulation in Hong Kong became relatively high again during 1971–4. For the period 1955–74 as a whole, Japan had the highest average growth rate of capital of over 9 per cent, and Hong Kong came second with a relatively high rate of nearly 7.6 per cent. Both Singapore and Taiwan achieved an overall average of over 6 per cent, while the overall rate for Korea was almost 6 per cent. These rates of capital accumulation should be considered high by all standards.

The growth rates of capital stock are of course related to the rates of increases in investment. The shares of gross domestic capital formation in gross domestic product (the investment share) are shown in Table 2.7.

TABLE 2.7 Investment Shares in Income, 1955–74
(percentages)

	Hong Kong	Japan	Korea	Singapore	Taiwan
1955–60 average	15.8	30.4	12.0	9.4[a]	17.2
1961–5 average	21.7	35.9	15.0	11.9	19.8
1966–70 average	18.7	38.5	25.8	17.7	25.1
1971–4 average	20.0	29.5	25.9	26.3	37.3
1955–70 average	18.6	34.6	17.3	14.3[b]	20.5
1955–74 average	18.9	33.5	19.1	16.8[c]	24.0

Investment share = Gross domestic capital formation as a percentage of gross domestic product.
[a]1957–60 average;   [b]1957–70 average;   [c] 1957–74 average

Sources: Appendix A, Tables A.1 – A.5.

In all cases there is a general tendency for the investment shares to increase over time. This can be clearly seen from the following results obtained from regressing $\ln I/Y$ on a time trend. The coefficients of t are positive and statistically significant in all cases.

Hong Kong:
$$\ln I/Y = -1.857 + 0.0157t \quad R^2 = -0.219$$
$$(0.0069)$$

Japan:
$$\ln I/Y = -1.512 + 0.0177t \quad R^2 = 0.526$$
$$(0.0039)$$

Korea: $\ln I/Y = -2.433 + 0.0599t$ $R^2 = 0.718$
                              (0.0088)

Singapore: $\ln I/Y = -2.624 + 0.0749t$ $R^2 = 0.809$
                              (0.0091)

Taiwan: $\ln I/Y = -1.903 + 0.0519t$ $R^2 = 0.949$
                              (0.0028)

In the case of Hong Kong, the average investment share for 1966–70 fell below that of 1961–5; in the case of Japan, the investment share for 1971–4 was lower than all the previous sub-periods. Nonetheless, the trend for the period 1955–74 as a whole in Hong Kong and Japan is still a significant upward one, as can be seen from the regression results shown above. Table 2.7 shows that Japan had by far the highest investment share in income. Even in the first sub-period 1955–60, Japan had already attained a very high investment share of 30 per cent, and there had been steady increases that it reached the high level of 40 per cent in 1969 and 1970. However, investment shares in Japan decreased considerably during 1971–4. Korea and Singapore started with relatively low investment shares in income, but both had been able to increase their shares rapidly over the period under study. Hong Kong and Taiwan already had moderately high investment shares at the initial period; but, while a steady increase in the shares occurred in the case of Taiwan, the investment share in Hong Kong tends to be levelling off at 20 per cent as from the early sixties. The political disturbances in 1966–7 had adverse effects on investment and resulted in investment shares being below 20 per cent during 1966–70.[9]

As far as theory goes, economists have different views on the importance of investment rates in the process of growth and development. On the one hand, Lewis (1955) maintains that a minimum of 12 per cent net investment rate is essential for any economy to 'take-off' in its process of development. Similarly, Rostow (1960) has mentioned a 10 per cent net investment rate as necessary for the 'take-off' stage of development to begin. On the other hand, in conventional neo-classical growth theory investment rates do not affect the long-run growth rate though they have effects on the absolute level of income attained. Inasmuch as the basic neoclassical growth model is not intended to describe the growth experience of developing economies, we can perhaps interpret the above-mentioned contradicting views in the following manner. Before the stage of sustained growth or maturity is reached, investment rates play an important role in the development process; however, once that stage has been attained the neoclassical implications become relevant. A comparison of Tables 2.1 and 2.7 indicates that while the rapid rate of output growth in Singapore and Korea and to some extent in Hong Kong and Taiwan is very much associated with the rapid increase in the shares of investment in income, the rapid growth in Japan is much less associated with an increase in investment shares.

Pooling time-series and cross-section data, we obtain the following regression equation for the relationship between the rate of growth and the investment share in the five economies under study over the sub-periods, 1955–9, 1960–5, and 1966–70.[10]

$$g = 4.117 + 0.212 \, I/Y \qquad\qquad R^2 = 0.426$$
$$(0.017)$$

There is a strong positive relationship between the rate of growth (g) and the investment share (I/Y) supporting our hypothesis that before the stage of maturity investment rates play an important part in the growth of output. We shall see later (Chapter 5) that the investment share can also influence the rate of growth through its influence on technical progress which is assumed to be endogenously determined.

Undoubtedly, the most popular and also the most controversial quantitative relationship in growth theory and development planning is the capital-output ratio and its variant, the incremental capital-output ratio (ICOR). The capital-output ratio can be measured gross or net, depending on whether GDP or NDP is chosen as the denominator. In practice, the trend indicated does not differ very much whether the gross or the net ratio is used. In the discussion that follows, unless stated otherwise, the capital-output ratio is gross. The capital-output ratio gives rise to controversy because of at least three reasons. First, there is the problem of measuring capital; secondly, many economists question the usefulness of the capital-output ratio as a concept in growth theory and development planning; and third, there is a lack of clear and universal trends of the ratio in time-series and cross-section data. For our present purpose, it is the third point which concerns us. While some economists take for granted that the capital-output ratio is constant[11] and some argue that it is constant at least in the long-run,[12] there are others who attempt to argue that the capital-output ratio varies with the level of development,[13] asserting that the ratio will rise during the 'take-off' period or in the post-take-off period. It is equally confusing when we look at the empirical evidence of individual countries. The long-run growth data of the developed countries in general do not show any definite trend in the movement of the capital-output ratio. The US experience has been a rise in the capital-output ratio until the 1920s and a steady decline since then, but the decline is by no means clear.[14] Matthews (1964) found modest fluctuations in the capital-output ratio of Britain since 1870 but with no overall trend. At the same time, Hoffmann (1965) found marked stability in the German ratio from 1850 to the later 1920s. For most western countries, this long-term stability has been disrupted in two periods, the depression of the 1930s and the post-war steady decline. The first deviation can be easily explained by the under-utilisation of capital during that period. The post-war decline is however more interesting. There has been little or no study of the long-term growth experience of the contemporary developing countries due largely to the lack of data. Being less ambitious, we shall now look at the rather short term behaviour of the capital-output ratio in the five economies under study during the period 1955–74.

TABLE 2.8 Capital–Output Ratios, 1955–74

	Hong Kong	Japan	Korea	Singapore	Taiwan
1955–60 average	1.63	2.54	2.96	1.74[a]	2.41
1961–5 average	1.40	2.34	2.55	1.45	1.97
1966–70 average	1.40	2.27	1.99	1.28	1.68
1971–4 average	1.28	2.23	1.86	1.34	2.19

[a] 1957–60 average.
Sources: Appendix A, Tables A.1 – A.5.

Table 2.8 shows the average capital-output ratio of sub-periods, 1955–60, 1961–5, 1966–70, and 1971–4. We observe that there is a steady fall in the ratio in all five economies. The only notable exception is Taiwan for the period 1971–4. This trend can be more easily seen by regressing $\ln K/Y$ on time for each economy during the period 1955–74.

Hong Kong: $\ln K/Y = 0.508 - 0.0145t$ $R^2 = 0.778$
(0.0018)

Japan: $\ln K/Y = 0.936 - 0.0079t$ $R^2 = 0.612$
(0.0015)

Korea: $\ln K/Y = 1.186 - 0.0324t$

                          (0.0016) $R^2 = 0.959$

Singapore: $\ln K/Y = 0.514 - 0.0175t$

                          (0.0035) $R^2 = 0.610$

Taiwan: $\ln K/Y = 1.122 - 0.0215t$ $R^2 = 0.777$

                          (0.0027)

The trend term in all cases bears a negative sign and is statistically significant. The greatest decline occurred in Korea and the lowest in Japan. In fact the decline has not been uniform, the decline in the first half of the entire period 1955–74 being faster than the second half. Indeed in the case of Hong Kong, the average capital-output ratio for the period 1960–5 is the same as the period 1966–70. When we regress $\ln K/Y$ on t and t^2, we find that the coefficients of t are significantly negative while those of t^2 are significantly positive, indicating that the capital-output ratio declined at a decreasing rate. We thus observe that the five economies share the experience of the Western countries in the steady decline of the capital-output ratio in the post-war years. Some reservations should perhaps be made with reference to Taiwan in view of its increase in the capital-output ratio in the recent years. We have yet to see whether this is just a short-term phenomenon. In general it seems that we cannot accept the hypothesis that the ratio tends to rise in the immediate post-take-off period. The decline in the ratio in both developed and developing countries seems to reflect the fact that output very often grew even more rapidly than capital in the post-war years. Such facts, in turn, are to be explained primarily by the acceleration of that part of growth achieved by technical improvement. In the developing countries, the declining of the capital-output ratio should be even more rapid. This is because in the process of development, the degree of capital under-utilisation will be reduced.[15] This at least partly explains the relatively slower decline in Japan, and the relatively faster decline in Korea.

    Let us now turn to consider the ICOR, which has been an even more controversial concept than the capital-output ratio. We in general observe even more confused trends of the ICOR in both time-series and cross-section data. It is however only to be expected that ICORs should fluctuate more than capital-output ratios. The latter is in fact but the cumulation of the former over the life-time of capital assets. Indeed the historical movement of the capital-output ratio is simply the trend of the ICOR smoothed over the life-time of capital. The two most important reasons for the divergence of the ICOR from the capital-output ratio are the cyclical variations in the intensity of capital utilisation and the intrasectoral variations of the ICOR. It is typical that the ICOR is above the capital-output ratio during a downswing and below it in the upswing. When we compare Tables 2.8 and 2.9, we observe that the capital-output ratios are invariably above the corresponding ICORs for the period 1955–70. This can be taken as a reflection of the fact that we are with the post-war upswing until the early 1970s. For the period 1971–4, the ICORs in Japan, Singapore, and Taiwan are above the corresponding capital-output ratios. Such a change signifies the end of an upswing and the beginning of a recession. Furthermore, the ICOR varies from sector to sector substantially. When there is a burst of investment in particular sectors there will be fluctuations in the aggregate ICOR. Another way of looking at the fluctuations of the ICOR is to express ICOR in terms of the ratio of the investment share (I/Y) and the rate of growth of output which is explained by technical progress, then the ICOR will emerge as a passive result of the interaction between the propensity to save and the rate of technical progress. Since it is difficult to see why these two magnitudes should hold a constant ratio to each other, one's expectation would then be for fluctuations in the ICOR. The ICOR will show clear trends if I/Y and dY/Y show definite divergent trends over time or across countries.

TABLE 2.9 Incremental Capital-Output Ratios (ICOR), 1955–74

	Hong Kong	Japan	Korea	Singapore	Taiwan
1955–60	0.93	1.89	1.50	–	1.07
1961–5	1.47	2.58	0.57	0.52	0.97
1966–70	0.54	1.82	1.68	1.04	1.62
1970–4	1.12	2.67	1.31	1.81	2.67
1955–70	1.24	2.11	1.16	0.85[a]	1.22
1955–74	1.17	2.20	1.35	1.25[b]	1.93

[a]1960–70; [b]1960–74
Sources: Appendix A, Tables A.1 – A.5.

The ICORs of the sub-periods, 1955–60, 1961–5, 1966–70 and 1971–4 are shown in Table 2.9. The ICOR of each sub-period is derived by regressing capital on output.[16] An examination of the data in Table 2.9 reveals that no observable time trend can be detected in any of the five economies. The lack of any definite trend in the movement of the ICORs over time is further evidenced by the results of regressing an ICOR on time. In all cases, the regression coefficients are statistically insignificant and the correlation coefficients are almost zero. In the case of Hong

Kong and Singapore, it seems that there is a close positive relationship between the rate of growth and the ICOR. There is however no such relationship (positive or negative) in Japan. In Korea and Taiwan, when we compare the first and the second sub-periods we observe that the fall in the ICOR is associated with a rise in the growth rates. However, when we compare the second and the third sub-periods we find that the ICOR and the growth rates are positively related. Thus, not only can we not trace some definite time trend of the ICOR in the five economies under study, but also we cannot establish any definite relationship between the rate of growth and the ICOR. Indeed, the relationship between the ICOR and the rate of growth has received considerable attention in the growth and development literature. Kuznets (1960, 1961) found that there is a general tendency for the ICOR to rise with income level both across space and over time. Vanek and Studenmund (1968) noted an inverse relationship of the ICOR to the growth rate of output. They explained this phenomenon by the simple fact that the replacement component in total investment is less important at a higher growth rate of output. Leibenstein (1966) also argued that there is an inverse relationship between the ICOR and the growth rates in the short run. He explained this by pointing out that output grows faster than capital in the short run because of more pronounced changes in noncapital inputs. Recently, Sato (1971) refined the methods used by Vanak and Studenmund and incorporated the responsiveness of the ICOR to the income level as observed by Kuznets into his model. He found that the relationship between growth rates and the ICOR is notable in economies with medium income, but not significant in economies with very low income and ambiguous in economies with high income. It has also been observed that the ICOR is positively related to the capital-output ratio.[17] By pooling time-series and cross-section data together, we obtain 14 observations for the five economies over the period 1955–70 which is sub-divided into three sub-periods. We wish to see how much of the variation in the ICOR can be explained by variations in growth rates and capital-output ratios. For this task, we regress the ICORs on growth rates (g), on capital-output ratio (K/Y), and on both.

$$\text{ICOR} = 0.371 + 0.106g \qquad\qquad R^2 = 0.238$$
$$(0.055)$$

$$\text{ICOR} = 0.447 + \mathbf{0.427}K/Y \qquad\qquad R^2 = 0.137$$
$$(0.308)$$

$$\text{ICOR} = -1.474 + 0.154g + 0.714K/Y \qquad R^2 = 0.575$$
$$(0.045) \quad\ (0.242)$$

Thus, while we find a positive relationship between the ICOR and the capital-output ratio, we do not find a negative relationship between the ICOR and the rate of growth. The latter result is contrary to the findings of most empirical studies. However, in both cases, we do not find the positive relationship very strong as the regression coefficients are insignificant at the 5 per cent level. Nevertheless, when we include both g and K/Y as the explanatory variables, we find that over half of the variation in the ICOR is explained. In fact, the regression coefficients of g and K/Y are both positive and statistically significant at the 5 per cent level.

The positive relationship between the ICOR and the growth rate as observed here should in fact be of no surprise to us inasmuch as we found earlier a strong positive relationship between the investment share and the growth rate. Such a positive relationship would of course imply a positive relationship between the ICOR and the growth rate. While the relationship between the ICOR and the growth rate may be negative in developed Western countries, there are good reasons to believe that in the fast-growing developing economies that relationship is positive. In developing countries, the role of capital in growth is in general greater than in developed economies.[18] Overall capital deepening in the process of development results in investment shares growing faster than output. The overall capital deepening is in turn the result of shifts of production to the more capital-using sectors (i.e. sectors with higher K/Y) in the process of economic development. Thus, it is the structural changes that occur in the process of rapid development that explain the positive relationship between the ICOR and the growth rate and the capital-output ratio.

3 The Patterns of Economic growth

In the last chapter, the dimensions and directions of the growth of output and inputs were discussed for the economy as a whole. In this chapter, we shall look at the 'development' aspects of the growth process, i.e. the structural changes which involve the inter-sectoral shift of resources. In the first section quantitative data concerning changes in the shares of the various major sectors in total employment and output are presented and discussed. The treatment follows the familiar Fisher-Clark-Kuznets approach.[1] Next, we shall examine the precise relationship between the changes in sectoral shares of national product and the process of growth by econometric methods along the lines of Chenery and associates.[2]

STRUCTURAL CHANGES

It has been widely observed that modern economic growth is accompanied by structural changes, especially by a movement away from agriculture.[3] In general, as economic growth takes place, there are shifts in the shares of the various types of production activities in the total product and in total productive resources used. Such shifts should not surprise us as it is most unlikely that the process of growth has equal impact on all kinds of activity. What has surprised us is the rapidity and magnitude of such shifts associated with modern economic growth. The simplest way to obtain some idea of the nature and extent of structural changes that have taken place is to divide the economy into three major sectors, viz. the primary, the secondary, and the tertiary sectors, and to observe how the shares of each major sector in total product and employment have shifted in the process of growth. Fisher, Clark, and Kuznets have slightly different definitions of the major sectors.[4] Nevertheless, the results are usually not very different from each other as the difference in definition involves only the relatively insignificant sectors. For our purpose the primary sector is designated to include agriculture and the associated activities of fishery, forestry, hunting, mining and quarrying. The secondary sector consists of manufacturing and construction. All the other sectors (transport and communication, utilities, commerce and trade, personal and community services) are grouped as tertiary.

Table 3.1 summarises the distribution of the domestic product among the three major sectors.[5] Broadly speaking, even within our rather short period of analysis (1955–75) the trend shown by all five economies under study follows quite closely the findings of Kuznets for the long term growth in developed economies. In all five economies, the share of the primary sector in total product declines in the process of growth.

TABLE 3.1 Distribution of Domestic Product among Major Sectors
(percentages)

	Hong Kong			Japan			Korea			Singapore			Taiwan		
	I	*II*	*III*	*I*	*II*	*III*	*I*	*II*	*III*	*I*	*II*	*III*	*I*	*II*	*III*
1955–60 average	3.4[a]	36.7[a]	59.9[a]	20.1	31.0	48.9	43.2	15.5	41.3	6.3[b]	11.0[b]	82.7[b]	33.5	21.7	44.8
1961–5 average	2.9	37.5	59.6	13.2	35.9	50.9	42.5	18.4	39.1	5.6	14.8	79.6	29.4	23.7	46.9
1966–70 average	2.1	37.6	60.3	10.3	37.1	52.6	32.1	24.6	43.3	3.8	21.5	74.7	23.8	27.4	48.8
1975	1.6	30.9	67.5	5.2	42.1	52.7	25.2	32.4	42.4	2.4	31.2	66.4	14.9	39.8	45.3

I – Primary Sector   [a] 1959–60 average   [b] 1957–60 average
II – Secondary Sector
III – Tertiary Sector

Sources: United Nations, *Statistical Yearbook of National Accounts*, various years.

Even in the case of Hong Kong and Singapore where the primary sector had already been very small even before industrialisation took place, the share of the primary sector in total product has declined continuously and very substantially. The almost unchanged share of the primary sector in total product in the case of Korea between the periods 1955–60 and 1961–5 is evidently the result of the lack of growth in the period of political instability and economic stagnation during the period 1958–62. Even in Japan where modern economic growth began much earlier than in the others, the share of the primary sector in total product dropped from 20.1 per cent in 1955–60 to 10.3 per cent in 1966–70, and to 5.2 per cent in 1975.

There had been substantial increases in the share of the secondary sector in total product in Japan, Korea, Singapore, and Taiwan throughout the period 1955—75. The increase in the case of Singapore is especially marked in the later years of the period. This is because Singapore began its full scale industrialisation only in the second half of the sixties. It should be noted that in the case of Hong Kong, owing to the lack of data, the 1955—60 average sectoral shares refer only to the 1959—60 average. Thus, the lack of appreciable changes in sectoral shares in Hong Kong as shown in the Table reflects only the situation for the period 1960—70. Industrialisation in Hong Kong began in the mid-fifties. There is little doubt that structural changes must have been quite substantial during the period 1955—9 and very much levelled off in the sixties. If data were available for the years before 1959, we should find that the share of the secondary sector in total product in the fifties in Hong Kong is substantially below that of the 1961—5 average of 37.5 per cent. Since the early seventies, there has been a rapid development of financial services in Hong Kong. By the mid-seventies, Hong Kong had become an international financial centre. Thus some resources of Hong Kong have been shifted from the manufacturing sector to the tertiary sector. At the same time, protectionist policies adopted by the countries providing markets for Hong Kong's export also have had the effect of deterring the growth of the manufacturing sector. Such developments in Hong Kong explain the decline in the share of the secondary sector in total product from the 1966—70 average of 37.6 per cent to 30.9 per cent in 1975.

When looking at the shares of the tertiary sector in total product, one observes a definite trend for the share of the tertiary sector to rise in Hong Kong and Japan and to fall in Singapore. No definite trend is exhibited in the cases of Korea and Taiwan. In the case of Hong Kong, the rising trend is apparent only after 1970 when the economy of Hong Kong began to diversify into the provision of financial services. In the case of Japan, the increasing share of the tertiary sector in total product, like other developed countries, is explained by the increasing demand for services provided by the tertiary sector as the income level increases. The continuous fall in the share of the tertiary sector in total product in Singapore should not be a surprise considering the peculiar nature of its economy. This is because *entrepôt* trade continued to be a major source of Singapore's income down to the early sixties, though its relative importance had been declining since much earlier. In this way, the composition of the tertiary sector of Singapore is quite different from the other economies under study.[6] Industrialisation in Singapore is therefore accompanied by shifts of resources from the tertiary sector to the secondary sector, or more specifically from *entrepôt* trade to manufacturing. In both Korea and Taiwan, there is no definite trend for the share of the tertiary sector in total product to change over time and in fact over the period 1955–75 the share has changed relatively little. However, the composition of the tertiary sector has changed considerably. The importance of utilities and commerce has increased at the expense of personal and administrative services. While the share of the secondary sector in total product has still been increasing rapidly in Korea and Taiwan, it is not to be expected that the share of the tertiary sector would increase significantly in these two economies. It has to be admitted that the stage of economic development attained by Korea and Taiwan is lower than that of the other three economies under study.

The shares of the major sectors in total employment are shown in Table 3.2. A comparison of Tables 3.1 and 3.2 can give interesting information on the relative movements of productivity in the various major sectors. This is because the ratio of a sector's share in total product to its share in total employment describes the ratio of the sector's productivity to country-wide productivity. If we express the changes in the share as relatives of initial levels, say k is the relative change for share in product and m is share in employment, then the ratio k/m describes the productivity rise of the sector relative to the countrywide rises.

TABLE 3.2 Distribution of Employment among Major Sectors (percentages)

	Hong Kong			Japan			Korea			Singapore			Taiwan		
	I	*II*	*III*	*I*	*II*	*III*	*I*	*II*	*III*	*I*	*II*	*III*	*I*	*II*	*III*
1955–60 average	8.1	48.3	43.6	37.6	24.8	37.6	71.3	8.2	20.5	7.4	20.9	71.7	61.6	13.0	25.4
1961–5 average	5.5	45.5	49.0	29.2	29.8	41.0	62.0	11.1	26.9	3.8	25.6	70.6	54.2	20.0	25.8
1966–70 average	4.3	53.7	42.0	20.8	33.3	45.9	54.6	15.2	30.2	2.5	33.1	64.4	42.2	22.9	34.9
1975	2.6[a]	50.7[a]	46.7[a]	12.8	34.2	53.0	44.5	22.0	33.5	2.4	29.4	68.2	37.6	21.9	40.5

[a] 1976

Sources: International Labour Office, *Statistical Yearbook*, various years.

In all countries, the shares of the primary sector in total employment fall. However, over 50 per cent of the labour force in Korea was still in the primary sector in the period 1966–70, and over 40 per cent in the case of Taiwan. There had been a drastic fall in the share of the primary sector in total employment in Singapore, Japan, and Hong Kong. When comparison is made with Table 3.1, it can be observed that with the exception of Singapore the shares of the primary sector in total employment are invariably greater than those in total product, implying that average labour product in the primary sector is below average. However, when the percentage changes in shares are compared, we observe that in all the economies the rise in productivity in the primary sector is greater than the rise in countrywide productivity. This is especially marked in Hong Kong and Singapore. The message here is that in the process of growth, the average product of labour in the primary sector has the tendency to catch up with that of the other sectors. Indeed, Kaldor has suggested that economic maturity should be defined as a stage at which the average and marginal labour product of all sectors are equal.[7] The experience of the economies under study seems to lend some support to his assertion.

With the exception of Hong Kong, there was a continuous rise in the shares of the secondary sector in total employment. With the exception of Singapore, there tends to be a slightly smaller rise in the productivity of the secondary sector than the countrywide rises. This phenomenon can well be explained by the fact that the prevailing industries in our five economies such as textiles, plastics, and electronics are basically labour-intensive. The rapid expansion of manufacturing output is usually accompanied by rapid increases in employment. Moreover, under-utilisation of the labour force often occurs in the secondary sector due to the need to absorb the large amount of rural-urban migrants. In consequence the productivity rises in the secondary sector tend to be below the countrywide level. This should of course be considered as a transitory phenomenon. In due course, the process of capital-labour substitution will occur in the secondary sector, and the excess labour force will be transferred to the tertiary sector. For some time, the productivity rise in the tertiary sector will thus be below the countrywide level. Again, in due course, the development of the modern sub-sectors in the tertiary sector will promote the rise in productivity in this sector. Finally, we should expect that the different relative productivity growths in the different sectors would eventually produce a mature economy in which the average and marginal labour product of all sectors are approximately equal.

Looking at the changes in the share of the tertiary sector in total employment among the five economies under study, we are unable to trace any universal trend. In Japan, Korea, and Taiwan, there is a clear trend of upward movement. In the case of Hong Kong, the share first rose, then fell and then rose again. In the case of Singapore, there is a clear trend of decreases in the share up to 1970, but not after 1970. In Japan, Korea and Taiwan, the rise in the share of the tertiary sector in total employment reflects the fact that the tertiary sector acts as the reservoir absorbing the labour moving away from the primary sector. This can be deduced from the drastic fall in the share of the primary sector in total employment in these economies. The amount of labour that cannot be absorbed by the secondary sector has to be absorbed by the tertiary sector. This is why it is often said that the rapid process of urbanisation in many developing countries makes the service sector the reservoir for disguised unemployment. In the case of Hong Kong and Singapore, on the other hand, the supply of labour to the secondary sector has to come from the service sector sooner or later as their primary sectors are of very small size. In both Hong Kong and Singapore, substantial amounts of labour resources were moved from the *entrepôt* trade services and the traditional services to the manufacturing sector. Thus, the differences in the basic economic structure of the groups of economies, Japan, Korea, and Taiwan on the one hand, and Hong Kong and Singapore on the other, explain the different trends of movement of the share of the tertiary sector in total employment.

THE PATTERN OF GROWTH AMONG ECONOMIES AND OVER TIME

In the last section, attention was drawn to the changes in sectoral shares of employment and output over time in the individual economies. In general we have observed a largely homogeneous pattern of movements in the sectoral shares. It is the purpose of this section to develop some general patterns of growth among the five economies and over the period 1955–70.

The shifts in sectoral shares of employment and output can largely be explained by differences in the income elasticities of demand for the products of different sectors. The shift away from agriculture is thus the result of the low income elasticity of demand for agricultural products. On the one hand, the low income elasticity of demand for agricultural products reflects the structure of human wants with respect to commodities such as food and clothing. On the other hand, the shift away from agriculture may also be the result of the greater inducement towards products of other sectors resulting from technological changes and shifts in the pattern of work and life closely associated with modern economic growth. The shift away from agriculture may further be reinforced by the gain of comparative advantage in industrial products over and loss of comparative advantage in agricultural production to the other economies. The tendency towards specialisation in international trade will further speed up the movement away from agriculture.

It is of great interest and importance to estimate the actual income elasticity of demand for the products of the major sectors. It is of special interest if we can estimate these elasticities from cross-country data. If we believe that there is a set of 'universal factors' governing the growth of all economies or at least a group of economies, then an estimation of income elasticities from cross-country data will reveal a uniform pattern of growth. The following set of 'universal factors' can be taken to produce this uniform pattern of growth:[8]

1. Common technological knowledge,
2. Similar human wants,
3. Access to the same market for imports and exports,
4. The accumulation of capital as the level of income increases,
5. The increase of skills as income increases.

As far as our five economies are concerned, it seems justifiable to assume the existence of Chenery's set of 'universal factors' governing a uniform pattern of growth in these economies. All these economies have a very similar cultural background and therefore similar human wants; and all have access to similar overseas markets for imports and exports. Though these economies have achieved different levels of technology, they have equal opportunity in the access to new technological knowledge; and of course in all these economies technical skill and capital accumulation take place as the level of income rises. To estimate the income elasticities and to establish a general pattern of growth, we can either use cross-section or time-series analysis,[9] or we can pool cross-section and time-series data together.[10] In this study, we shall use the method of pooling cross-section and time-series data together. We fit our data to the following two equations

$$\ln X_i = \text{constant} + b\ln y + d\ln N \tag{1}$$

and $$\ln X_i = \text{constant} + b'\ln y + c(\ln y)^2 + d'\ln N \tag{2}$$

where X_i is the share of the ith sector in total product,
$i = 1$ (primary sector), 2 (secondary sector), and 3 (tertiary sector);
y – per capita income in 1970 US \$;
N – thousands of population.

The logarithmic form was chosen as it invariably gave a better fit than the ordinary linear case in the trial runs. In equation (1), the sectoral share is not only a function of per capita income but also of the size of population. The size of population is conventionally used to indicate market size. However, a further implication of the size of population should be noted. The change in the size of population also reflects the change in the actual or potential labour supply. In the growth models with unlimited supplies of labour, the expansion of the industrial sector is supported by increases in the labour supply which in the long run depends on natural increases in population and in the short run on inter-sectoral shifts of labour or immigrants from neighbouring territories.[11] Thus, a positive coefficient of ln$N$ can imply the important role of market size in industrial growth or the importance of the unlimited supplies of labour. In equation (2), an additional explanatory variable $(\ln y)^2$ is introduced; this makes the relationship between X_i and y a non-linear one, thus allowing for changes in elasticity with changing levels of income. The non-linear relationship leading to equation (2) is then:

$$X_i = e^a . y^{(b' + c\ln y)} N^{d'} \tag{3}$$

where a is a constant, and the income elasticity, $\dfrac{dX_i}{dy} . \dfrac{y}{X_i}$, is equal to $(b' + 2c\ln y)$.

In both the cases of the secondary and tertiary sectoral shares, equation (2) gives much better fit than equation (1). In the case of the primary sectoral share, however, the linear specification is the more appropriate. Table 3.3 summarises the estimates of the production patterns generated from equation (2), together with the results for the primary sectoral share estimated from equation (1). All the coefficients of ln$y$ are of the expected sign, and are statistically significant (at the 5 per cent level) with the exception of the primary sector estimated from equation (2). The results show that as the level of income rises, the share of the primary sector in total product will fall while that of the secondary and tertiary sectors will rise. Furthermore, we observe that the coefficients of the non-linear term $(\ln y)^2$ bear a negative sign in all cases. In the case of the primary sector, this means that the fall of its share in total product will be at an increasing rate as income increases. In the cases of the secondary and tertiary sectors, the negative coefficient implies that their share increases at a decreasing rate when income rises. The negative coefficient in the case of the primary sector is small and statistically insignificant; and in view of the fact that the linear relationship gives a better fit, we may conclude that there is a constant income elasticity in the case of the share of the primary sector in total product. The negative coefficient is

TABLE 3.3 Estimates of Production Patterns: Five Economies
Regression Results of Equations (1) and (2)

	Regression Coefficient with Respect to:				
Sector	intercept	In y	$(\ln y)^2$	In N	R^2
Primary	4.486	−1.047		0.463	0.904
		(0.052)		(0.027)	
Primary	4.086	−0.919	−0.0106	0.466	0.903
		(0.783)	(0.0895)	(0.033)	
Secondary	−4.927	2.136	−0.153	0.0961	0.485
		(0.827)	(0.068)	(0.0249)	
Tertiary	2.397	0.651	−0.0381	−0.101	0.871
		(0.268)	(0.0221)	(0.008)	

Figures in brackets are standard errors.
y−per capita income; N−size of population.

statistically significant at the 5 per cent level in the case of the secondary sector and at the 10 per cent level in the case of the tertiary sector; and also the coefficient of $(\ln y)^2$ in the former case is of much higher value than the latter. This means that while there is a definite and rather marked trend of an increasing share at a decreasing rate in the secondary sector, the trend is much less clear in the case of the tertiary sector. However, it should be noted that the secondary sector has a much higher coefficient of $\ln y$ than the tertiary sector implying that the secondary sector has a much stronger response to changes in the level of income. All the coefficients of the size of population are highly statistically significant. The sign is positive in the case of the primary and secondary sectors indicating the existence of economies of scale and possibly a positive response to increases in the labour supply in these two sectors. When there are economies of scale in production, an increase in market size lowers costs and thus permits expansion of the sector. Our results indicate that the primary sector has a much higher income elasticity with respect to market size than does the secondary sector. This is perhaps related to the outward-looking tendency of the manufactured products in the economies under consideration. For the manufacturing sector it is the expansion of foreign markets rather than home markets that is more relevant to growth in all these economies. In the tertiary sector, the coefficient of $\ln N$ bears a statistically significant negative sign. This is a rather surprising result at first sight. We can perhaps explain the unimportance of scale economies in these economies by the dominance of many kinds of traditional services which are best done by small or medium rather than large size operations. The coefficient of determination is relatively high for the primary and the tertiary sectors. Thus, 90 per cent of the variations in the share of the primary sector and 87 per cent of that of the tertiary sector can be explained by changes in income and population size. On the other hand, only 49 per cent of the variations in the share of the secondary sector can be explained by changes in income level and population size. This is either due to the exclusion of important explanatory variables or the lack of a single growth pattern of the secondary sector for all the five economies. We shall divide the economies into more homogeneous groups and consider the impact of export performance on the changes in the share of the secondary sector in total output later in this chapter.

We shall now try to infer some general patterns of growth from the estimations shown in Table 3.3. We shall try to trace how the sectoral shares in total output change with changes in the level of income. Setting the population at 30 million,[12] the share of the primary sector in total output is 85 per cent in the linear case and 84 in the non-linear case when the economies are at the low level of development with per capita income of US $100. As income increases, the fall in the share of the primary sector will be slightly more rapid according to the results derived from equation (1) which has a higher coefficient of $\ln y$. Thus, at the income level of US $500 the linear case gives the share of the primary sector equal to 15.7 per cent and the non-linear case 16.0 per cent. In both cases, it can be seen that the fall in the share of the primary sector in total output is quite drastic. However, at rather high income levels, the fall becomes slightly more rapid in the non-linear case as the regression equation has a negative coefficient of $(\ln y)^2$. Thus at the rather high income level of US $1400, both equations (1) and (2) generate equal shares of 5.3 per cent; and as income goes up to US $2000 the share equals 3.7 per cent in the linear case and 3.6 per cent in the non-linear case. In general, the growth pattern in our economies is one which shows a very drastic fall in the share of the primary sector in total output, from over 80 per cent at the beginning of development to less than 8 per cent after the income level of US $1000 (which has been used as a dividing line between developing and developed countries) has been attained.

The growth pattern in the secondary sector is one which has an increasing share in total product as the level of income rises. However, the increase is at a decreasing rate. Setting the size of population at 30 million, the share of the secondary sector is only 14 per cent at the per capita income level of US $100; it increases to 30.8 per cent at the level of US $500, and to 33.7 per cent at the level of US $1100. However, from this level on, the share starts to fall, though at a very slow rate. At the high income level of US $2000, the share is 31.8 per cent. Surprisingly, our results in this respect are very similar to those of Chenery and Taylor (1968) whose sample consisted of 54 countries, both developed and developing. They found that the levelling off of the share of the secondary sector occurs at the per capita income level of US $1000, which is almost identical with the results obtained from our small sample of five fast growing Asian economies. There seems to be really a universal pattern of growth existing in the behaviour of the share of the secondary sector in total product. The share of the tertiary sector behaves very similarly to that of the secondary sector, i.e. it increases with rises in the level of income but at a decreasing rate and the levelling off also occurs at the per capita income level of US $1100. However, there are two major differences. First, after the income level of US $1100 the share of the tertiary sector still continues to rise though the rate is very slow. In fact, according to our results, the share of the tertiary sector will not fall until the extremely high income level of US $5000 is reached. Secondly, the share of the tertiary sector is always greater than that of the secondary sector at comparable income levels. Thus, at the low income level of US $100, the share of the tertiary sector is 35 per cent; it increases to 57 per cent at the income level of US $1100 and to 60 per cent at the level of US $2000. In Figure 3.1, the share of the various sectors at different levels of per capita income (from US $100 to US $2000) are plotted on graphs, from which we can clearly see the production patterns in the three major sectors in the course of development.

To sum up, we have come up with an interesting growth pattern of the five fast-growing Asian economies. This pattern indicates a continuous shift of the shares in output from the agricultural sector to the secondary and tertiary sectors as growth proceeds. The shift has however been at a decreasing rate as the per capita income level rises. The shift to both the

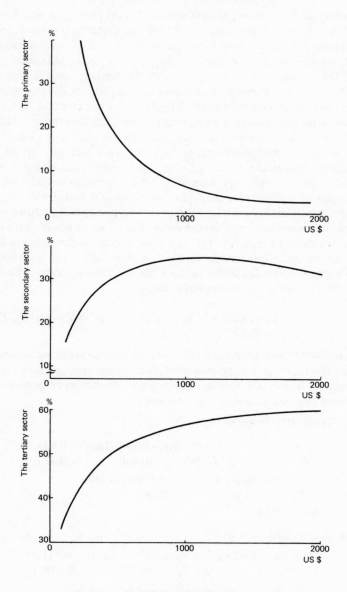

Figure 3.1   Growth patterns: five economies

secondary and the tertiary sectors levels off at the per capita income level of US \$1100, which can then be taken as the dividing line between the developing and fully developed stages in the course of development. In the developing stage, the share of the primary sector falls drastically while the shares of the secondary and the tertiary sectors rise very rapidly. In the developed stage, the share of the primary sector continues to fall but only at a very slow rate. The share of the secondary sector has a falling tendency though the rate is again very slow. On the other hand, the share of the tertiary sector continues to rise at a slow rate.

As we have mentioned many times in this chapter, in all five economies industrial production is to a greater or lesser extent export-oriented. Thus, export performance which depends largely on the expansion of the overseas market is an important factor affecting the changing share of the secondary sector in total product. Accordingly, we include the manufacturing export ratio (E_m/Y) as an additional explanatory variable in equation (2). We also include the investment ratio (I/Y) as an additional variable because we think that increases in investment favours the expansion of the secondary sector. Thus, we have the following regression equation:

$$\ln X_2 = \text{constant} + \text{b''}\ln y + \text{c'}(\ln y)^2 + \text{d''}\ln N + \text{e}\ln (E_m/Y) + \text{f}\ln(I/Y) \tag{4}$$

Data of the city economies and the other economies are fitted separately to equation (4) as we believe that the production pattern of the secondary sector is different in some ways between the two groups. The following regression results are obtained:

Hong Kong and Singapore:

$$\ln X_2 = -23.29 + 9.497\ln y - 0.741 \ (\ln y)^2 - 0.839 \ \ln N$$
$$\qquad\qquad (4.269) \qquad (0.406) \qquad\quad (0.429)$$
$$\qquad + 0.580\ln \ (E_m/Y) + 0.396\ln \ (I/Y) \tag{5}$$
$$\qquad\quad (0.140) \qquad\qquad (0.061)$$
$$R^2 = 0.984$$

Japan, Korea, and Taiwan:

$$\ln X_2 = -0.879 + 1.079\ln y - 0.066(\ln y)^2 - 0.0115\ln N$$
$$\qquad\qquad (0.337) \qquad (0.026) \qquad\quad (0.0193)$$
$$\qquad + 0.0401\ln \ (E_m/Y) - 0.0591\ln \ (I/Y) \tag{6}$$
$$\qquad\quad (0.0134) \qquad\qquad (0.0569)$$
$$R^2 = 0.954$$

The results indicate that the statistical fit has been improved by including the manufacturing export ratio and the investment ratio as additional explanatory variables, especially in the case of the city economies. There are several points which are worth noting. First, the regression coefficient of the manufacturing export ratio is positive and highly statistically significant in both equations (5) and (6). However, the magnitude of the coefficient is much larger in the case of the city economies indicating their heavier dependence on export performance and thus the expansion of overseas markets. Secondly, the coefficient of the population size now becomes negative in both equations (5) and (6), though it is statistically insignificant. Thus in the case of the city economies, the coefficient of $\ln N$ turns from a high positive value to a negative value as a result of adding further explanatory variables in the estimating equation. The message here is that export performance in the city economies far outweighs the importance of population growth in the expansion of the industrial sector. Lastly, we note that the regression coefficient of the investment ratio is positive and highly statistically significant in the city economies but bears a negative sign (though statistically insignificant) in the cases of Japan, Korea, and Taiwan. This means that while the expansion of the secondary sector in the city economies depends very much on the overall investment rates, this is not so in the other economies under study. This can perhaps be explained by the fact that in the city economies investment concentrates on the industrial sector while in the other economies a substantial proportion of overall investment is directed to the primary sector.

PART II

The Causes of Growth

4 Factor Inputs, Capital–Labour Substitution, Technical Progress and Economic Growth

THE ESTIMATION AND AGGREGATION OF PRODUCTION FUNCTIONS

In Part II, we shall analyse the causes of rapid economic growth in the five economies under study. The present and the next chapters are devoted to the causes of growth in connection with the structure of production. Specifically, we shall examine such questions as the role of returns to scale, growth of factor inputs, the ease of factor substitution, and the rate of technical progress. These are the kind of questions that may be answered by the study of production functions. The production function is supposedly a purely technological relationship independent of economic and behavioural factors such as prices, structure of industry, institutional and historical relationships. Of course, production function studies can answer the above questions only if we can identify the production function. The identification problem would of course have implications on the method of estimation to be used. A production function may or may not be identified; if identified, there is still the problem of obtaining unbiased and consistent estimates of the parameters in the production function. For our purpose of studying economic growth, there is an additional problem of aggregation. Our study in this and the next chapter depends very much on the legitimate use of the notion of an aggregate production function with aggregate labour and capital inputs and an aggregate output.[1] Even if microeconomic production functions can be identified, there is no guarantee that such production functions retain their identifiability when aggregated over firms and industries.

In brief, there are two major objections to the use of production functions in studying economic growth; first, it is the problem of identifiability and the associated problems of estimation, and second, it is the question of the existence of the aggregate production function. In the following discussion, we shall look at these two problems more closely and try to justify as far as possible the use of aggregate production functions in our study of the five fast-growing Asian economies. Nevertheless, we must emphasise that we do recognise the limitations in the use of production functions to study economic growth. It is only that we feel that given the 'neoclassical' economic environment[2] in these economies and the existence of some theoretical justification for a carefully and logically specified model of production, it is permissible to adopt the aggregate production function approach to study economic growth in view of its explanatory power relating to many important issues in growth and development. Thus, we are willing to acknowledge the deficiencies of the aggregate production function approach while using it to generate useful empirical results.

(1) *The Problem of Identification and Estimation*

The problem of identification and estimation in the study of production functions arises from the fact that we cannot treat the production function as a relationship independent of the other relationships in the entire economic model. In other words, we must consider the production function side by side with the entrepreneurial behaviour relations. Marschak and Andrews (1944) showed that the classical ordinary least squares (OLS) estimates of Cobb-Douglas parameters are biased and inconsistent in the context of a model of firm behaviour. Given the Cobb-Douglas production function:

$$Y = AL^\alpha K^\beta \tag{1}$$

where Y is output, L and K are labour and capital inputs respectively, A, the technical parameter, and α and β are the output elasticities of labour and capital respectively.

Profit maximisation leads to the following factor employment equations:

$$Y/L = w/(\alpha p) \tag{2a}$$
and $$Y/K = r/(\beta p) \tag{2b}$$

where w is the wage rate, r is the rate of return to capital, and p, the price of output.

Assuming (1) and (2) are subject to random disturbances that are lognormally distributed, they can be written in a form suitable for empirical estimation as follows:

$$\ln Y - \alpha \ln L - \beta \ln K = \ln A + v_1 \tag{3a}$$
$$\ln Y - \ln L = \ln(w/p\alpha) + v_2 \tag{3b}$$
$$\ln Y - \ln K = \ln(r/p\beta) + v_3 \tag{3c}$$

The interpretation of the random disturbances v $(j = 1, 2, 3)$ is that v_1 is a 'technical' disturbance in the production function, while v_2 and v_3 are 'entrepreneurial' disturbances that reflect an inability to achieve exact profit maximization.[3] Equations (3a) to (3c) constitute a system of simultaneous equations in which Y, K, L, are jointly determined. It can be seen that if w, r, and p are treated as constants (e.g. in the case of cross-section studies of firms in a competitive industry), the production function is *underidentified*. This follows from the rank and order conditions.[4] The problem here is, of course, that there are no exogenous variables in the system. However, in time-series studies where w, r, and p will change over time, then the production function can be identified as in this case w, r, and p can be used as exogenous variables. But, even if the production function can be identified there is still the problem of estimating the parameters in equation (3a). Rewriting (3a) to (3c) as a set of reduced form equations in terms of Y, K, and L respectively, we observe that:

$$E(Lv_1) = E(Kv_1) = \sigma_1^2(1 - \alpha - \beta) \neq 0$$

This means that K and L are not independent of v_1, the 'technical' disturbance. Hence, the estimation of (3a) by OLS will generally be biased and inconsistent.

It should however be noted that the above analysis is made in the context of the conventional model of a firm. Such results may not follow from models with different assumptions. Specifically, if we assume that a firm is operating under uncertainty and therefore can only maximise expected profits but not actual profits, then it can be shown that the estimation of equation (3a) by OLS method is unbiased and consistent.[5] In such a model of the firm, the 'technical' disturbance in the production function is attributable to random influences such as weather, unpredictable variations in the performance of inputs, etc., which are not known to the entrepreneur when he makes his decisions. As a result, output and hence profits are uncertain, and a plausible behavioural assumption under this situation is maximisation of the expected value of profits. This model of the firm can be summarised as follows: If the 'technical' disturbance u_1 is assumed to be normally distributed, the expected value of Y is

$$E(Y) = AL^{\alpha}K^{\beta}e^{(\frac{1}{2})\sigma_1^2} \tag{4}$$

where σ_1^2 is the variance of u_1.

Maximization of the expected value of profits gives rise to the following equations for factor employment:

$$Y/L = (w/\alpha p)e^{u_2}e^{u_1 - (\frac{1}{2})\sigma_1^2} \tag{5a}$$
$$Y/K = (r/\beta p)e^{u_3}e^{u_1 - (\frac{1}{2})\sigma_1^2} \tag{5b}$$

where u_2 and u_3 are the 'entrepreneurial' disturbances.

Taking logarithms, the production model of maximizing expected profits can be represented by the following equations:

$$\ln Y - \alpha\ln L - \beta\ln K = \ln A + u_1 \tag{6a}$$
$$\ln Y - \ln L \qquad = \ln(w/\alpha p) - \tfrac{1}{2}\sigma_1^2 + u_1 + u_2 \tag{6b}$$
$$\ln Y - \ln K \qquad = \ln(r/\beta p) - \tfrac{1}{2}\sigma_1^2 + u_1 + u_3 \tag{6c}$$

In this model, if it is assumed that the 'technical' disturbances are not correlated with the 'entrepreneurial' disturbances, i.e. $E(u_1 u_2) = E(u_1 u_3) = 0$, it can be shown that K and L are independent of the 'technical' disturbances u_1 by rewriting (6a) to (6c) in their reduced forms. That the 'technical' and 'entrepreneurial' disturbances are independent of each other should be a reasonable assumption as the former is attributable to the vagaries of nature and the latter to entrepreneurial inertia and miscalculations. Thus, as we can show that $E(Ku_1) = E(Lu_1) = 0$ in this model of the firm, the OLS estimates of equation (3a) or (6a) are unbiased and consistent.

The elasticity of substitution in the Cobb-Douglas production function is constant and equal to one. A less restrictive class of production function is the CES (constant elasticity of substitution) production function in which the elasticity of substitution is still constant but can take any positive value. More about the estimation problems of CES production function will be discussed in later sections. Here it is sufficient to point out that the identification and simultaneous equation problems of fitting the Cobb-Douglas function carry over to the CES production function. However, in the estimation of CES production functions, nonlinearity of the function has initially posed a bigger problem than the simultaneous-equation aspect. The problem of estimating the parameters of a set of simultaneous equations where one of these is nonlinear in parameters and the others are linear or log-linear is rather difficult to tackle. Theoretically, the argument of specifying a model of maximizing expected profits rather than actual profits to overcome the simultaneous-equation problem in the Cobb-Douglas case can easily be extended to the CES case.[6]

Inasmuch as the nature of profits is essentially stochastic, the model of maximizing expected profits seems to be more plausible than that of maximizing actual profits. Hence the OLS estimates of the production relationship between inputs and output may not be biased and inconsistent. In view of this, the simpler OLS method is used in obtaining parameter estimates of the production function in this study. The use of OLS method is further justified by Hildebrand and Liu's finding that the use of direct and two-stage least squares methods in estimating production functions generate very similar results.[7]

(2) *The Problem of Aggregation.*

The problem of aggregation in the study of production has been known to economists for quite a long time. The matter of capital aggregation in a production function was extensively discussed in a debate in *Econometrica* in 1946–48. Work in the field has also been summarised by Green (1964). However, the most elaborate work on the aggregation problem of a production function has been done by Fisher (1969). Fisher has shown that the existence of aggregate production functions depends on very stringent conditions, viz. capital augmentation of all technical differences among firms, absence of specialisation in employment (i.e. all firms must hire the same mix of labour types), and absence of specialisation in production (i.e. all firms must produce the same basket of outputs). It is clear that these conditions can seldom be fulfilled in the real world economy. But, it must be recognised that such stringent conditions for legitimate aggregation under all circumstances may not be of much real significance. What we really care about is whether aggregate production functions provide an adequate approximation to reality over the values of the variables that occur in practice. This is especially so for the empirical studies of technical progress, growth, and related subjects. Both Fisher (1969) and Blaug (1975) thought that the aggregation problem produces less damage to a study of technical progress and economic growth where factor prices are assumed to be competitively determined than one which uses aggregate production functions in testing the theory of price determination as in the early work of Cobb and Douglas. Furthermore, there may be something working behind the existing discussion on the aggregation problem which reduces the dimensionality of the aggregation problem. For example, Fisher admitted that if firms invested in approximately fixed ratios and produced products or hired labour in approximately fixed proportions, then an approximate aggregate of capital, output and labour would exist.[8] More recently, Sato (1975) points out that the Fisher aggregation problem is what kind of interfirm differences in efficiencies permits exact aggregation for any distribution of efficiencies. As we indicated before, the condition is that differences in efficiencies should be purely capital-augmenting. Sato inverts the question and asks what distribution of efficiencies would permit exact aggregation for an arbitrary pattern of interfirm efficiency differences. The answer to this new question, according to Sato, reveals that even if the Fisher condition is not satisfied, one may still have aggregate production function with capital and labour aggregates in the short run if the distribution of efficiencies is 'well-behaved'. Changes in the distribution do not as a rule leave the aggregate production function invariant, but if the change happens not to disturb the basic form of the distribution, the aggregate production function would also remain invariant in form. In fact, Sato argues that this is the only way one can justify the use of a single aggregate production function over time. In short Sato has attempted to derive a much less restrictive condition for exact aggregation than the Fisher condition and in so doing has given great comfort to those who use aggregate production functions in empirical research.

Thus, while one must recognise the deficiencies of the aggregate production function approach, one must also realise that some aggregation is necessary for empirical work. Perhaps one could agree partially if not wholly with Solow (1966) that we cannot think of 'the macroeconomic production as a rigorously justifiable concept . . . it is either an illuminating parable, or else a mere device for handling data, to be used as long as it gives good empirical results, and to be abandoned as soon as it doesn't, or as soon as something better comes along.' Thus, insofar as the use of the aggregate production function gives sensible and meaningful empirical results in the study of our fast-growing Asian economies, we could perhaps regard its use in the present study as justifiable.

THE CONCEPT OF TECHNOLOGICAL CHANGE

Capital accumulation had long been taken as the dominant determinant of economic growth. Not only was it the belief of the classical economists like Ricardo that productivity is increased principally where capital per worker is increased,[9] it was also the general belief of economists in the forties and fifties. This is witnessed, for instance, in the work of Lewis (1955) and Rostow (1960), both of whom stressed the importance of capital accumulation in initiating economic growth.[10] The work of Abramovitz (1956) and Solow (1957) has however drastically changed this point of view. It is found that the increase in output per worker is far greater than what can be accounted for by increases in capital per worker. Indeed, Solow found that 90 per cent of the increases in output per worker in the United States during the period 1909–49 cannot be explained by increases in capital per worker. Solow's work was further supported by the studies of Massell (1960), Aukrust (1959), Nittamo (1958), and Reddaway and Smith (1960), among others. Even after allowing for detailed quality changes in capital and labour inputs, economies of scale, inter-sectoral shifts of resources, Denison (1962) still found that 40 per cent of the changes in productivity in the United States during the period 1909–57 are left unexplained. To this unexplained growth in output per worker, Solow gave the name technological change.

Nevertheless, the name of technological change given to that part of unexplained growth in productivity is a misleading one. To Solow (1957), slowdowns, speedups, improvements in the education of the labour force, and all sorts of other things[11] are lumped together to appear as technological change. Domar (1961) thought a more appropriate name for technical change to be 'the residual'. Accordingly, very much of the effort in studying the economics of technological change since Solow's seminal paper has been spent on narrowing down this 'residual' so that it can be more accurately used to describe the advance of knowledge itself instead of everything lumped together. The most notable attempt in this direction must be Jorgenson and Griliches (1967). They carried out a complete set of checks on the index number problems involved in measuring technical change as a residual from an

aggregate production function. They also sought an economic behavioural explanation for all observed changes in outputs, inputs, prices
and incomes rather than just for technical change. Jorgenson and
Griliches måde the following adjustments for contributions of input
growth to output growth: (1) disaggregating the price index for capital
to obtain a better measure of capital input; (2) correcting for utilisation
of input stocks; and (3) taking flow prices for capital and labour services
into account to obtain even better measures of capital and labour inputs.
After these corrections Jorgenson and Griliches found that very little
'residual' (only 3.3 per cent) remained. Their study seems to suggest that
the study of technical change in economic growth is meaningless as
technical change is due almost entirely to mis-measurement and
therefore does not in fact exist. This interpretation is, however, in my
opinion not really acceptable. One can argue that many of the
adjustments made to reduce the contribution of the 'residual' are likely
to be related to the conventionally defined 'embodied' and 'disembodied' technical progress. For example, changes in capacity utilisation
could be related to new methods of production, management, and
organisation. Similarly, changes in the quality of capital and labour
inputs are related to investment activities and learning by doing which
are forms of endogenous technical progress. Above all, changes in flow
prices are governed by interest rates and depreciation rates and must be
related to investment activities, inventions and improved organisations.
Thus many of the adjustments to measurements of inputs are in fact due
to technical progress. Whether one classifies these changes as technical
change or input contributions to growth is then largely a matter of
definition. Hence, it is not without reason that the measuring of
technical progress from aggregate production functions has continued
to survive despite Jorgenson and Griliches' discouraging results.

It is undoubtedly true that in the decade following Solow's 1957
paper, the attention of economists has very much been diverted from the
effect of capital accumulation to that of technological change in
examining the process of economic growth. It is, on the other hand,
interesting to note that the recent trend has been the switching of
attention back to the importance of capital accumulation. This,
however, does not mean that technological change has been discredited
as an important source of growth. The new argument suggests that
technological change itself is closely related to capital accumulation,
either by being embodied in the new capital goods or by being advanced
as a result of increases in the rate of investment.

The essential quantitative effect of technological change is to shift the production function enabling greater output to be produced with the same volume of inputs, or the same output with less input. This can be illustrated by the following diagram:

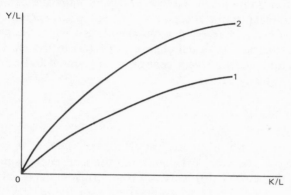

Figure 4.1

The shift of the production function from 1 to 2 represents technological change.[12] Strictly speaking, such a shift also includes the effects of returns to scale, inter-sectoral shifts in resources, and other things. In general, technological change and increasing returns to scale are thought to be the most important forces in shifting the production function. In Figure 4.1, constant returns are however assumed as the general form of the production $Y = f(K, L)$ is represented by $Y/L = f(K/L)$.

Technological change has another set of measurable properties. It can be classified as neutral or non-neutral (biased). In the literature, there are three ways of classifying technological change in this connection. The divergence in classification arises from the fact that technological change shifts the entire production function; this results in an index-number problem as to which point on the old production function should be compared with which point on the new one. The Hicks (1932) definition of neutrality is based on comparing points on the new and old production functions where the K/L ratio is constant. Technological change is said to be Hicks-neutral if the ratio of the marginal product of capital to that of labour remains unchanged at a constant K/L ratio when the production function shifts. Hicks-neutral technical progress can be represented by the following production function:

$$Y = A(t)f(K, L)$$

where $A(t)$, the efficiency index, is a function of time; Y is output and K and L are capital and labour inputs respectively.

On the other hand, the Harrod (1947) definition of neutrality is based on comparing points where the K/Y ratio is constant. If the rate of profit (or the marginal product of capital assuming the existence of a perfectly competitive factor market) remains unchanged when the production function shifts, technological change is neutral in the Harrod sense. Harrod-neutral technological change is represented by the following production function:

$$Y = f(K, A(t)L)$$

Thus Harrod-neutral technological change can be said to be labour-augmenting, as technological change has the same effect as population growth in the sense that it increases the effective units of labour.

The third definition of neutrality is that of Solow (1963). This is simply the mirror-image of Harrod's definition. Solow's definition is based on comparing points with the same L/Y ratio. Technological change is said to be Solow-neutral if wage per worker is constant and therefore the distribution of income is constant at a given L/Y ratio when the production function shifts. Solow-neutral technical progress is represented by this production function:

$$Y = f(A(t)K, L)$$

Thus, Solow-neutral technical progress is capital-augmenting, i.e. it increases the effective units of capital.

The three definitions of neutral technological change will be the same only if the distribution of income at a given K/L, K/Y or L/Y ratio is all the same. This happens for instance when the production function is of the Cobb-Douglas type.[13] In empirical studies Hicks-neutral technical progress is the commonly used assumption owing to the simplicity in its specification in the context of production functions. On the other hand, in the theoretical discussion of growth models Harrod-neutral technical progress is as a rule specified. This is due to the fact that only Harrod-neutrality is compatible with steady state growth in the conventional growth models.

Conventionally, technological change is by and large treated as exogenous, i.e. it is independent of the other variables in the growth model. Two categories of exogenous technological change have emerged in the literature: the disembodied type and the embodied or vintage type. In the disembodied models, plants built at different times (i.e. of different vintages) are of the same productivity. Technological change takes place like manna from heaven in the form of better methods and organisation that improve the efficiency of both new and old capital alike. We can find examples of disembodied technological change in the various advances in industrial engineering (e.g. the development of time and motion studies) and operational research (e.g. the development of programming techniques). The earlier attempts to measure technological change are very often confined to this kind of model because of the relative simplicity in estimation procedures.

No one can deny the importance of such disembodied technological change. It is however true that many changes in technology are embodied in new machinery and equipment. This means that plants built at different times cannot be treated as homogeneous but are of different productivities. Vintage-capital models have been developed by Johansen (1959) and Solow (1959) and are elaborated by Phelps (1962), Matthews (1964), Bliss (1968), and Bardhan (1973), among others. However, in these models embodied technical progress is still purely a function of time and is therefore exogenous.[14] There are various kinds of vintage models classified according to the presence or absence of *ex ante* and *ex post* substitutability of the factors of production. In the terminology of Phelps, we have putty-putty, putty-clay, and clay-clay models. In the theoretical treatment of growth, the greatest attention has been placed on putty-clay models as they seem to have the most realistic assumption among all. On the other hand, in empirical work, the putty-putty models are much more popular because of simplicity in the estimation procedure. Among the few attempts to estimate an aggregate putty-clay relation, the most notable is Mizon (1974) which uses very complex non-linear estimation techniques for such a purpose. Mizon's putty-clay model is non-linear in parameters and variables and there is no simple transformation that can reduce it to linear form. Accordingly he uses a well-established minimisation routine to estimate the structural parameters in his model.

Unfortunately, there are many inherent problems in the estimation of the rate of embodied technical progress. In the estimation of putty-putty models almost invariably the estimation of the rate of embodied technical progress depends crucially on some arbitrarily assumed values of the output elasticity of capital and the rate of capital depreciation. In addition, the rate of disembodied technical progress has also to be assumed if technical progress is regarded as only partially embodied in the model under consideration.[15] Thus in estimating the rate of embodied technical progress, we have first to find by the method of trial and error a combination of the assumed values which would give the best fit to the specified relationship. This procedure can sometimes give rise to unreasonable estimates of the rate of embodied technical progress associated with some unreasonable assumed values of other parameters.[16] In other cases,[17] different values of the rate of embodied technical progress are assumed and the rate which gives the best fit to the specified production relationship is taken as the true rate of technical progress. Thus, the technique of estimation is entirely arbitrary. As a matter of fact, the empirical results have not been in the support of the embodiment hypothesis. Wickens' (1970) estimation results for the United States for the period 1900–60 failed to support the embodiment hypothesis but the disembodiment hypothesis was accepted. A recent study of the United States for the period 1929–68 also came to similar conclusions.[18] Furthermore, if we follow Nelson's (1964) derivation that embodiment is represented by changes in the average age of capital, we find that in practice such changes are usually small and so the effect of embodiment cannot be of great importance.[19]

Neither have the few attempts of estimating the putty-clay relation produced satisfactory results. In Mizon's 1974 study of the United Kingdom, estimates of the putty-clay model are obtained only at the expense of huge amount of computer time as the convergence was found to be very slow. More importantly, the poor parameter estimates on both economic and statistical grounds in Mizon's study are very discouraging. Owing to these estimation problems and the absence of satisfactory empirical results supporting the embodiment hypothesis in the literature and the lack of data (e.g. on the age distribution of capital), we shall not make any attempt to measure the rate of embodied technical progress in the present study.[20] On the other hand, we believe that it is important to take the view that technical progress is at least partially endogenously determined. It must be largely true that changes in some crucial variables such as investment and capital growth rates will affect the rate of technical progress. We shall discuss this issue in the next chapter.

In the rest of this chapter, we will look at the role of disembodied technical progress, scale economies, factor inputs and substitution elasticities in economic growth. We shall first estimate a Cobb-Douglas production function for the purpose of examining the importance of technical progress and scale economies. Next, we will use Denison's national income accounting approach to analyse the role of factor inputs. Such an approach implies the existence of a Cobb-Douglas production function if the factor shares are assumed to be constant over time. Lastly, we will turn our attention to a more general form of production function, the constant elasticity of substitution or CES production function. Here, we attempt to examine the part played by substitution elasticities and the modifications we need to make to our Cobb-Douglas results when substitution elasticity is no longer assumed to be fixed at unity.

TECHNICAL PROGRESS AND ECONOMIES OF SCALE:
Estimation of the Cobb-Douglas Production Function

If we accept that an economy or a sector of the economy can be approximated by an aggregate Cobb-Douglas production function, it is possible to estimate the economic parameters of returns to scale and the rate of technical progress. Assuming that technical progress is Hicks-neutral and grows at a constant exponential rate, the aggregate Cobb-Douglas production function used for estimation can be written

$$Y_t = A_0 e^{\lambda t} K_t^b L_t^a e^u \qquad (7)$$

where Y_t, K_t, and L_t are output, capital input and labour input at time t respectively. To avoid the problem of intermediate products, Y_t refers to valued added rather than total output, K_t is normally taken as gross capital stock unless the rate of capital utilisation is known, and L_t represents either number of workers employed or number of man-hours. The other symbols are

A_0–the level of technology at the initial time
λ–the rate of disembodied technical progress
a–output elasticity of labour
b–output elasticity of capital
e^u–the multiplicative error term.

Taking the logarithm on both sides of equation (7), we have the following equation which is suitable for estimation:

$$\ln Y = \ln A_0 + \lambda t + b \ln K + a \ln L + u \qquad (8)$$

In this form, the sum of the output elasticities, a and b, define the degree of returns to scale; a sum of greater than one implies increasing returns and a sum of less than one, decreasing returns. An alternative version of equation (8) is to subtract $\ln L$ from both sides. Then we have

$$\ln Y/L = \ln A_0 + \lambda t + b\ln K/L + (a + b - 1)\ln L + u \qquad (9)$$

According to equation (9), the coefficient of $\ln L$ equals the sum of the output elasticities minus one, and its sign therefore indicates increasing or decreasing returns to scale. In comparison with (8), equation (9) has the advantage that the statistical significance of returns to scale can be tested directly, for testing whether the coefficient $\ln L$ is significantly different from zero is a test for constant returns to scale. On the other hand, if equation (8) is used, the statistical significance of the sum of output elasticities (i.e. $a + b$) can only be tested indirectly.

However, in estimating equation (9) it must be noted that even if we neglect the aggregation problem and assume that firms maximise expected profits, and therefore the simultaneous-equation problems do not arise, it is only legitimate to estimate such an equation by the OLS (ordinary least squares) method when the following assumptions are made. First, it must be assumed that u is normally distributed and with zero mean. Second, u is with constant variances, i.e. its probability distribution remains the same over all observations of the explanatory variables. This is known as the assumption of homoscedasticity. Third, we must assume that the successive values of u are temporally independent. This is the assumption of no autocorrelation or serial correlation. Fourth, there must be an absence of perfect multicollinearity among the explanatory variables. Fifth, the explanatory variables, K and L, are measured without error. For these five assumptions, there is no way of testing the assumption of zero mean and the problem of heteroscedasticity in assumption two should not be serious in our case which is a time-series study of individual countries. In addition, though it must be true that K and L tend to move together over time, it is unlikely that they are perfectly linearly correlated. Consequently, in the context of our problem, the two assumptions that need more detailed treatment are autocorrelation and errors in the measurement of variables.

Autocorrelation may be a serious problem in our present study as we are dealing with time-series data. Most of the published time-series data involve some interpolation and 'smoothing' processes which tend to average the true disturbances over successive time periods and consequently the successive disturbances could be interrelated. Also, even purely random factors exert influences that are spread over more than one period of time, and hence the disturbances over the affected periods will be interrelated. When autocorrelation does exist, the value, as well as the standard errors, of the parameter estimates is affected. This means that (1) OLS parameter estimates are unbiased but (2) the conventional formula for OLS variances (as given by a standard computer regression programme) is incorrect and may give too small a variance so that reliability could be overstated. (3) In any case there will exist a different estimator that will have smaller variance than that of ordinary least squares correctly calculated. There are various tests available for the presence of autocorrelation. The most-widely used in empirical research is undoubtedly the Durbin-Watson test.[21] It has the advantage of simplicity in calculation and applicability to small samples. In the present study the Durbin-Watson statistic is given for all the regression equations. However the Durbin-Watson test has the drawback that it is inconclusive.[22] The d statistic used in the test has values lying between zero and four. There is a range of d values over which we cannot reject or accept the null hypothesis of no autocorrelation. This uncertain range is defined by d_L, the lower bound values of d, and d_U, the upper-bound values of d; d_L and d_U in each case are determined by the total number of observations and the number of explanatory variables and, of course, the chosen level of significance. Thus when the empirical d is equal to, or greater than, d_U, we can accept the null hypothesis of zero autocorrelation, and reject it if the empirical d is equal to or smaller than d_L. In the present study, we shall consider the problem of autocorrelation damaging our results when the empirical d is equal to or less than d_L. In such cases, we re-estimate the parameters with transformed data using the estimated autocorrelation parameters obtained by Durbin's 'two-step' method.[23] In view of the fact that we do not re-estimate the cases where the empirical d falls in the inconclusive region, we take a stricter level of significance of 5 per cent in performing the Durbin-Watson test. In the original calculations of Durbin and Watson, tables of 5 per cent and 1 per cent levels of significance were produced. It is to be noted that in the Durbin-Watson test a 5 per cent level of significance means a smaller region of accepting the null hypothesis than a 1 per cent level, and hence a 5 per cent level of significance is more likely to accept that there is serial correlation than a 1 per cent test. So far no Durbin-Watson table of higher than 5 per cent level of significance has been produced. In almost all cases this means that we carry out re-estimation based on transformed data when the empirical d is smaller than the critical value of d_U for a 1 per cent test.

Another important issue we must consider is the inevitable errors of measurement in the factor inputs in the production function. This is especially true for capital. The average prices of capital goods (measured at constant prices) change over time and newer capital goods embody a more recent and efficient technology. Hence a given book dollar value of capital at the present period as a rule means 'more' or 'less' capital than the previous periods.[24] This type of error in quality measurement also applies to labour inputs. Over time the quality of labour changes as a result of changes in the sex-age distribution and educational and training attainment of the labour force. The sheer measurement of the number of workers employed has neglected these aspects of quality changes.[25] Another possible measurement error in capital results from our using the stocks in existence instead of the service flows.[26] Fortunately, within the context of estimating the Cobb-Douglas or CES production function, the parameter estimates will remain unbiased if the utilisation rate of capital is not correlated with the magnitude of gross capital stock and the volume of employment.[27] In addition, it should be noted that the under-utilisation rate of capital in the economies under study was relatively low in comparison with most of the developing economies. The low level of capital under-utilisation can at least partially be justified by the low levels of unemployment of the labour force in these economies during the period under study. Thus the discrepancy between capital stock in existence and capital service flows should not be very large in the cases under study. In a number of cases (all sectors of Japan, and the manufacturing sector of Singapore and Taiwan), the volume of employment has been adjusted by indices of hours of work per week.[28] However, in no case have we attempted to construct quality indexes for labour with regard to age-sex composition and education level attained. In the first place, we do not have the necessary information to compute such indexes and secondly, even if information were available we would still need to make some bold assumptions such as that 40 per cent of the differences in earnings between workers of the same age are due to factors other than differences in level of education attained.[29]

Lastly, we must also consider the possibility of mis-specifying the production function by including only two inputs, capital and labour. Land must also be an important factor of production. In this context we mean land to be residential land, commercial and industrial land, agricultural land, and natural resources. As we have relied heavily on the perpetual inventory method to estimate capital stock, and as the gross investment estimates we have used include very little, if any, net purchases of land (since sales and purchases cancel out), our capital stock series are very unlikely to have included the value of residential, commercial and industrial land.[30] And, of course, agricultural land and natural resources are entirely omitted if we include only capital and labour as inputs in the production function. Nevertheless, in the production function analysis below we have left out land as a separate factor of production despite the fact that we realise its existence in practice. Our justification is that so far as we are solely concerned with *changes* in inputs in our production function studies, the omission of land is probably unimportant. This is because changes in land inputs occur very slowly and our period of analysis is only 16 years. Viewed from this angle, it seems possible for us to agree with Denison that the error resulting from the exclusion of land as a factor input in the analysis of the sources of growth cannot be very serious.[31]

With the above qualifications and justifications on our methodology, we can now proceed to the estimation of equation (9). This equation is applied to the manufacturing sector of Hong Kong and Singapore for the period 1960–70, and the various sectors (namely the economy as a whole, the agricultural sector, the manufacturing sector and the non-farm sector) of Japan, Korea, and Taiwan. Unless stated otherwise, the period covered for Japan and Taiwan is 1955–70, while that for Korea is from 1960–70. The estimation of equation (9) is by the OLS method. The results are shown in Table 4.1. Despite the good overall fit as revealed by the high R^2s, the results are not satisfactory in many ways. First, none of the estimates for the returns-to-scale parameter (i.e. the coefficient of $\ln L$) is significantly different from zero at the 5 per cent level, and in many cases the magnitude of the regression coefficient of $\ln L$ is unacceptable on *a priori* grounds. Second, some of the estimates for the output elasticity of capital are also intuitively implausible; this must to some extent be related to the unreasonable scale parameter estimates. In view of the fact that we cannot reject the hypothesis that there are constant returns to scale in all cases and that the standard errors of many of the regression coefficients are large, possibly because of the high correlation between $\ln L$ and $\ln (K/L)$, we turn to a constant-returns-to-scale form of equation (9). This can be done simply by dropping the term $\ln L$. Thus we have the following equation for estimation:

$$\ln Y/L = \ln A_0 + b \ln K/L + \lambda t + u \tag{10}$$

Table 4.2 reports the regression results of equation (10) which specifies a constrained Cobb-Douglas production function for the various sectors of the five economies. When compared with the results shown in Table 4.1, it can be seen that in all cases the statistical fit has been much improved in the sense that the F-value is invariably higher in the constrained form of the production function than the unconstrained form. The standard errors of the regression coefficients (especially those of the trend term) have become smaller, and except in two cases the estimates for the output elasticity of capital fall within plausible limits.

TABLE 4.1 Cobb-Douglas Production Function with Variable Returns: Regression Estimates of Equation (9)

		b	$v-1$	λ	R^{-2}	F	D$-$W
Hong Kong	M	0.1133 (0.1899)	-0.04139 (0.04850)	0.0633 (0.0373)	0.974	128	2.445
Japan	E	0.3151 (0.2780)	0.2929 (2.0792)	0.0574 (0.0449)	0.994	860	0.896
	A	0.4360 (0.9184)	-0.1207 (0.1464)	-0.0102 (0.0306)	0.980	250	0.943
	M	0.1784 (0.4131)	0.5342 (0.9436)	0.0461 (0.0525)	0.981	265	1.371
	N	0.0844 (0.5619)	0.0651 (0.1357)	0.0941 (0.0817)	0.970	583	1.008
Korea	E	0.4677 (0.2130)	-0.0427 (0.1205)	0.0605 (0.0397)	0.987	311	1.069
	A	1.625 (1.3170)	5.4051 (3.3967)	-0.0134 (0.0468)	0.851	200	2.031
	M	0.5748 (0.1131)	0.0805 (0.1798)	0.0455 (0.0193)	0.923	409	1.648
	N	1.4422 (0.3997)	1.4065 (0.8198)	-0.0273 (0.0503)	0.841	16	1.409
Singapore	M	1.3134 (0.5886)	0.5663 (0.4197)	-0.0399 (0.0563)	0.860	22	1.461
Taiwan	E	1.0153 (0.4103)	0.0662 (0.0393)	0.0489 (0.0086)	0.982	290	0.910
	A	-0.2047 (0.9303)	0.8261 (1.4745)	0.0228 (0.0447)	0.802	19	0.977
	M	0.3619 (0.1761)	0.2219 (0.4439)	0.0415 (0.0272)	0.971	171	1.476
	N	0.8617 (0.3358)	-0.0619 (0.0297)	0.0808 (0.0104)	0.974	200	1.438

E $-$ economy as a whole   A $-$ agricultural sector
M $-$ manufacturing sector   N $-$ non-farm sector
$v = a + b$, i.e. the sum of the output elasticities of labour and capital

TABLE 4.2 Cobb-Douglas Production Function with Constant Returns: Regression Estimates of Equation (10)

		b	λ	$\overline{R}^2$	F	D – W
Hong kong	M	0.2620 (0.0742)	0.0321 (0.0069)	0.975	199	2.236
Japan	E	0.3061 (0.2397)	0.0631 (0.0189)	0.995	1395	1.017
	A	1.1701 (0.2227)	− 0.0285 (0.0207)	0.981	385	1.028
	M	− 0.0737 (0.3137)	0.0874 (0.0290)	0.982	400	1.344
	N	0.171 (0.159)	0.0709 (0.0286)	0.975	930	1.364*
Korea	E	0.389 (0.081)	0.0544 (0.0035)	0.988	512	1.970
	A	0.269 (0.370)	0.0223 (0.0180)	0.851	24	1.538
	M	0.6117 (0.0735)	0.0370 (0.0032)	0.931	68	1.592
	N	0.696 (0.0830)	0.0620 (0.0037)	0.979	38	1.964
Singapore	M	0.5530 (0.1791)	0.0359 (0.0049)	0.877	28	1.332
Taiwan	E	0.371 (0.102)	0.0458 (0.0119)	0.915	384	1.373*
	A	0.264 (0.548)	0.0174 (0.0192)	0.893	30	1.650
	M	0.3484 (0.1590)	0.0537 (0.0117)	0.973	272	1.313
	N	0.496 (0.136)	0.0482 (0.0075)	0.489	176	1.401*

* Results obtained after correcting for first-order serial correlation.

The exceptions are the agricultural and manufacturing sectors of Japan. In the former case, the estimate is unreasonably high (1.17) and in the latter it bears a negative sign though statistically insignificant. These unreasonable results suggest possible mis-specification of the production relationship. In the next chapter, we shall see that the misspecification in the case of Japanese manufacturing lies largely in the specification of technical progress; when technical progress is assumed to be partially endogenously determined, the estimates for the output elasticity of capital are in line with our intuition. In the case of Japanese agriculture, the misspecification seems to have come from the assumption of unit elasticity of substitution in the Cobb-Douglas case. In the later CES function estimations in this chapter, the parameter estimates are more satisfactory.

When looking at the estimates for the output elasticity of capital, one may also realise that in some cases (in fact in 6 out of 14 estimates), they are not statistically significant at the 5 per cent level. This tends to suggest that changes in capital per worker do not explain very much of the change in output per worker in these cases, notably in the agricultural sector of Korea and Taiwan. However, it should be noted that in the manufacturing sector of Hong Kong, Korea, and Singapore and the economy as a whole in Korea and Taiwan, increases in capital per worker play a significant role in explaining productivity growth as the regression coefficient of $\ln K/L$ in these cases are statistically significant.

Turning to the estimates for the rate of disembodied neutral technical change which is represented by the regression coefficient of the trend term, we find that in all except three cases the estimates are statistically significant. All the exceptions are found in the agricultural sectors. We must, however, note that in the case of Japanese agriculture, the negative estimated rate of technical progress should not be taken seriously as there is a strong indication of mis-specification as revealed by the implausibly high estimate of the output elasticity of capital. In general we find that technical progress has been important in the non-agricultural sectors of the economies under study in the present context of a Cobb-Douglas aggregate production function. The Japanese economy as a whole achieved a relatively high rate of technical progress of 6.3 per cent per annum which is considerably higher than the 5.4 per cent enjoyed by Korea and the 4.6 per cent achieved by Taiwan. The rate of technical progress of 8.7 per cent in Japanese manufacturing must be considered as quite outstanding by all standards. At the same time the 5.4 per cent enjoyed by the Taiwan manufacturing and the 6.2 per cent achieved by the Korean non-farm sector are also worth noting.

It is of interest to note that the Cobb-Douglas results suggest that the manufacturing sectors of both Hong Kong and Singapore may have experienced only very moderate rates of technical progress (of 3.2 per cent and 3.6 per cent respectively) when compared with the high rates enjoyed by the manufacturing sectors of Japan and Taiwan. Considering the highly statistically significant regression coefficient of the capital per worker variable and the fact that growth in capital input was very rapid in these two city economies, we tend to think that capital accumulation was at least as important as technical progress in explaining productivity growth in the manufacturing sector of Hong Kong and Singapore. Similarly, as growth in capital was very rapid in all sectors in our group of economies, capital accumulation should be regarded as an important contributing factor to growth whenever the regression coefficients of the capital per worker variable are statistically significant.

We must however be very cautious in interpreting our estimation results in connection with the importance of economies of scale in the economies under study. It is true that in the context of our two-input production functions, economies of scale do not seem to be important. But, we must bear in mind that we have omitted land as a factor input, the income share of which is probably quite substantial in our economies (even in the cases of Hong Kong and Singapore). The implication is that if land had been included in the production function analysis, the sum of the output elasticities of all inputs will probably substantially exceed one suggesting that economies of scale are of considerable importance in the economies under study.

FACTOR INPUTS AND RESOURCES REALLOCATION: *The National Income Accounting Approach*

In the last section when we estimated the Cobb-Douglas production function, we discussed briefly the importance of factor inputs in explaining productivity growth in terms of the statistical significance of the estimated output elasticity of capital. In this section we will discuss in detail the separate contributions of capital and labour.[32] In the above econometric estimations, there is no way to examine the role of resources reallocation in economic growth, which is believed to be an important contributing factor to growth in those fast-growing countries (such as the economies under study) which have experienced rapid structural changes. Also because of the lack of a continuous time-series on Y and L for the whole economy in the cases of Hong Kong and Singapore (though data at five-year intervals are available), we cannot carry out the Cobb-Douglas function estimation in these two cases. By adopting the well-known Denison national income accounting approach, it is possible to separate the individual contributions to growth of capital and labour, to study cases where data are available for the beginning and end of a period only, [33] and to isolate the effect of resources reallocation.[34] It is for these reasons that the present section will employ growth accounting as our methodology in analysing some of the causal factors of economic growth. We shall confine our analysis to the economy as a whole. It must be pointed out that in essence there is no real conflict between the Cobb-Douglas function estimation and the growth accounting approach as far as the fundamental methodology is concerned. An explanation of the growth accounting method and its relation to the Cobb-Douglas production function follows.

The essence of the growth accounting method is to use the factor shares in national income as weights when combining the individual factor inputs to form an index of total factor input, and to define that part of output growth which cannot be explained by increases in factor inputs as total factor productivity. This total factor productivity is therefore the same as the 'residual' or technical progress defined in the early part of this chapter. This approach has been most often associated with the names of Denison, Solow, and Kendrick,[35] and it is Denison who has made the most elaborate study of this type. This approach of weighting inputs by factor shares can be explained as follows. Assuming a neo-classical production function, we have

$$Y = F(K, L, t) \tag{11}$$

where Y is output K and L are capital and labour inputs respectively, and t is time.

Differentiating equation (11) with respect to time, we have

$$\frac{dY}{dt} = \frac{\partial F}{\partial K} \cdot \frac{dK}{dt} + \frac{\partial F}{\partial L} \cdot \frac{dL}{dt} + \frac{\partial F}{\partial t}$$

Dividing the above through by Y gives

$$\frac{dY/dt}{Y} = \frac{\partial F/\partial K}{Y} \cdot \frac{dK}{dt} + \frac{\partial F/\partial L}{Y} \cdot \frac{dL}{dt} + \frac{\partial F/\partial t}{Y}$$

Denoting the proportional growth rates of output, capital, and labour as

$$\dot{Y}\left(= \frac{dY/dt}{Y}\right), \dot{K}\left(= \frac{dK/dt}{Y}\right), \text{and } \dot{L}\left(= \frac{dL/dt}{Y}\right) \text{respectively, we obtain}$$

$$\dot{Y} = \frac{(\partial F/\partial K)K}{Y} \cdot \dot{K} + \frac{(\partial F/\partial L)L}{Y} \cdot \dot{L} + \frac{\partial F/\partial t}{Y}$$

$(\partial F / \partial t)/Y$ is the proportional rate of shift of the production function. It is taken to represent total factor productivity or technical progress. Denoting it as $\dot{A}$, we have

$$\dot{Y} = \frac{(\partial F / \partial K)K}{Y} \cdot \dot{K} + \frac{(\partial F / \partial L)L}{Y} \cdot \dot{L} + \dot{A}$$

or $$\dot{A} = \dot{Y} - \frac{(\partial F / \partial K)K}{Y} \cdot \dot{K} - \frac{(\partial F / \partial L)L}{Y} \cdot \dot{L} \qquad (12)$$

$\dfrac{(\partial F / \partial K)K}{Y}$ and $\dfrac{(\partial F / \partial L)L}{Y}$ are the share of capital in income and the share of labour in income respectively. If we assume that income shares are constant over time, equation (12) is reduced to:

$$\dot{A} = \dot{Y} - \beta_K \cdot \dot{K} - \beta_L \cdot \dot{L} \qquad (13)$$

where β_K and β_L are capital and labour shares in income respectively. Equation (13) constitutes the basic equation used by growth economists to calculate the sources of growth. It can be seen that equation (13) is in fact the same as the Cobb-Douglas production function expressed in log-linear form. As far as the experience of the industrialised countries is concerned, the factor shares in income have been quite stable, and hence most of the studies employ equation (13) in which β_K and β_L are constants. It is in this way that most of the studies of the sources of growth in the literature imply a Cobb-Douglas production function, though any form of the neoclassical production function should be compatible with this approach. If other production functions, such as the CES, are assumed, then the weights β_K and β_L will change over time, i.e. different weights must be used in calculating total factor productivity at different moments of time.

Total factor productivity as represented by $\dot{A}$ in equation (13) is a catch-all phrase embodying all those changes in factor inputs. Nevertheless, the general approach of using equation (12) or (13) to study the sources of growth does help to throw light on the relative importance of the factor-input contributions and non-factor-input contributions to growth. The relative importance of these two different sources of growth often offers an explanation of the rate of growth, and the different levels of income and productivity attained by different countries.

In the calculation of the sources of growth in the different economies, we shall use equation (13) in which the factor shares in income are treated as constants, thus implying a Cobb-Douglas production function.

Furthermore, β_K is assumed to equal 0.4 and β_L 0.6 in the cases of Hong Kong, Korea, Singapore, and Taiwan. This is based on the estimated output elasticities of capital of around 0.4 (see Table 2) for the economy as a whole of both Korea and Taiwan obtained from the earlier Cobb-Douglas estimations. No factor share data on Hong Kong and Singapore are available, but we believe that Hong Kong and Singapore should not differ from Korea and Taiwan greatly in this aspect. We therefore also use the 0.4 and 0.6 figures for factor shares in Hong Kong and Singapore. For Japan, β_K is set at 0.3 and β_L at 0.7, which are again based on the Cobb-Douglas estimation results obtained earlier in this chapter. It must be pointed out again that although we assume that the sum of the output elasticities of capital and labour is one, this does not imply the absence of economies of scale in our economies. This is because we have left out land as a factor input in the production function, and the income share of land can be quite substantial in the these economies.

Our objective is to explain the sources of growth of output instead of those of output per worker. The sources-of-growth literature has been largely concerned with the latter. This is perhaps justified in part by the interest of development economists in the level of per capita output. However, such a measurement of the sources of growth is very sensitive to the rate of labour force expansion. In the study of the developed countries in which the rate of labour force growth is low, it makes relatively little difference whether one is calculating the sources of growth of output or the sources of growth of productivity. On the other hand, for the developing nations in which population growth is generally high, it is much more informative and suited to our purpose if we concentrate on the sources of output, rather than productivity, growth.

In the sources-of-growth literature, there are two contrasting patterns of empirical evidence. Firstly, for a considerable period of time since the early work of Abramovitz and Solow, the findings have almost been invariably that total factor productivity constitutes by far the most important source of growth. For example, Denison found that in all the eight European countries he studied (Belgium, Germany, Netherlands, Norway, Denmark, France, Italy, and the United Kingdom) over 50 per cent of output growth cannot be explained by increases in inputs even after allowance for quality changes in labour inputs. We must however note that all these findings are related to the industrialised economies. A somewhat contrasting pattern of findings has emerged from the experience of the developing economies. The application of the sources-of-growth methodology to developing countries has only been done very recently.[36] In these studies of the developing economies, it has been found that the contributions of factor inputs to growth have been much more important than those of total factor productivity. These findings are in fact in line with an earlier but somewhat neglected study on the post-war Israeli economy.[37] In fact, even before such empirical evidence was provided, some economists had doubts about the relevance of the sources-of-growth experience of developed countries to the less developed economies. For instance, Hicks (1965) remarked that 'It is very wrong to give the impression to a poor country, which is very far from equilibrium even on a past technology that capital accumulation . . . is a matter of minor importance.' Nonetheless, little attention has so far been devoted to explaining such contrasting patterns of sources of growth in the developed and developing countries. Our purpose here is to add to the existing evidence the experience of these five Asian economies,[38] and go a step further in explaining the differences in the patterns of sources-of-growth.

The sources of growth of real output for the economy as a whole for the five economies are shown in in Table 4.3. Over the entire period 1955–70, total factor productivity accounted for a considerable proportion of growth of output for the economy as a whole. It accounted for slightly less than 50 per cent of growth in Hong Kong, slightly over 60 per cent in Japan, and just over 50 per cent in the other three economies. When compared with other findings, our results suggest that the importance of total factor productivity in explaining growth in the five economies lies somewhere between the two existing contrasting patterns of sources of growth of the developed and developing countries. Moreover, if we exclude Japan, which is comparatively much more developed, the four remaining economies form a rather homogeneous group with regard to the role of total factor productivity in growth, ranging only from 46 per cent to 56 per cent. Japan, the economy in our group for which there have been previous similar studies, showed considerable increases in the importance of total factor productivity when compared with earlier findings for an earlier period.[39] Our findings indicate that the percentage growth of output explained by total factor productivity is much higher in our economies than in other developing economies. For Correa's nine Latin American countries for the period 1950–62, an average of 34 per cent of output growth is explained by total factor productivity.[40] Bruton's study of five Latin American countries for the period 1940–64 shows an even lower percentage of 28.[41] For some Asian economies not included in the present study, it is 39 per cent for the Philippines (1955–70), 31 per cent for Israel (1950–65), and 24 per cent for India (1950–

TABLE 4.3 The Sources of Growth of Real National Income:
The Economy as a Whole
(percentage points with percentage distribution in brackets)

| Country | Period | Explanation of Sources of Growth | | | Rate of Growth of Income |
		Capital Input	Labour Input	Total Factor Productivity	
Hong Kong	1955–60	1.87 (22.7)	3.98 (48.2)	2.50 (29.1)	8.25
	1960–6	4.33 (41.0)	1.97 (18.6)	4.27 (40.4)	10.57
	1966–70	1.11 (16.1)	1.49 (21.6)	4.30 (62.3)	6.90
	1955–70	3.12 (33.5)	1.86 (20.0)	4.33 (46.5)	9.31
Singapore	1957–66	0.72 (13.4)	0.94 (17.5)	3.70 (69.0)	5.36
	1966–70	3.76 (32.3)	2.78 (23.9)	5.10 (43.8)	11.64
	1957–70	1.44 (22.0)	1.50 (22.9)	3.62 (55.2)	6.56
Korea	1955–60	0.87 (20.6)	1.35 (32.0)	2.00 (47.4)	4.22
	1960–6	0.67 (9.7)	2.14 (31.0)	4.10 (59.3)	6.91
	1966–70	3.67 (36.3)	1.38 (13.6)	5.06 (50.1)	10.11
	1955–70	2.12 (24.0)	1.73 (19.6)	4.99 (56.4)	8.84
Japan	1955–60	2.03 (22.2)	1.05 (11.5)	6.06 (66.3)	9.14
	1960–6	3.11 (34.8)	0.92 (10.3)	4.91 (54.9)	8.94
	1966–70	2.90 (24.1)	0.86 (7.1)	8.28 (68.8)	12.04
	1955–70	2.78 (27.5)	0.98 (9.7)	6.36 (62.8)	10.12
Taiwan	1955–60	1.07 (20.4)	1.05 (20.0)	3.12 (59.6)	5.24
	1960–6	1.79 (19.3)	1.45 (15.6)	6.04 (65.1)	9.28
	1966–70	3.07 (38.0)	3.18 (39.4)	1.82 (22.6)	8.07
	1955–70	2.00 (24.9)	1.72 (21.5)	4.30 (53.6)	8.02

60).[42] For our group of five fast-growing Asian economies, the average is 55 per cent including Japan and 52 per cent excluding Japan. This average is however lower than the 64 per cent obtained for the advanced Western countries for the period 1950–62.[43] Thus, our results for the five economies under study complicate the findings of previous studies. When we include our results in the existing findings, the two contrasting patterns of sources of growth between developed and developing countries become much less clearcut. Our group of economies (with the exception of Japan) is by no means more developed than the Latin American countries or Israel and yet they have shown a sources-of-growth pattern more similar to the developed countries than other developing nations. It then seems that it is more than the stage of economic development attained that has determined the role of total factor productivity in explaining the growth of output.

Our results suggest that about 50 per cent of output growth in the economies under study is accounted for by increases in factor inputs. For the period 1955–70 as a whole, the contribution of capital to growth is in general greater than that of labour. The only exception is Singapore where the contributions of capital and labour are roughly equal. The greater importance of capital in explaining growth is most marked in Japan, and least marked in Taiwan. For the earlier period 1955–66, the contribution of labour is greater than that of capital in Korea. Over the three successive periods, the contributions of capital and labour in Taiwan are more or less equal in each period. Over time, the percentage contribution of total factor productivity increases in the case of Hong Kong (and that of factor inputs decreases accordingly), but decreases in the case of Singapore. In Japan and Korea, the percentage has been reasonably stable over the successive periods. In Taiwan, the percentage contribution of total factor productivity declines noticeably in the most recent sub-period 1966–70.

Considering the changes in actual percentage points, we observe that total factor productivity ranges from over 6 per cent per annum in Japan to 3.6 per cent in Singapore. For Japan, Korea and Taiwan, the present estimates are very close to the Cobb-Douglas function estimates obtained earlier in this chapter. This is of course not a surprise as the fundamental methodology of the two sets of estimates is similar. For Hong Kong and Singapore, the present estimates give valuable information which we could not obtain by a Cobb-Douglas estimation due to the lack of sufficient data. In all cases increases in total factor productivity are high by any standard. They compare very favourably even with the countries with top scores in Denison's study (3.97 for Germany and 4.16 for Italy) and all the five countries have achieved a higher measure in percentage points of total factor productivity than all the Latin American and other Asian countries which have been studied by similar methods. Over the successive sub-periods, there is a general tendency for total factor productivity to rise in the economies under study, except for the fall in Taiwan in the sub-period 1966–70. In general the five also have very high percentages for capital's contribution to growth, especially in the cases of Hong Kong and Japan. This experience is shared only by Israel which has a 4.1 per cent contribution of capital to growth during the period 1950–65. The actual percentage of labour's contribution to growth has been high in Hong Kong in the earlier period and in the more recent periods in Singapore and Taiwan. Like the other developed countries, Japan has a relatively low measure of labour's contribution in percentage points. Over time, the contribution of labour declines in Hong King and Japan, and rises in Singapore and Taiwan, while in Korea it is reasonably stable. It is to be expected that in a mature economy like Japan, the contribution of labour would decline slowly. In Hong Kong, it is due to the slowing down of the inflow of labour from the Chinese Mainland and possibly the use of more capital-intensive methods of production. In Korea and Taiwan where urban-rural migration is still going on and the rate of population growth is high, labour's contribution to growth has not shown any sign of decline. In Singapore, the large-scale inflow of labour force from Malaysia in the sixties is largely responsible for the considerable increase in the contribution of labour to growth. Except for the most recent sub-period 1966–70 in Hong Kong, the contribution of capital generally increases over time.

Let us now consider the role of resources reallocation among sectors; this has been considered as one of the most important factors in explaining the differences in growth rates among countries.[44] Considering the nature of general disequilibrium in developing economies, it is expected that resources reallocation must have played an even more important role than in developed countries. According to the method we have used, the gains from resources reallocation lump together with total factor productivity or the 'residual'. Unfortunately there are numerous problem associated with the concept and measurement of resources reallocation. Firstly, there is the problem of which kind of resources we should consider. Traditionally, land is treated as fixed and therefore plays little or no part in resources reallocation. However, the reallocation of agricultural land for industrial and commercial use might be of great importance to urban economies like Hong Kong and Singapore. One way of taking land into consideration is of course to treat land as a form of capital. Many economists are interested in studying the flow of capital resources between agricultural and non-agricultural sectors in the process of development. Some hold the view that the supply of agricultural surplus to the non-agricultural sector is a prerequisite for rapid economic development,[45] while others maintain that there is a tendency of inflow into the agricultural sector in the process of development, especially in the case of Asian countries.[46] There is however always the problem of how to measure the resource flow and the items to be included in the flow. On the other hand, some economists concentrate their attention on the outflow of rural workers to the non-agricultural sector in the process of economic development. Such discussions are found in the dualistic models of growth associated with the names of Lewis, Fei-Ranis, and Jorgenson.[47] In studying the post-war growth experience of nine Western countries Denison attempts to measure the gains from the reallocation of labour force from the agricultural sector to the non-agricultural sector, and concludes that such a reallocation of resources constitutes one of the major factors explaining the differences of growth rates among the Western countries he has studied. Inasmuch as rural-urban migration is a dominant phenomenon in the economies under study, the reallocation of labour from one sector to another should have been the most important form of resources reallocation in these economies. We accordingly follow Denison's method in isolating the gains of resources reallocation from the 'residual', and see how much of total factor productivity is due to the reallocation of labour from the agricultural to the non-agricultural sector. The basic idea is to calculate the amount by which the initial year national income would have been higher if the final year employment pattern had prevailed. We divide the period under study 1955–70 into three sub-periods, and we arrive at the following results:

TABLE 4.4 The Gains from Reallocation of Resources

Country	Hong Kong	Japan	Korea	Singapore	Taiwan
1955–60					
% points		1.00	1.71		0.86
as a % of $\dot{A}$		18.10	85.50		27.60
as a % of $\dot{Y}$		10.90	40.50		16.40
1960–6					
% points	0.24	0.90	1.28	0.17	1.38
as a % of $\dot{A}$	5.60	22.50	31.2	4.60	22.80
as a % of $\dot{Y}$	2.30	10.10	18.50	3.20	14.90
1966–70					
% points	0.16	1.03	1.43	0.27	1.02
as a % of $\dot{A}$	3.70	13.80	28.30	5.30	56.00
as a % of $\dot{Y}$	2.30	8.60	14.10	2.30	12.60

$\dot{A}$ — percentage of total factor productivity growth;
$\dot{Y}$ — rate of income growth.
For the detailed procedures in derivation, see Appendix B.

The results in Table 4.4 suggest that resources reallocation of labour in those countries with a relatively large agricultural sector (Japan, Korea, and Taiwan) plays an important part in explaining the growth of output. Understandably, the two urban economies, Hong Kong and Singapore, gain little from such a reallocation as the agricultural sector had been extremely small even before modern economic growth took place. However, the reallocation of land use might have played an important part though we have no way of quantifying its contribution. Among the other three economies under study, Korea with the most backward and relatively largest agricultural sector has benefited most from the reallocation of labour force, especially during the early sub-period of 1955–60. During this period in Korea, 86 per cent of the total factor productivity and 41 per cent of output growth is explained by the reallocation of labour force. Japan with the least backward and relatively small agricultural sector benefits only moderately from such a reallocation. Taiwan also benefits only moderately. This is perhaps due to the fact that in Taiwan the most rapid reallocation of labour force took place before 1955. Nevertheless, it is in relative terms that we say Japan and Taiwan gain moderately from the reallocation of labour. In absolute terms, both countries gained about a percentage point per annum for each of the sub-periods, which should be regarded as very high. Of course the gain of about 1.5 percentage points for each of the sub-periods by Korea is extremely high by any standard. It is also of interest to note that among the five economies under study, Korea with the largest proportion of output explained by total factor productivity is also the economy that gains most from reallocation of labour resources. At the same time, Hong Kong with the smallest proportion of output growth explained by total factor productivity is the economy that gains the least from resources reallocation. It then seems that the greater the extent of resources reallocation, the more important is total factor productivity as a source of growth. This explains at least partially why the estimated rates of technical progress we obtained for Hong Kong and Singapore in the last section are relatively low.

To sum up, our growth accounting exercise applied to the economy as a whole has revealed some interesting contrasts in the patterns of sources of growth between developed and developing countries. The experience of the developed Western countries shows that irrespective of the rate of growth of output, a large proportion of output growth, say well above 50 per cent, is explained by total factor productivity. The relatively minor role of factor inputs in explaining growth of output can largely be accounted for by the following factors:

1. In most of the developed Western countries, the rate of population growth is low and as a result the contribution of labour growth to output growth is small.
2. Given that the growth rate of capital is greater than that of labour (which is usually the case in the developed and the fast-growing developing countries), a smaller capital share in income (which is the weight used in calculating the percentage point contribution of capital to

growth) will give rise to a lower weighted sum of the growth rate of inputs,[48] and hence a higher total factor productivity. Generally speaking developing countries tend to have a higher capital share in income than developed countries because of higher marginal product of capital in the former. Developing countries usually have capital share within the range of 0.4–0.5 while the corresponding range for developed countries tends to be 0.25–0.3. The higher marginal product of capital in the developing countries can be explained by the fact that there exist numerous 'gaps' in the capital structure of the developing countries. To a considerable extent investment represents efforts to fill in these gaps, i.e. to make the capital structure more comprehensive. In the developed countries with an already extensive capital structure, investment is much more in the form of replacing and duplicating existing capital. Consequently it adds little to the capacity of the economy.

Moreover, in the developed Western countries, there is a close association between the rate of growth of output and total factor productivity, i.e. those countries experiencing higher total factor productivity are also those countries with higher rate of growth of output. According to Denison's study, the advance of knowledge (which is defined by Dension as the 'residual' of total factor productivity) is only a minor component of total factor productivity. It is the reallocation of labour from agriculture to non-agricultural sectors and economies of scale (which, for Denison, result from expansion of the national market and independent expansion of local markets) that are the dominant components of total factor productivity. Furthermore, by and large the relative gains from resources reallocation and economies of scale determine the relative growth rates of the developed Western countries. It then seems that the models of surplus-labour economies are not only applicable to the developing countries but also to the contemporary growth experience of Western countries.[49] From this point of view, there seems to exist a general theory of growth which can be used to describe developed as well as developing economies.

In developing countries, on the other hand, the sources-of-growth patterns are characterised by a greater importance of the contribution of factor inputs to growth. Among the developing countries with sources-of-growth data available, we can identify two sub-groups: those countries with a relatively higher and those with a relatively lower contribution of total factor productivity to growth. The former group comprises the five economies under study plus Venezuela and Peru, and the latter group includes Israel, USSR, Brazil, and the Philippines. With the exception of Israel, the rate of growth of the former group is greater than that of the latter. This observation seems to suggest that among the developing countries, those with a higher contribution of total factor productivity to growth are those which have enjoyed faster rates of growth. In this respect, the experience of the developing countries is similar to that of developed nations. However, as we do not find scale economies important in the growth of our group of economies, the major component of total factor productivity in developing countries should be advances of technical knowledge and gains from resources reallocation. To summarise, our results suggest that while total factor productivity could be both the necessary and sufficient condition for rapid growth in developed nations, it is only a necessary one for developing countries.

ELASTICITY OF SUBSTITUTION AND TECHNICAL PROGRESS:*Estimation of the CES Production Function*

At least since the time of Marshall's *Principles* the notion of substitutability between factors of production has been recognised as the core of neoclassical production and supply theory. But a precise measure of the degree of input substitutability was not developed until Hicks' *Theory of Wages* (1932) and Mrs. Joan Robinson's *Economics of Imperfect Competition* (1933). Following Hicks, the elasticity of substitution is defined as the percentage change in the K/L ratio with respect to a given percentage change in the marginal rate of technical substitution, given the state of technology. In spite of the precision of the definition, production functions had for a long time been confined to the restrictive cases of the Cobb-Douglas function (where the elasticity of substitution is one) and the Leontief fixed-proportion function (where the elasticity of substitution is zero). It was not until the study of Arrow *et. al.* in 1961 that the CES production function was derived allowing the elasticity of substitution to assume any value. The significance of this development is that elasticity of substitution can be estimated as a constant within a given industry, a given economy, or a given period of time, but it may vary across industries, economies, and time periods.

The CES production function derived by Arrow *et. al.* is as follows:

$$Y = A \left[b(K)^{-\rho} + (1-b)L^{-\rho} \right]^{-1/\rho} \tag{14}$$

where Y is output,
             K, capital input,
             L, labour input,

A, the efficiency parameter which indicates the level of technology,

b, the distribution parameter which indicates the capital intensity,

ρ, the substitution parameter, where $1/1 + \rho = \sigma$, the elasticity of substitution.

In the form shown above, the production function is homogeneous of degree one, i.e. it exhibits constant returns to scale. Hicks-neutral technical change and non-constant returns to scale can be easily introduced into (14) which can then be written as:

$$Y = A_0 e^{\lambda t}[b(K)^{-\rho} + (1-b)L^{-\rho}]^{-v/\rho} \tag{15}$$

where λ is the rate of Hicks-neutral disembodied technical change, and v is the scale parameter. When $v > 1$, there is increasing returns, and when $v < 1$, decreasing returns, and when $v = 1$, constant returns. Taking the logarithm of (15) on both sides, we have:

$$\ln Y = \ln A_0 + \lambda t + -v/\rho \ln[b(K)^{-\rho} + (1-b)L^{-\rho}] \tag{16}$$

It can be seen that b and ρ enter into (16) in a non-linear way, and thus the parameters of the CES production function cannot be estimated by the ordinary linear least squares method. Accordingly, several alternative methods for estimation have been proposed. Clearly, the parameters can be estimated by the use of non-linear least squares.[50] The basic idea is to make initial guesses concerning the values of b, A, ρ, and v, and to obtain a predicted output. The sum of squares of differences between predicted and actual output becomes a function of the values assigned to these parameters. One then attempts to minimise this error sum of squares by iterative estimation until the parameter estimates appear to converge to a particular set of values. This method is however not followed in the present study for two reasons. First, on practical grounds, the iterative estimation requires rather complicated procedures; and secondly, on econometric grounds, the method is not desirable as the finite sample properties of such estimates are not known, though if convergence exists, the estimates will have the desirable asymptotic properties ·of efficiency, consistency, unbiasedness and sufficiency.

Another method very often used in empirical research is Kmenta's single-equation method based on linear approximation of the CES production function.[51] The essence of Kmenta's method consists of expanding the logarithm of the CES function in a Taylor series about an initial value of ρ. Excluding terms of the third and higher order, he arrived at the following approximation of the CES function:

$$\ln Y/L = \ln A_0 + (v-1)\ln L + v(b)\ln K/L - \tfrac{1}{2}\rho v b(1-b)$$
$$(\ln K/L)^2 + \lambda t \qquad (17)$$

or the following if constant returns to scale are assumed:

$$\ln Y/L = \ln A_0 + (b)\ln K/L - \tfrac{1}{2}\rho b(1-b)(\ln K/L)^2 + \lambda t \qquad (18)$$

Thus the estimating equation comes to nothing more than the addition of a 'correction term' involving $(\ln K/L)^2$ as a variable to the standard Cobb-Douglas estimating equation. Estimations based on equation (17) and (18) suffer from two serious drawbacks. First, we need a large sample and significant disperson in the K/L series to be able to say anything about the sign and magnitude of the coefficient $(\ln K/L)^2$ with some degree of confidence. In practice, it is often the case that the range of sample variations in K/L is so small that the standard error of the regression coefficient is usually too large to permit rejection of the Cobb-Douglas hypothesis that the coefficient of $(\ln K/L)^2$ is zero.[52] Secondly, in the Kmenta method of estimation, the parameter of elasticity of substitution can only be obtained indirectly. The estimated elasticity of substitution depends not only on the regression coefficient of $(\ln K/L)^2$ but also on that of $\ln K/L$. The consequence is that the calculated value for elasticity of substitution from such an estimation very often lie outside the plausible limits. In order not to miss any meaningful results, we did in fact try to estimate equations (17) and (18) with our data. However, in 12 out of 14 cases, we find that the regression coefficient of the 'correction term' is statistically insignificant, and furthermore, in many cases the calculated values for elasticity of substitution fall into implausible limits. The estimation results are therefore not discussed here but reported in Appendix C, Table A.15.

The CES production function can also be estimated by employing the first-order profit-maximisation conditions of the firm. This is in fact the method proposed originally in the seminal paper of Arrow and others. Another possibility is to use the constrained linear least squares. A side equation assuming cost minimisation subject to a constraint is first set up for estimating the values of b and ρ which are then fit into (16) so that A_0, λ and v can be estimated by the conventional method. In theory, it has been argued that the cost-minimisation approach has certain advantages over the profit-maximisation approach.[53] First, the regression estimates obtained from the profit-maximisation approach are very sensitive to returns to scale and the form of market structure. Unbiased estimates can only be obtained if there is a perfectly competitive market and constant returns to scale prevail. On the other hand the cost-minimisation approach is not sensitive to the nature of returns to scale or variations in the elasticity of demand for the product (which is dictated by the form of market structure). In the cost-minimisation approach, the basic behavioural assumption is only that an entrepreneur attempts to produce on the expansion path in the long-run. It is thus also compatible with a variety of non-profit-maximising hypotheses of the firm, and as a result it is somewhat more general than the profit-maximisation approach. But, we must note that in our present context the cost-minimisation approach need not be better because we have *not* found any indication of variable returns and the markets in general are very competitive in the economies under study. Moreover, we should also note that the cost-minimisation approach requires two more sets of data, the rate of return to capital and the capital stock, both of which are not always available and if available are possibly subject to wide margins of measurement errors. Under these circumstances only the profit-maximisation approach of estimating the CES production function will be employed in the present study.

The profit-maximisation method can be explained as follows. Given the CES production function with no technical progress, homogeneous of degree one,[54]

$$Y = A[bK^{-\rho} + (1-b)L^{-\rho}]^{-1/\rho} \tag{14}$$

we can divide through by L and obtain:

$$Y/L = A[b(K/L)^{-\rho} + (1-b)]^{-1/\rho} \tag{14a}$$

Raising both sides of (14a) to the ρ power, we have:

$$(Y/L)^{\rho}A^{-\rho} = [b(K/L)^{-\rho} + (1-b)]^{-1} \tag{14b}$$

Differentiating (14) partially with respect to L yields:

$$\partial Y/\partial L = A(1-b)[b(K/L)^{-\rho} + (1-b)]^{(-1/\rho)-1} \tag{14c}$$

Substituting (14a) into (14c), we have:

$$\partial Y/\partial L = Y/L \ (1-b) \ [b(K/L)^{-\rho} + (1-b)]^{-1} \tag{19}$$

Substituting (14b) into (19) gives:

$$\partial Y/\partial L = Y/L \ (1-b) \ (Y/L)^{\rho} A^{-\rho} \tag{20}$$

After simplification and transforming, we have:

$$(Y/L)^{1+\rho} = \partial Y/\partial L . A^{\rho} \ (1-b)^{-1} \tag{21}$$

Let us now introduce a side equation assuming profit-maximixation. Assuming perfect competition in both the product and factor markets, the first-order profit maximisation condition is given by:

$$\partial Y/\partial L = w \tag{22}$$

where w is the wage rate.

Substituting (22) into (21), we obtain the following single equation:

$$(Y/L)^{1+\rho} = A^{\rho} (1-b)^{-1} w \tag{23}$$

Taking logarithm of (23) and dividing through by $(1+\rho)$, we finally obtain the following estimating equation:

$$\ln (Y/L) = \sigma \ \text{In} \left[A^{\rho} \ (1-b)^{-1} \right] + \sigma \ \text{lnw} \tag{24}$$

or we can write:

$$\ln (Y/L) = a_0 + a_1 \ \text{lnw} + u \tag{25}$$

where a_0 is a constant,
      a_1, the elasticity of substitution,
      u, the error term with usual assumptions.

Technological change can be easily introduced into (25). Assuming that $A = A_0 \ e^{\lambda t}$, (25) turns into:

$$\ln (Y/L) = a'_0 + a_1 \text{lnw} + a_2 t + u' \tag{26}$$

where, a_1 as before is the estimate of the elasticity of substitution, $a_2 = \lambda(1 - \sigma)$, enables λ, the rate of Hicks-neutral disembodied technical progress, to be calculated as $a_2/(1 - a_1)$.

Equation (26) has the advantage that capital data are not required in its estimation. This not only proves to be extremely helpful when capital data are unreliable or unavailable, it is also sometimes desirable to use a model which does not require capital data even if such data are available. This is because it is argued that in models of technical progress and growth it is the amount of capital which is in use, and not the amount of capital that is in existence, that is important. In practice, it is virtually impossible to have an accurate measure of the capital in use; any capacity utilisation index employed has to be arbitrary. Furthermore, equation (26) has the advantage that the estimate for the elasticity of substitution is obtained directly from the regression coefficient of $\ln w$, while as we have already mentioned the complicated manner that ρ enters into the coefficient of $(\ln K/L)^2$ in the Kmenta method often causes the resulting calculated estimates of the elasticity of substitution to fall within implausible limits. However we must also note than in equation (26) the regression coefficient of the trend term divided by one minus the estimated elasticity of substitution gives the unbiased estimate of the rate of neutral disembodied technical progress. However, in practice, the resulting estimate of the rate of technical progress will fall within sensible limits only if the estimated elasticity of substitution is rather low. As the estimated elasticity of substitution approaches unity from above or below, the computed rate of technical progress approaches minus or plus infinity. In addition, when the estimated elasticity of substitution is greater than one, the computed rate of technical progress will be negative even if the regression coefficient of the trend term is positive, which would indicate that there is some net increase in labour productivity apart from that explained by wage increases. Thus the computed rate of technical progress in the estimation of equation (26) depends crucially on the estimated elasticity of substitution. When the estimated elasticity of substitution is near or greater than one, we cannot then put too much weight on the computed rate of technical progress.

It is to be noted that equation (26) assumes the ability of firms to achieve instantaneous changes in labour productivity when wage rate changes. If we follow Nerlove's assumption of an exponentially distributed lag,[55] we have the following alternative equation for estimation:

$$\ln{(Y/L)_t} = \text{constant} + l\sigma\text{1n}w_t + (1-l)\text{1n}(Y/L)_{t-1}$$
$$+ l(1-\sigma)\lambda t \qquad\qquad (26a)$$

where l is the elasticity of adjustment which indicates the fraction of the desired adjustment that is completed in the course of a single year.

Owing to the absence of data on wage rates in some of the sectors, equations (26) and (26a) are only fitted to eight sectors of the five economies under study. They are the M sector of Hong Kong, the A and M sectors of Japan, the A and M sectors of Korea, the M sector of Singapore, and the A and M sectors of Taiwan. The regression results of equation (26a) show that in not a single case was the regression coefficient of $\ln{(Y/L)_{t-1}}$ statistically significant, implying that $l = 1$, i.e. the adjustment was likely to be almost instantaneous. Consequently, the results of equation (26a) will not be discussed but just given in Table A.16 in Appendix C. The results of equation (26) are given in Table 4.5.[56] The overall statistical fit is good but in a few cases the standard errors are relatively large making the regression coefficients statistically insignificant. Looking at the estimated elasticities of substitution, we find that in all cases the estimates fall into very plausible limits, though the range over which the estimates spread is quite wide. The estimates of elasticities of substitution vary from 1.156 in the manufacturing sector of Hong Kong and 0.91 in the agricultural sector of Taiwan to the rather low value of 0.169 in Korean agriculture and 0.258 in Taiwan manufacturing. In three out of the eight estimations, the elasticities of substitution are statistically indistinguishable from zero. This occurs in the manufacturing sector of Japan, Singapore and Taiwan. In the former two cases (the M sector of Japan and Singapore) the estimated elasticities of substitution are also statistically different from one implying that the Cobb-Douglas specification of the production function can largely be rejected. In addition, in three other cases, viz. the A sector of Japan, and the A and M sectors of Korea, the estimated elasticities of substitution are also statistically different from one. In view of the fact that in a considerable number of cases, the unity substitution elasticity assumption can largely be rejected, we would like to find out in what ways and to what extent the Cobb-Douglas results obtained earlier have to be re-interpreted. Fortunately, we can show that the existence of non-unit elasticity of substitution may not be as disastrous to the Cobb-Douglas results as it appears to be. This issue will be dealt with towards the end of this section.

Empirical evidence on factor substitution possibilities suggests that

TABLE 4.5 CES Production Function—Profit-maximisation Approach: Regression Estimates of Equation (26)

			a_1	a_2	R^2	$D-W$	σ	$\lambda(\%)$
Hong Kong	M	1960–70	1.1560 (0.4367)	−0.0104 (0.0247)	0.933	2.767	1.156	6.68
Japan	A	1955–70	0.4970 (0.2396)	0.0399 (0.0250)	0.957	1.706	0.497	7.93
	M	1955–70	0.2807 (0.2270)	0.0650 (0.0129)	0.986	1.342	0.281	9.04
Korea	A	1962–70	0.1691 (0.0406)	0.0258 (0.0219)	0.842	1.686	0.169	3.11
	M	1960–70	0.3339 (0.0856)	0.0131 (0.0045)	0.816	1.546	0.334	1.97
Singapore	M	1960–70	0.3451 (0.2620)	0.0276 (0.0058)	0.739	1.617	0.345	4.21
Taiwan	A	1955–65	0.9098 (0.1173)	0.0073 (0.0044)	0.964	2.323	0.910	8.09
	M	1955–70	0.2580 (0.2478)	0.0666 (0.0183)	0.965	1.272	0.258	8.98

$a_1 = \sigma$ $a_2 = (1-\sigma)\lambda$

there are differences in substitution elasticities between the agricultural sector and the manufacturing sector and between economies at different stages of economic development. In general it is found that the agricultural sector has higher elasticities of substitution than the manufacturing sector, typically greater or equal to one in the agricultural sector and less than one in the manufacturing sector.[57] The reason for this difference in sectoral substitution elasticities is that the agricultural sector uses relatively simple technology which offers greater flexibility in input combinations. On the other hand, in the manufacturing sector the use of more complicated modern technology often means that the range of substitution possibilities is limited. This is especially true in developing economies where the scope of product mix is limited and the modern technology directly imported from abroad is inflexible. Such technology is inflexible because it is not designed in accordance with the peculiar situation prevailing in the developing economies. Thus, at an early stage of economic development, we expect that there is a rather wide difference between the elasticities of substitution of the A sector and M sector; but as development proceeds such differences will narrow, because at higher stages of development the elasticity of substitution will become lower in the A sector and higher in the M sector as a result of increased product mix in the M sector and the diffusion of more sophisticated machinay into the A sector. Of course, at higher levels of income, the industrial structure can cope with imported technology better and there is therefore greater flexibility in using the modern technology. In our three economies which have a significant agricultural sector, we find that our hypothesis of higher substitution in the A sector can be accepted in the cases of Japan and Taiwan. While the substitution elasticity is very near one in the A sector of Taiwan, it is only around one half in Japanese agriculture. This supports our belief that at higher stages of development the substitution elasticity in the agricultural sector will fall. However, the hypothesis that the substitution elasticity of the manufacturing sector will increase in the process of development does not seem to hold as our results suggest that the manufacturing sector of Japan has the second lowest substitution elasticity among the five economies under study. There is no explanation we can offer to these results without further investigation; we shall return to this issue shortly. In the case of Korea, our study suggests that the M sector has a higher elasticity of substitution than the A sector, though that of the M sector is not itself high. The very low substitution elasticity of the A sector in Korea perhaps reflects the fact that agricultural production in Korea still depends almost entirely on manual operations which offer very little possibility of factor substitution with the prevailing economic and social organisation in the rural areas. On the other hand, with the land reform and attempts of mechanisation agricultural production in Taiwan has entered the early stage of farm mechanisation during which production is often characterised by high substitution elasticity.

As we are dealing with a relatively short period of growth, it is difficult to trace the changes in the elasticities of substitution over time. In fact, so far we have assumed that in the period of our analysis the parameters in the production function remain constant. To test the validity of this assumption and the hypothesis that the substitution of elasticity will increase in the M sector and decrease in the A sector in the process of development, we shall now apply some sort of stability analysis to our estimations.[58] What we do is to fit equation (26) to a small number of observations in each case first, and then increase the number of observations gradually to see whether there is any structural break in each case. In other words, we wish to find out whether the production function is stable for the observations we have for each sector of the economies under study. By stability of the production function, we mean that the parameters of the function do not change significantly during the period. A structural break is said to have occurred when the parameters of the production function that prevail in the t years are no longer valid in the year $t + 1$. The operational procedure for finding the structural break is to fit equation (26) to a period of n observations, and then to $n + m$ observations. Two sets of estimates are therefore obtained, one from n observations, and another from $n + m$ observations. At this point we perform an F-test on the sum of squared residuals of the two regressions to test the hypothesis that the two regressions are generated from the same structure. If we can accept the hypothesis at a pre-specified 5 per cent level of significance, we proceed to run another regression with more observations, and perform a new F-test in a similar way. We shall go on until we come to the point where we can reject the hypothesis. In fitting equation (26) to the eight sectors of the five economies and applying our procedure of finding the structural break, we find that only in two cases, viz. the M sector of Hong Kong and Japan can we reject the hypothesis that the observations we have in each case are generated from the same structure. In the case of Hong Kong, the structural break occurs in 1966, and in the case of Japan it occurs in 1959. Thus, in these two cases it is better to divide the entire period into two sub-periods and fit the sub-period observations to equation (26). In doing so, the following results are obtained.

HONG KONG

1960 − 6: ln Y/L = constant +0.3251nw +0.0516t
$$(0.725) \qquad (0.0278)$$
$$R^2 = 0.973 \qquad D - W = 2.10$$
$$\sigma = 0.325 \qquad \lambda = 7.65\%$$
1966 − 70: ln Y/L = constant +1.2611nw −0.0255t
$$(0.586) \qquad (0.0702)$$
$$R^2 = 0.694 \qquad D - W = 2.28$$
$$\sigma = 1.261 \qquad \lambda = 9.77\%$$

JAPAN

1955 − 9: ln Y/L = constant +0.2111nw +0.0693t
$$(0.636) \qquad (0.0192)$$
$$R^2 = 0.984 \qquad D - W = 2.18$$
$$\sigma = 0.211 \qquad \lambda = 8.78\%$$

1959 − 70: ln Y/L = constant +0.7361nw +0.0263t

(0.253)   (0.0129)

$R^2 = 0.987$ $D - W = 1.33$

$\sigma = 0.736$ $\lambda = 9.97\%$

The regression results indicate that the major source of structural break is the change in the value of the substitution elasticity in the two sub-periods. In the case of Hong Kong manufacturing, there is an increase of substitution elasticity from 0.694 to 1.261, and in the case of Japanese manufacturing it increased from 0.211 in the first sub-period to 0.736 in the second period. In both cases, the estimated elasticities of substitution are statistically different from zero in the later period but not in the earlier period. These results suggest that there is a tendency for the elasticity of substitution to increase over time in the manufacturing sector of Hong Kong and Japan. Thus, we may argue that although the estimated elasticity of substitution for the manufacturing sector of Japan during the period 1955–70 as a whole was relatively low, it does not reflect the true picture as it has not taken into consideration the changes in the substitution elasticity during that period. In the period 1959–70 the manufacturing sector of Japan apparently had a higher substitution elasticity than Singapore, Korea, and Taiwan. In the period 1966–70 Hong Kong manufacturing had in fact a greater-than-one estimated elasticity of substitution; this perhaps reflects the great increases in product mix and the remarkable adaptability of the economy to modern technology in the recent years in Hong Kong. However, it is very important to note that one must not accept these results without reservation. This is due to the fact that the number of observations in each sub-period is too small to give any reliable parameter estimates. The estimated substitution elasticities in the later period though statistically significant have relatively large standard errors which do not enable the estimates to be statistically different from even 0.5, not to mention 1. The message here is that we should not take the value of 1.261 and 0.736 very seriously. What we could establish is at most that the substitution elasticities in Hong Kong and Japanese manufacturing in the sixties were greater than those in the fifties; we certainly cannot accept the drastic increases in the elasticities of substitution over such a short time period in Hong Kong and Japanese manufacturing as indicated by the magnitude of the regression estimates.

The estimates for the rate of technical progress from equation (26) are considerably higher than those obtained from the Cobb-Douglas case of equation (10) in most cases. This is largely the result of the different specification of the production function. The Cobb-Douglas production function assumes that elasticity of substitution is euqal to one. Misspecification of the substitution parameter will lead to biases in the estimate of technical change if capital and labour grow at different rates. In most of our cases, capital grows faster than labour. If this is the case and the substitution elasticity is specified as one when it is actually less than one, there will be an overestimation of the contribution of capital to growth and underestimation of the rate of technical change. On the other hand, if substitution elasticity is specified as one while it is actually greater than one, an overestimation of technical change will be the result. This can be explained intuitively by the fact that the smaller the elasticity of substitution the more difficult it is to achieve increased output simply by increasing one factor relative to another. Thus, an overstated elasticity of substitution will overstate the contribution of increases in the capital-labour ratio to productivity increases. Rigorously, this can be shown by rewriting the Kmenta approximation of the CES production function {equation (17)} in the following form:[59]

$$\frac{dA}{A} = \frac{dY}{Y} - vb\frac{dK}{K} - v(1-b)\frac{dL}{L} - \tfrac{1}{2}b(1-b)\frac{\sigma-1}{\sigma}\left(\frac{dK}{K} - \frac{dL}{L}\right)^2 \quad (17')$$

It can be readily seen from equation (17′) that when the elasticity of substitution (σ) has been overstated, dA/A (the rate of technical progress) will be understated, and vice versa. In addition the extent of bias in the estimate of the rate of technical progress when the substitution elasticity is misspecified depends on the magnitude of $dK/K - dL/L$. If $dK/K - dL/L = 0$, the rate of technical progress will not be affected by the value of elasticity of substitution. As far as our economies are concerned the K/L ratio did not rise very rapidly during the period under study. This is due to the fact that although capital grew very rapidly the growth in the labour force was also very fast. In addition, the period under consideration is relatively short so that the change in K/L ratio cannot be too large under any circumstances. Thus, even though we found in a number of cases that elasticities of substitution are significantly different from one, the results obtained from the Cobb-Douglas estimations can still largely be retained. On the other hand, we must also recognise that estimations of CES functions are still important and useful endeavours because they enable us to obtain information of substitution elasticities which are important in many ways other than their impact on the estimated rates of technical progress. Looking at our results we nonetheless observe that the rising K/L ratio in our economies coupled with the resulting lower-than-unity estimated substitution elasticities have given rise to higher estimated rate of technical progress than the Cobb-Douglas estimates in most cases. However, it can also be observed that although the Cobb-Douglas function and the CES function give rise to estimates of technical progress of different magnitude, the two sets of estimates in most cases are quite similar in relative terms. Specifically, a sector which has a relatively high estimated technical progress in the Cobb-Douglas case usually also has a relatively high estimate in the CES case. The greatest differences between the two sets of estimates of technical progress occur in the cases of Hong Kong manufacturing, Japanese and Taiwan agriculture. In the case of Hong Kong, however, the estimated rate of technical progress is not statistically significant in the present CES estimation, and furthermore the estimated rate of technical progress in this case is bound to be unreliable as the estimated elasticity of substitution is greater than one. As we have pointed out before, when the estimated elasticity of substitution approaches one, the calculated rate of technical progress will approach infinity in the estimation of equation (26). For the same reason, we should not take the present CES estimates of technical progress in Taiwan agriculture seriously as the estimated elasticity of substitution is very close to one. In these two cases, we should therefore only consider the Cobb-Douglas estimates. In the case of Japanese agriculture, Cobb-Douglas estimations give rise to unreasonable parameter estimates of both output elasticity of capital and technical progress. From the much more plausible estimates obtained from the present CES estimation, it seems that Cobb-Douglas functions are not appropriate for Japanese agriculture to the extent that their use will seriously distort the parameter estimates. This is perhaps due to the fact that Japanese agriculture has experienced a more rapid increase in capital per worker than both Korea and Taiwan, and consequently the misspecification of the substitution elasticity leads to serious errors in the estimates. Thus, in the case of Japanese agricultural, we should only take the present CES estimates into consideration.

More recently, the CES production function has been further generalised to allow for variable elasticity of substitution between inputs. These generalised production functions are now known as the variable elasticity of substitution (VES) production functions.[60] In the VES production functions, it is usually assumed that the substitution elasticity is a function of the capital-labour ratio. Thus, as long as the capital–labour ratios do not fluctuate over a wide range, the CES and

VES production functions normally generate very similar results. As a crude test of the empirical relevance of the VES production function to the economies under study, we attempt to fit data of our economies to a time-series version of the LIU-HILDEBRAND VES production which is specified as:

$$Y/L = Ae^{\lambda t}[b(K/L)^{-\rho} + a(K/L)^{-m\rho}]^{-1/\rho} \qquad (27)$$

Using the method described above {equations $(14) - (26)$}, the following equation suitable for estimation can be obtained from (27):

$$\ln Y/L = a_0 + a_1 \ln w + a_2 \ln K/L + a_3 t \qquad (28)$$

where $a_1 = 1/(1 + \rho)$
$a_2 = \rho m/(1 + \rho)$
$a_3 = \lambda/(1 - \sigma)$

The variable elasticity of substitution in the above equations is defined as: $\dfrac{1}{(1 + \rho) - (\rho m/S_k)}$, where $m = a_2(1 + \rho)/\rho$, and S_k is capital's share in income.[61] It can be seen that equation (28) differs from equation (26) only in the inclusion of the term, $\ln K/L$. Thus, a test of the statistical significance of the regression coefficient of $\ln K/L$ indicates whether the VES production function should be preferred to the CES function. The regression results of equation (28) with data of our economies show that in no case was the regression coefficient of $\ln K/L$ statistically significant at the 5 per cent level. In consequence, the results are not discussed but just reported in Appendix C, Table A.17.

With so much on the estimation of production functions assuming exogenously determined technical progress, we shall consider endogenous technical progress in the next chapter.

5 The Determinants of Technical Progress

INTRODUCTION

In the last chapter, we examined in some detail the role of technical progress in the economic growth of the five economies in our study. We attempted to measure the rate of technical progress by alternative methods. Without exception, we found that technical progress has played an important part in the rapid growth of all the economies during the subject period. However, the estimation of the rate of technical progress has so far been confined to the assumption of exogenous technical progress. We assumed that technical progress just appears like manna falling from heaven; it is costless and does not depend on other economic variables in our model. It is perhaps true that many of the factors that govern the rate and direction of technical progress are outside the usual boundaries of economics. Nevertheless, the treatment of technical progress as entirely exogenous is clearly unrealistic. Some factors we customarily include as variables in economic models may influence the rate of technical progress in important ways. In particular, it is very likely that technical progress can be influenced by investment activities. In the last decade or so, some attempts have been made to construct macro-economic models with the assumption of endogenous technical progress. This brighter side of the story has unfortunately not penetrated the empirical literature on growth and distribution. Extremely little has been done to test the endogenous technical progress hypotheses and apply them to describe the growth experience of developed and developing economies. This is especially astonishing when we at the same time observe the ever-increasing empirical work based on the assumption of exogenous technical progress. The purpose here is to test the various endogenous technical progress hypotheses with the data of the five economies. In doing so, we shall be able to throw some light on the determinants of technical progress in these fast-growing Asian economies.

ENDOGENOUS TECHNICAL PROGRESS HYPOTHESES

In this section, we shall briefly review the literature on endogenous technical progress.[1] We shall however confine our review to material on the testable endogenous technical progress hypotheses which we are going to discuss. We shall therefore omit the induced bias theories and those theories which relate the rate of technical progress to the resources devoted to research and development. We are leaving out the induced bias theories because at present we are mainly interested in the rate rather than the direction of technical progress. We are leaving out the theories incorporating resources devoted to research and development because the research sector is as a rule not identifiable, except perhaps in the case of Japan. For instance, in the case of Hong Kong, a research sector hardly exists; technology is mainly imported from abroad. Moreover, data on research inputs are in general very deficient. Nevertheless, in one of the theories we describe below, research and development activities are implicitly involved.

It was Kaldor (1957) who first introduced the notion that technical progress is to be explained by the process of investment itself. He postulated that the proportionate growth rate of output per worker ($\dot{y}$) is an increasing function (but with decreasing slope) of the proportionate growth rate of capital per work (K/L), i.e.

$$\dot{y} = F(K/L) \qquad \text{and} \quad F' > 0; \qquad F'' < 0; \qquad F(0) > 0$$

Assuming that technical progress is completely labour-augmenting, the above equation is a technical progress function expressing the rate of technical progress as a function of the proportionate growth rate of capital per worker. The tehcnical progress function is assumed to exhibit some kind of diminishing returns, and when capital per worker is constant, technical progress will depend on exogenous drift.[2] Assuming that the postulated relationships are linear, Kaldor's technical progress function can be expressed as

$$\lambda = a + b \ (K/L) \tag{1}$$

Where λ is the rate of technical progress which is both exogenously and endogenously determined; a is the rate of exogenous technical progress, similar to the symbol λ defined in Chapter 4 where technical progress is always treated as exogenous.

Learning as a process of acquiring knowledge has long been studied by psychologists and production management scientists. There exists empirical evidence of increased productivity due to learning from experience. The best evidence is the finding of Wright (1936) who observed that the number of man-hours required to produce an airframe was a decreasing function of the number of airframes of the same type previously produced. Such a relationship was found to be very precise; the amount of labour required to produce the Nth airframe is equal to $aN^{-1/3}$, where a is a constant. There are also other studies which attempt to relate labour productivity to learning-by-doing in some specific production processes, mainly in the defense industries.[3] However, it was not until Arrow's (1962) seminal paper that the concept of learning by doing was incorporated into a macroeconomic model. Arrow's aim was to build up a neoclassicial growth model in which at least part of technical progress does not depend on the passage of time as such but develops out of experience gained within the production process itself. In relating technical progress to experience, Arrow chose cumulative gross investment as the index of experience while previous studies favoured cumulative output as an index. Arrow argued that the appearance of new machines provides more stimulation to innovation while cumulative output (say output growing at a roughly constant rate) is very uninspiring to innovation.[4] Arrow's growth model is built upon the assumptions of a fixed coefficient production function, embodying labour-augmenting technical progress, full employment, constant exponential growth of its labour force and a constant saving ratio. The notion of a learning by doing is incorporated in the assumption that a labour efficiency index associated with workers of a particular vintage is a strictly increasing function of cumulative gross investment. Such a relationship is expressed as

$$A_t = A_0 . G_t^{c} \tag{2}$$

where A_t is the level of technology of time t;
A_0, the initial level of technology;
G, the index of learning, measured by cumulative gross investment;
c, the learning coefficient, or in other words it is the elasticity of A_t with respect to the index G.

Thus, both Kaldor (1957) and Arrow (1962) related the rate of technical progress to investment activities. More recently, Eltis (1971,

1973) has analysed the entrepreneurial decision on research and development expenditure, and used the results to link investment with technical progress at the macroeconomic level. Instead of relating technical progress to the growth rate of the capital-labour ratio, or investment per worker, or cumulative gross investment, Eltis sees the share of investment in income as the crucial factor affecting the rate of technical progress.[5] Eltis' analysis can be shown by the following diagram:

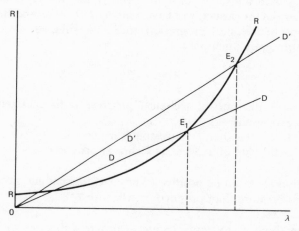

Figure 5.1

The vertical axis measures the annual research and development expenditure (R) and the amount of expected earnings from successful research and development activities. The horizontal axis measures the annual rate of cost reduction (λ) which is an index of technical progress (both exogenous and endogenous). RR shows the relationship between research and development expenditure and the rate of cost reduction; it cuts the vertical axis above the origin indicating that there is a setup cost of research and development. Moreover, RR is upward sloping and convex from below $(dR/d\lambda > 0;\ d^2R/d\lambda^2 > 0)$, meaning that a higher rate of cost reduction has to be brought about by a higher R, and it becomes increasingly expensive to reduce cost at a higher proportional rate. Assuming that the expected earnings from successful research and development activities are proportional to the annual rate of cost reduction resulting from the discovery, and to the total expected sales of equipment, we can draw DD, the expected earning curve, as a straight line passing through the origin. Thus the *DD* curve will shift to the left when there is a rise in the expected sale of equipment. The intersection of the *RR* and *DD* curves at E_1 represents a position of long run profit maximisation in an industry where entry is the likely consequence of abnormal profits. When there is an increase in the share of investment in income, the demand for equipment will be increased and as a result the *DD* curve will shift to $D'D'$. A new equilibrium will be established at E_2, at which a higher rate of cost reduction is attained. Thus, in two economies with the same constant labour force, the economy with a higher share of investment will have a higher *DD* curve, and therefore a higher rate of technical progress. Hence Eltis suggests the following technical progress function:

$$\lambda = a + b(I/Y) \tag{3}$$

where λ is the rate of technical progress both endogenous and exogenous;

I/Y is the share of investment in income;

a, the rate of exogenous technical progress.

In equation (3) a can be positive or negative, depending on whether λ varies less or more than proportionately with I/Y.

All the above endogenous technical progress theories we have just reviewed are however confined to a closed economy. They are therefore applicable only to the advanced economies which do not rely on foreign technology. In almost all developing economies, the inflow of foreign technology constitutes the major source of technical progress. The foreign trade sector as an engine of technical progress is a neglected topic in the theories of growth and development. For instance, all five economies of this study rely heavily on imported foreign technology for their economic growth. Even in the case of Japan, the inflow of foreign technology plays an important part in her post-war economic growth.[6] Thus, any satisfactory endogenous technical progress function describing the developing countries must take the borrowing of foreign technology into account. In this study, the amount of imported capital goods (M') is taken as an indicator of imported foreign technology.[7] There are several justifications for choosing imported capital goods as our index. In the first place, modern technology is very often embodied in the machinery and equipment imported by the developing countries. Secondly, the installation and working of such machinery and equipment require special skill and very often changes in organisation and management. Thus the importation of disembodied technical progress in the form of improvements in organisation, management and skill are also reflected by the amount of capital goods imported. Thirdly, even the importation of the same type of machinery and equipment over time will contribute to technical progress as it will help to diffuse technical skill over the whole economy. The more widespread the use of particular techniques, the higher will be the overall rate of technical progress in the economy. Evidently, the absolute amount of capital goods import is not a satisfactory variable to be included in the technical progress function. A more preferred index should be the proportion of capital goods import in total import (M'/M), or that of capital goods import in gross investment (M'/I). On *a priori* grounds, the latter, i.e. M'/I, should be a more meaningful index as M' is directly related to investment and hence increases in the importance of imported technology should be reflected by increases in the proportion of imported capital goods in total investment. On the other hand, if the trend of total import has been a steadily increasing one, then the increased proportion of imported capital goods in total import could also be a good indicator of technology import. Under these circumstances, both indices, i.e. M'/I and M'/M, will be used and the choice between the two in each case will be judged on economic and statistical criteria. With the inclusion of the technology import component, the Kaldor technical progress function becomes

$$\lambda = a + b(K/L) + m(TM) \tag{4}$$

and the Eltis technical progress function is now represented by:

$$\lambda = a + b(I/Y) + m(TM) \tag{5}$$

where TM is technology import represented by either M'/M or M'/I.

The original and the above modified forms of the Kaldor-Eltis technical progress functions will be used in the testing of endogenous technical progress hypotheses to be presented in the next section.

THE ESTIMATING EQUATIONS

We shall use basically the same estimating methods as we employed in

Chapter 4. Specifically, we shall estimate the Cobb-Douglas production function by the usual log-linear method.[8] Of course, in the present case technical progress is no longer confined to the trend term, but is also affected by other economic variables in the model. This, however, only amounts to some minor modifications of the estimating equations with which we have already dealt.

(1) Learning By Doing

Assuming Hicks-neutral technical progress,[9] and that technical progress is partly exogenous and partly the result of learning by doing, the relationship between inputs and output can be represented by:

$$Y_t = A_0 e^{at} G_t^c f(K_t, L_t) \tag{6}$$

where A_0 is the initial level of technology,
         G, the index of experience,
         c, the coefficient of learning,
         a, the rate of exogenous technical progress.

Similarly, if technical progress is assumed to be wholly the result of learning by doing, the production relationship is:

$$Y_t = A_0 G_g^c f(K_t, L_t) \tag{7}$$

Specifying a constant-returns-to-scale Cobb-Douglas production function and taking logarithms on both sides, we have the following estimating equations (9) and (10) corresponding to equations (6) and (7):[10]

$$\ln Y/L = \text{constant} + \beta \ln K/L + at + c\ln G \tag{8}$$
$$\ln Y/L = \text{constant} + \beta \ln K/L + c\ln G \tag{9}$$

In estimating equations (8) and (9), we shall try both cumulative output and cumulative gross investment as an index of experience. There is no *a priori* reason to believe which one is more appropriate for our purpose.

(2) Kaldor-Eltis Technical Progress Functions

A production function with Hick-neutral technical progress is represented by:

$$Y_t = A_0 e^{\lambda t} f(K_t, L_t) \tag{10}$$

Incorporating the endogenous technical progress functions of Kaldor and Eltis of equations (1) and (3) into (13) and omitting the time subscripts, we have the following:

$$Y = A_0 e^{(a + bK/L)t} f(K, L) \tag{11}$$
$$Y = A_0 e^{(a + bI/Y)t} f(K, L) \tag{12}$$

In the Cobb-Douglas case, the following estimating equations are obtained:

$$\ln Y/L = \text{constant} + \beta \ln K/L + at + b(K/L)t \tag{13}$$
$$\ln Y/L = \text{constant} + \beta \ln K/L + at + b(I/Y)t \tag{14}$$

Now, if we take imports of capital goods as an index of the inflow of foreign technology, i.e. we substitute equations (4), and (5) into equation (10), we obtain the following additional estimating equations:

$$\ln Y/L = \text{constant} + \beta \ln K/L + at + b(K/L)t + m(TM)t \tag{15}$$
$$\ln Y/L = \text{constant} + \beta \ln K/L + at + b(I/Y)t + m(TM)t \tag{16}$$

In addition we hypothesise that technical progress in the five economies of the study is entirely the result of the inflow of technology from abroad. We then have

$$\ln Y/L = \text{constant} + \beta \ln K/L + at + m(TM)t \tag{17}$$

EMPIRICAL RESULTS

Data on the manufacturing sector of the five economies under study are fitted to equations (8) and (9) for testing the learning by doing hypothesis, and to equations (13) to (17) for testing the Kaldor-Eltis technical progress functions.

(1) Learning By Doing

Table 5.1 reports the regression estimates of equations (8) and (9), the Cobb-Douglas estimations of learning by doing. In all the estimations, the statistical fit has been extremely good,[11] and there is no indication of serial correlation as revealed by the Durbin-Watson statistic. There seems to be no discrimination in using the index of cumulative gross investment or cumulative output as the goodness-of-fit in the two cases are more or less the same. At the same time, the two indices do not give rise to contradictory results with regard to our significance tests.[12]

TABLE 5.1 Testing the Learning By Doing Hypothesis

	In K/L	*t*	*In ΣI*	*In ΣY*	*D − W*	$\bar{R}^2$
		The regression coefficient of				
Hong Kong	0.413 (0.145)	0.0480 (0.0148)	− 0.0847 (0.0705)		2.30	0.984
	0.391 (0.121)	0.0448 (0.0117)		− 0.0894 (0.0683)	2.15	0.984
	0.147 (0.176)		0.1186 (0.0471)		1.51	0.959
	0.220 (0.185)			0.1261 (0.0632)	1.36	0.951
Japan	0.036 (0.396)	0.0821 (0.0437)	0.0075 (0.0035)		1.34	0.984
	− 0.107 (0.407)	0.0923 (0.0472)		0.0083 (0.0062)	1.35	0.984
	0.689 (0.095)		0.0683 (0.0335)		1.12	0.979
	0.666 (0.110)			0.0849 (0.0406)	1.14	0.979
Korea	0.544 (0.091)	0.0530 (0.0138)	− 0.0537 (0.0450)		1.59	0.954
	0.568 (0.098)	0.0460 (0.0132)		− 0.0363 (0.0516)	1.55	0.948
	0.715 (0.131)		0.1147 (0.0166)		1.33	0.857
	0.733 (0.132)			0.1373 (0.0197)	1.30	0.859
Singapore	0.375 (0.261)	0.0147 (0.0230)	0.0569 (0.0605)		1.33	0.881
	0.365 (0.239)	0.0043 (0.0278)		0.0911 (0.0791)	1.33	0.890
	0.241 (0.152)		0.0948 (0.0124)		1.33	0.884
	0.337 (0.149)			0.1032 (0.0127)	1.33	0.896
Taiwan	0.120 (0.260)	0.0981 (0.0404)	− 0.120 (0.105)		1.44	0.973
	0.134 (0.337)	0.0892 (0.0495)		− 0.0944 (0.1277)	1.44	0.972
	0.695 (0.125)		0.124 (0.035)		1.21	0.964
	0.713 (0.110)			0.1290 (0.0333)	1.21	0.967

From the results shown in Table 5.1, we can divide the five economies into three categories in accordance with the importance of learning effects: (1) Hong Kong, Korea and Taiwan, showing little or no learning effect, (2) Singapore, where learning effects have some influence on technical progress, and (3) Japan, indicating considerable effects of learning by doing.

For Hong Kong, the learning coefficient bears a negative sign (though not statistically significant) when both the trend term and the learning variable are included in the regression. Even when technical progress is assumed to be completely dependent on learning effects, the learning coefficient is positive but only marginally significant. However, as the F-value in fact declines significantly when the trend term is dropped, the model with both exogenous and learning effects on technical progress is the more relevant. Thus our results do not suggest that learning by doing effects are significant in the manufacturing sector of Hong Kong. The results for Korea are in general very similar to those obtained for Hong Kong. In the estimation of equation (8) in which both the time trend and the learning index are included, the learning coefficients bear a negative sign (though statistically insignificant) while the coefficients of the trend term remain highly significant. However, when only the learning variable is included, the learning coefficients turn out to be positive and highly significant. Yet, we should not put too much weight on this result as the goodness-of-fit is much worsened when the trend term is dropped from the regression. Thus evidence is still in favour of the proposition of negligible learning effect in the manufacturing sector of Korea.

The results for Taiwan are again very similar to Hong Kong and Korea. The learning coefficients when standing by themselves alone are statistically significant. However, once when the time trend is also included in the estimation, the learning coefficients become negative though not statistically significant. On the other hand, the regression coefficients of the trend term remain statistically significant (though only marginally) when learning effects are assumed to be present. Thus in the case of Taiwan, exogenous technical progress has relatively stronger effects than learning by doing on productivity growth.

In the case of Singapore, the estimated rate of exogenous technical progress and learning coefficient are both positive but statistically insignificant at the five per cent level. This indicates that technical progress is subject to some learning effects as the statistical significance of the conventional trend term coefficient in this case cannot survive the addition of a learning variable. The presence of learning effects is further confirmed by the estimation of equation (10) in which the trend term is dropped. In such an estimation the learning coefficients become highly significant and in fact the statistical fit is better for equation (10) than equation (9). Thus, we may conclude that technical progress is to a considerable extent affected by learning by doing; however, the learning effect should not be over emphasised as the learning coefficients are not statistically significant in the presence of the conventional trend term.

It is in the case of Japan that we find very strong effects of learning by doing on the rate of technical progress. From Table 5.1 we can see that the trend term coefficients become insignificant when a learning variable is included in the regression, and the learning coefficient is statistically significant when cumulative gross investment is used as an index. When we exclude the trend term in the regression we obtain highly significant learning coefficients. Indeed, the statistical fit is much better in the cases where technical progress is partly exogenous and partly affected by learning than the case in which technical progress is completely exogenous. We can therefore conclude that in the manufacturing sector of Japan, learning by doing is more powerful in explaining the shift of the production function than the conventional trend term.

Our whole exercise of testing the learning-by-doing hypothesis seems to suggest that the relative importance of the effects of learning on productivity increases depends very much on the relative level of technology already achieved. Our results indicate that the higher the level of technology already achieved, the greater will the effects of learning by doing be. Japan, with a great deal of technical heritage and having achieved a relatively high level of technology even before the War, has therefore greater learning effects on technical progress. On the other hand, the learning-by-doing hypothesis is to a great extent not applicable to the other four economies which commenced on their path of rapid growth and structural change only in the sixties and have achieved a relatively much lower level of technology. At the same time, we observe that in Singapore relatively stronger learning effects are present than in Hong Kong, Korea and Taiwan. There are reasons for us to believe that Singapore had achieved a higher absolute level of technology than Hong Kong, Korea and Taiwan at the beginning of the period under study. Singapore even before her full industrialisation programme in 1961 had some sophisticated industries with advanced technical skill such as food processing, petroleum refining, engineering and transport equipment. There were a considerable number of pioneer foreign firms taking the lead in developing modern technology even in the fifties. Taiwan benefited to some extent from the technological foundation built by the Japanese during her Colonial period. But the extent of benefit could not have been very important. Korea benefited much less from the period of Japanese rule. A considerable amount of modernisation and development did take place under the Japanese, but primarily in the Japanese sector designed to serve Japanese rather than Korean objectives.[13] In addition, Korea suffered from a period of war (1950–4), and economic and political instability (1958–62). Her period of rapid growth can be taken to have started only from 1963. Hong Kong, unlike Singapore, had no sophisticated industries demanding high skills before the sixties. She relied almost entirely on indigenous and labour-intensive methods of production in the manufacturing sector which produced mainly textile and plastic goods. There were also fewer pioneer foreign firms in industry, and there has been a lack of government support and encouragement for research and development. The rate of technical progress might have been rapid in Hong Kong manufacturing during the period under study, but it must be quite true that its absolute level of technology achieved was relatively low at the beginning of the period.

The hypothesis that the relative importance of learning effects is related to the level of technology already achieved at the beginning of the period is not without appeal to common sense. It is very likely that the more advanced and efficient a production process, the better the chance for the sheer repetition of that process to give rise to further increase in productivity. Most of the studies on learning by doing in the literature deal with defence industries, in particular the aircraft industry. These are usually the industries which embrace the most advanced skill and knowledge of the time and therefore reveal strong learning effects on productivity increases. On the other hand, in most underdeveloped economies, in spite of the long period of engagement in a particular line of production, e.g. spinning and weaving, productivity remains low. The absence of learning effects in these case may then be attributable to the low level of technology used at the very beginning.

(2) Kaldor-Eltis Technical Progress Functions

Table 5.2 reports Cobb-Douglas estimates of equations (13) to (17). As expected, in most of the cases the use of M'/I as an index of imported technology gives better statistical fits than the index M'/M. The only exception is the case of Hong Kong. Consequently, the results reported in Table 5.2 are with reference to M'/M in the case of Hong Kong and with reference to M'/I in all other cases. However, it should be noted that even in the case of Hong Kong the differences in the use of the two set indices are purely statistical. The use of M'/M and M'/I gives similar results as far as testing the importance of imported technology in productivity growth is concerned. The regression results suggest the division of the five economies under study into three groups, though the countries are not necessarily grouped in the same way as the learning-by-doing case. The three categories are: (1) Japan, in which the endogenous technical progress hypothesis strongly holds with reference to the propositions of Kaldor and Eltis, i.e. technical progress is related to investment activities, (2) Hong Kong, Singapore and Taiwan, in which technical progress is related to the importation of foreign technology rather than investment activities, and (3) Korea, in which the endogenous technical progress hypothesis can be rejected with reference to either investment activities or importation of foreign technology.

Examining the case of Japan in Table 5.2, we observe that the coefficients of the trend term (which denote exogenous technical progress) become statistically insignificant whenever I/Y is included in the regression irrespective of whether M'/I is also included or not. On the other hand, the coefficients of I/Y are highly significant. However, the coefficients of the trend term continue to be significant when K/L or M'/I are built into the model, though the coefficient of K/L is statistically significant whether M'/I is excluded or included. In all cases, the coefficients of M'/I are insignificant, and bear a negative sign. Indeed, when K/L and/or M'/I are present the estimated capital coefficients turn out to be negative or exceedingly small suggesting their inapplicability to the model.[14] Our regression results suggest that I/Y is by far the most important determinant of technical progress in Japanese manufacturing; the effects of K/L are also considerable but those of M'/I are of minor importance. We can therefore reject the assumption that technical progress is wholly exogenously determined in the manufacturing sector of Japan, but accept the hypothesis that technical progress is largely determined by investment activities.

From the results of the estimation for Hong Kong shown in Table 5.2, we observe that the coefficients of the trend term remain highly significant irrespective of whether I/Y, or K/L, is included in the technical progress function. However, while the coefficient of I/Y is insignificant, that of K/L is significant; this indicates that to some extent the rate of technical progress is related to the rate of changes in capital per worker. Nevertheless, once we introduce the import of capital goods into the model (in this case represented by M'/M), the coefficients of the trend term become insignificant and even bear a negative sign in two estimations. At the same time, when M'/M is present the coefficients of I/Y and even that of K/L are statistically insignificant. On the other

TABLE 5.2 Testing the Kaldor-Eltis Technical Progress Functions

Country	ln K/L	t	Investment activities	Technology Import	$\bar{R}^2$	D – W
Hong Kong	0.3801 (0.0720)	−0.0291 (0.0239)		0.2756 (M'/M)t (0.1050)	0.986	2.46
	0.2622 (0.0791)	0.0314 (0.0113)	0.0021 (I/Y)t (0.0250)		0.972	2.24
	0.2012 (0.0701)	0.414 (0.0062)	0.0486 (K̇/L)t (0.0162)		0.986	2.65
	0.3814 (0.0772)	−0.0310 (0.0269)	0.0046 (I/Y)t (0.0192)	0.2765 (M'/M)t (0.1128)	0.983	2.68
	0.2524 (0.1561)	0.0233 (0.0492)	0.0383 (K̇/L)t (0.0329)	0.0707 (M'/M)t (0.0907)	0.984	2.53
Japan	0.0084 (0.2975)	0.0926 (0.0272)		−0.1170 (M'/I)t (0.0692)	0.984	1.30
	0.2448 (0.1724)	0.0236 (0.0185)	0.0978 (I/Y)t (0.0164)		0.995	2.76
	−0.4469 (0.4110)	0.1123 (0.0380)	0.0962 (K̇/L)t (0.0414)		0.984	1.91
	0.2450 (0.1799)	0.0247 (0.0210)	0.0965 (I/Y)t (0.0195)	−0.0063 (M'/I)t (0.0462)	0.995	2.76
	0.0081 (0.4148)	0.0915 (0.0357)	0.0929 (K̇/L)t (0.0372)	−0.1293 (M;/I)t (0.6733)	0.987	2.34
Korea	0.7175 (0.0809)	0.0548 (0.0091)		−0.0077 (M'/I)t (0.0038)	0.950	2.02
	0.5937 (0.0782)	0.0430 (0.0080)	−0.0231 (I/Y)t (0.0281)		0.928	1.80
	0.4513 (0.1117)	0.0299 (0.0058)	0.0335 (K̇/L)t (0.0212)		0.948	1.46
	0.6993 (0.0835)	0.0606 (0.0109)	−0.0225 (I/Y)t (0.0234)	−0.0077 (M'/I)t (0.0038)	0.950	2.18
	0.6297 (0.1482)	0.0513 (0.0142)	0.0126 (K̇/L)t (0.0228)	−0.0071 (M'/I)t (0.0044)	0.959	1.77
Singapore	0.7378 (0.1612)	0.0213 (0.0072)		0.0117 (M'/I)t (0.0048)	0.903	2.03
	0.7916 (0.1911)	0.0586 (0.0118)	−0.0419 (I/Y)t (0.0205)		0.890	1.34
	0.1714 (0.2153)	0.0249 (0.0059)	0.0228 (K̇/L)t (0.0029)		0.751	1.85
	0.7858 (0.1879)	0.0348 (0.0242)	−0.0175 (I/Y)t (0.0296)	0.0085 (M'/I)t (0.0065)	0.893	1.90
	0.8262 (0.1605)	0.0059 (0.0045)	−0.0608 (K̇/L)t (0.0209)	0.0180 (M'/I)t (0.0035)	0.951	2.57
Taiwan	0.2926 (0.1518)	0.0451 (0.0111)		0.0089 (M'/I)t (0.0041)	0.979	1.80
	0.4509 (0.1271)	0.0669 (0.0093)	−0.0474 (I/Y)t (0.0135)		0.986	1.95

continued on p. 104

Table 5.2 *(Contd.)*

			Regression Coefficient of			
Country	In K/L	t	Investment activities	Technology Import	$\bar{R}^2$	$D-W$
	0.2784 (0.2129)	0.0612 (0.0151)	−0.0119 (K /L)t (0.0202)		0.970	1.70
Taiwan	0.4797 (0.1537)	0.0709 (0.0147)	−0.0544 (I/Y)t (0.0236)	0.0022 (M'/I)t (0.0059)	0.984	1.93
	0.1038 (0.1989)	0.0532 (0.0135)	0.0216 (K /L)t (0.0230)	0.0121 (M'/I)t (0.0054)	0.978	1.57

hand, the coefficients of M'/M are invariably positive and statistically significant in two out of our three estimations; the exception occurs when both K/L and M'/M are included in the technical progress function.[15] It then seems that investment activities have relatively little impact on the rate of technical change in Hong Kong manufacturing, though we cannot perhaps ignore altogether the effect of the rate of change in capital per worker. By far the most important determinant of technical progress is the import of foreign technology as represented by the proportion of capital goods imports in total imports.

In the case of Singapore, the results suggest that even to a greater extent than Hong Kong technical progress is not at all related to investment activities. The coefficients of the trend term survive very well the inclusion of I/Y and K/L into the model; they remain highly statistically significant in both cases. On the other hand, four of the five regression coefficients associated with I/Y and K/L bear a negative sign and some of them are even statistically significant. This insignificance of investment activities in the technical progress function holds true no matter whether the index of imported technology (represented by M'/I) is included in the technical progress function or not. Looking at the effects of imported technology on technical progress, we find that the regression coefficients of M'/I are positive and statistically significant at the 5 per cent level in two estimations and at the 25 per cent level in the estimation where I/Y is also included as an explanatory factor of technical progress. We can thus conclude that like Hong Kong the most important determinant of technical progress in Singapore manufacturing is the inflow of technology from abroad.

In some ways similar to Hong Kong and Singapore, the results for Taiwan also show that technology import as represented by M'/I exerts significant influence on technical progress. The regression coefficients of

M'/I are statistically significant in two estimations but insignificant in the case where I/Y is also included as a determinant of technical progress. Very much like Singapore, it is certain that investment activities have little influence on technical progress in Taiwan manufacturing; the regression coefficients of K/L and I/Y bear a negative sign in three out of the four estimations performed, and in the remaining case the coefficient is positive but hardly significant. On the other hand, it is worth noting that the regression coefficients of the trend term remain positive and highly statistically significant in every estimation no matter which of our determinants of technical progress are included. This suggests that besides the considerable effects of imported technology on technical progress, the exogenously determined technical progress cannot be ignored in Taiwan manufacturing.

The results for Korea are quite surprising. It should be expected that if the Korean experience were to be different from the other three economies under study it should still be very close to that of Taiwan. Specifically, as both Korea and Taiwan received massive foreign aid and imports of capital goods during their period of modern growth, it is expected that technical progress in these two countries should be closely related to the import of foreign technology. On the contrary, the results for Korea show that technology import as represented by M'/I (or M'/M which gives similar results but a worse statistical fit) is not at all a determinant of technical progress. Indeed, it is disturbing to find that all regression coefficients of M'/I are negative and in one estimation even significantly negative. Also, there is no indication that investment activities are important determinants of technical progress. On the other hand, like the case of Taiwan the regression coefficients of the trend term remain highly statistically significant in all estimations. It seems that we have no way of explaining these statistical results but must instead resort to alternative specification of the index representing technology import. This will be done towards the end of this chapter.

The results we have obtained so far for Japan, Hong Kong, Singapore and Taiwan are very much in line with our intuitive expectations. Japan, being a developed nation with the high level of technology already achieved, naturally depends for her technical progress on her own effort more than from borrowing technology from abroad. She might have relied heavily on inflow of technology in the first decade after the War, but since the late fifties she has emerged as a net exporter rather than importer of technology. Even if technology is imported, it is modified and improved to suit the best interests of Japanese production. This has been called 'the art of improvement engineering'. Hong Kong and

Singapore are both tiny city economies with little natural resources, and both economies were lacking skill and technical man power at the beginning of economic development. Manufacturing establishments are generally small in size, and hence cannot afford to undertake research and development activities. In Hong Kong, the practice of a laissez-faire policy deprives research and development and technical training of any government support and encouragement. This was much less true in Singapore in the sixties when the government was determined to launch an industrialisation programme. However, even in Singapore government support in the development of indigenous techniques is indirect. The government's attention rather is focused on attracting pioneer foreign firms by means of legislation, e.g. tax concessions and stricter labour laws. As a result of high growth rates and high saving propensities neither Hong Kong nor Singapore have a shortage of capital resources. However, foreign investment is very much encouraged and welcomed for the sake of introducing foreign technology into the economy. All in all, it is therefore not surprising to find that the import of capital goods used as an index of foreign technology inflow constitutes the single most important determinant of technical progress in Hong Kong and Singapore. The inflow of foreign technology should be even more crucial to the productivity growth of Hong Kong manufacturing inasmuch as neither learning effects nor investment activities have an important influence on the rate of technical progress. On the other hand, learning has been found to have had a considerable effect on the productivity growth of Singapore manufacturing. As we have explained, the difference between the two city economies in the importance of learning effects is due to the probably higher absolute level of technology in Singapore manufacturing at an early stage of development. This probably higher level is in turn related to the nature of the industries established at the initial stage of development and government policy encouraging the inflow of foreign technology at the beginning of industrialisation. Similarly, finding imported technology to be important in Taiwan manufacturing is hardly surprising. Taiwan, with its low initial level of technology and lack of resources and skill with which to develop that technology at the early stages of development, had no choice but to rely on foreign technology. Fortunately for Taiwan, the massive inflows of United States loans and aid greatly facilitated its importing of technology from abroad. On the other hand, it is very difficult to explain the results for Korea. Like Taiwan, Korea also received massive aid and private capital inflows during its period of industrialisation; there is therefore no conceivable reason to explain the unimportance of imported technology as a determinant of technical progress. We suspect, therefore, that the unexpected results for Korea are due not to the misspecification of the technical progress function but the wrong choice of index to represent the inflow of foreign technology. On second thought, we might think that owing to a more disrupted economy and lower level of technology than Taiwan, Korea at the early stages of development and growth relied not just on imported capital goods but on imports of complete plants and planned-in-detail projects. From this point of view, the inflow of technology can perhaps be better represented by the amount of direct aid to the manufacturing sector. To test this hypothesis, we will specify the following technical progress functions:

$$\lambda = a + b(I/Y) + g(F/Y) \tag{18}$$
$$\lambda = a + b(K/L) + g(F/Y) \tag{19}$$

where (F/Y) is the share of official foreign aid directed to the manufacturing sector in total manufacturing output; thus (F/Y) instead of M'/I or M'/M is used as an index of the inflow of foreign technology.

Substituting (18) and (19) into a Cobb-Douglas production function with Hick-neutral technical progress and taking logarithms, we have the following estimating equations:

$$\ln Y/L = \text{constant} + \beta \ln K/L + at + b(I/Y)t + g(F/Y)t \tag{20}$$
$$\ln Y/L = \text{constant} + \beta \ln K/L + at + b(K/L)t + g(F/Y)t \tag{21}$$

In addition, (F/Y) is assumed to be the only endogenous economic variable influencing technical progress, and we have the following estimating equation:

$$\ln Y/L = \text{constant} + \beta \ln K/L + at + g(F/Y)t \tag{22}$$

Data on the manufacturing sector of Korea are fitted to equations (20) to (22). The regression results, which are reported in Table 5.3, support this hypothesis. The coefficients of F/Y are highly statistically significant in all the regressions performed.

The coefficients of the trend term are also highly significant indicating that the exogenous component of technical progress is also considerable. Despite the fact that technical progress has been shown to be partially exogenously determined, our study suggests that official aid plays a dominant role in determining technical progress in Korea. From our

TABLE 5.3 Capital Inflows and Technical Progress: Korea

The Regression Coefficient of

ln K/L	*t*	*(F/Y)t*	Investment activities	R^2	$D-W$
0.576	0.0282	0.148		0.979	2.32
(0.049)	(0.0033)	(0.043)			
0.552	0.0354	0.154	$-0.0289(I/Y)t$	0.987	2.98
(0.044)	(0.0048)	(0.038)	(0.0157)		
0.566	0.0292	0.145	$-0.0023(K/L)t$	0.983	1.95
(0.068)	(0.0038)	(0.058)	(0.0198)		

F/Y = the share of official foreign aid directed to the manufacturing sector in total manufacturing output
Source of data on F – Economic Planning Board, *Korea Statistical Yearbook*, 1971.

a priori knowledge, inflow of foreign technology should be closely associated with such official capital inflows into the manufacturing sector. Thus, in all cases of Hong Kong, Korea, Singapore, and Taiwan, we have found the inflow of foreign technology to be an important determinant of technical progress, though the inflow of technology might have taken different forms in different economies.

6 Export Performance and Economic Growth

THE GROWTH AND CHANGING STRUCTURE OF FOREIGN TRADE

All five economies have experienced spectacular development of foreign trade in the course of their rapid growth. Nevertheless, there are some differences in the pattern of foreign trade development. In Japan, rapid expansion of foreign trade began in the early twentieth century. Owing to the lack of natural resources, Japan's industrialisation process relies heavily on imports which have to be financed by expanded exports. Ever since the early stage of modern economic growth, it seems that Japan has never doubted its export capabilities and in consequence it has always adopted an outward-looking policy in its process of growth in the modern era. Both Korea and Taiwan, on the other hand, had reservations about their export capabilities at the beginning of their industrialisation. As a result, it was not until the late fifties in the case of Taiwan and the early sixties in the case of Korea that they turned their attention from import substitution to export orientation. The cases of Hong Kong and Singapore are rather special. Before industrialisation took place, they were *entrepôt* trade economies taking advantage of their geographical location and fine harbours. It was largely historical factors (Communist takeover in China, Korean War, etc.) that caused Hong Kong to switch from *entrepôt* trade to manufacturing industries.[1] Owing to the small home market, Hong Kong's manufactured products are mostly for exporting. In Singapore, on the other hand, both industrialisation and outward-looking policies are to a large extent the result of deliberate government action. Moreover, while the importance of *entrepôt* trade declines very rapidly after the beginning of industrialisation in Hong Kong, it has retained considerable importance in the Singapore economy.

Let us now look at some of the key indicators in the growth and changing structure of foreign trade in the five economies. In Table 6.1

statistics on the export and import ratios, the proportion of manufacturing exports and imports of capital goods in total exports and imports respectively, and the growth rates of total exports .and imports, manufacturing exports and capital goods imports are presented for three sub-periods, 1955–60, 1960–5, and 1965–70.[2] Looking at the export and import ratios, we find that the trade sector is very large in Hong Kong representing over 50 per cent of national output, and it is quite significant in Taiwan. On the other hand, the trade sector of Japan is not as large as one would have expected. As expected, the trade sector is also relatively large in Singapore but there is a wide discrepancy between the export and import ratios implying a huge deficit on the visible trade account. This reflects the fact that Singapore has a huge surplus on its net export of services and significant inflows of both short and long-term capital. A similar discrepancy between the export and import ratios can also be observed in the case of Korea. Here the net

TABLE 6.1 The Growth and Changing Structure of Foreign Trade
(in percentages)

Country	Period	$\dfrac{X}{Y}$	$\dfrac{M}{Y}$	$\dfrac{Xm}{X}$	$\dfrac{M'}{M}$	$\dot{X}$	$\dot{X}m$	$\dot{M}$	$\dot{M}'$
	1955–60	31.5	63.7	87.9	10.3	19.7	19.5	12.0	17.6
Hong Kong	1960–5	41.0	67.0	89.9	13.5	11.1	12.1	9.0	14.6
	1965–70	52.3	66.7	94.0	16.5	15.0	15.5	9.9	12.9
	1955–60	9.2	9.0	83.5	12.1	10.8	11.0	6.8	19.4
Japan	1960–5	8.6	8.1	84.6	14.8	10.2	10.5	6.5	5.2
	1965–70	9.4	7.4	87.8	13.2	12.2	12.7	12.2	18.0
	1955–60	0.6	10.7	14.4	17.2	−1.2	−0.4	−8.7	−13.7
Korea	1960–5	2.9	14.1	33.0	20.3	42.0	77.7	14.5	19.1
	1965–70	7.9	22.6	69.0	33.5	21.8	27.2	20.6	31.8
Singapore	1960–5	26.4	59.2	16.5	11.3	4.7	14.0	4.4	22.4
	1965–70	29.1	70.2	24.9	13.9	13.9	20.5	19.2	21.6
	1955–60	10.9	14.7	16.4	30.0	11.5	39.3	10.1	20.5
Taiwan	1960–5	15.1	16.5	41.9	34.5	18.7	24.6	12.4	9.8
	1965–70	23.1	22.2	57.1	43.4	18.3	29.0	17.6	21.2

X – export of goods
M – Import of goods
Xm – Export of manufactured goods
M' – Import of capital goods
$\dot{X}$, $\dot{X}m$, $\dot{M}$, and $\dot{M}'$ are exponential growth rates obtained by regressing
ln Z (where Z = X, Xm, M, M') on t (where t = time).

Sources: See Appendix A, Tables A.1–A.5.

surplus in the export of services is limited and the deficit has been mainly financed by the inflow of capital. As to the composition of exports, we observe that some 90 per cent of Hong Kong's exports and over 80 per cent of those of Japan are manufactured products. As early as the period 1955–60 manufactured products constituted 88 per cent of total exports in Hong Kong and the percentage has increased to 94 per cent for the period 1965–70. This shows that right from the very beginning manufactured products are for exports in the case of Hong Kong. Even in Japan the proportion of manufactured products has been steadily growing. In the cases of Korea, Singapore and Taiwan, the proportion of manufactured goods in total exports has been growing rapidly over the sub-periods. The increase is particularly dramatic in the late sixties in Korea and in the early sixties in Taiwan. While manufactured goods accounted for 69 per cent of total exports in Korea and 57 per cent in Taiwan for the sub-period 1965–70, they still only constituted 25 per cent in Singapore. However, given the strong emphasis of the government currently on industrialisation and outward-looking policies, one might expect manufacturing exports to expand very rapidly. For the import of capital goods, the proportion in total imports is relatively low in Hong Kong, Japan and Singapore, though in the cases of Hong Kong and Singapore the proportion has been increasing. The relatively low proportion of capital goods imports in Hong Kong and Singapore is largely explained by the fact that they import a relatively high proportion of raw materials and food-stuffs. The differences between these two urban economies and Korea and Taiwan are much less when we look at the M'/Y ratios instead of the M'/M ratios. For Japan, the low proportion of imports of capital goods is of course explained by the fact that Japan does not have to rely on them. In Korea and Taiwan, the proportion of capital goods imports is not only relatively high but also increases substantially over the sub-periods. The pattern is similar for the growth rates of total exports and imports, manufacturing exports and capital goods imports. We shall therefore not discuss them as we do for the foreign trade ratios and the ratios of manufactured products (capital goods) in total exports (imports). It is sufficient to note that the growth rates (except for the sub-period 1955–60 in Korea) are extremely high by all standards and there is little doubt that the foreign trade sector must have played an important part in the rapid growth of these economies in the post-war years.

What is then the secret of success of these economies in export expansion? Their experience seems to support the hypothesis that the free working of market forces is necessary for success in the expansion of manufacturing exports. In Korea and Taiwan, the government authorities have taken many important measures to remove the impediments to the smooth working of the price mechanism. An analysis of these policies and their effects would be of great interest and importance. It is, however, not the purpose of the present study to discuss such policies in detail. There has already been a large volume of literature on such discussions.[3] In brief, in Taiwan a series of measures was taken by the government in the late fifties to liberalise controls over imports and raise many tariffs. At the same time export incentives were strengthened by the extension of the scope of tax rebates to include materials used for export production, and by the initiation of low-cost export loans. More importantly, the administrative procedures of exporting and importing were also greatly streamlined and simplified. In Korea the history of exchange rate and trade policy can be divided into two time periods. From 1958—64 the improved performance of exports was primarily the result of devaluing its overvalued foreign-exchange rates. Since 1965 export promotion has mainly been associated with increases in export subsidies and liberalisation of import restrictions. This programme of export promotion has included the reduction of the interest rate on export loans, increases in tax benefits by granting accelerated depreciation privileges on plant and equipment improvement used for export production, and exemption of custom duties on imported materials and capital equipment for export production. In Hong Kong, Japan and Singapore, the free market environment had already been established at the time of industrialisation and export expansion, and consequently there was no need for the government authorities to take measures to remove the impediments to the smooth working of the price mechanism. Thus in these cases industrialisation was followed immediately by export expansion while in the cases of Taiwan and Korea there was a stage of import substitution preceding the stage of export expansion.

From this brief introduction to the growth and changing structure of foreign trade in these countries, let us now move on to consider the relations between export expansion and economic growth. We shall first review the existing theoretical models and then construct an export-led model of growth which can ascertain the intermediate links relating the expansion of exports to the growth of national output. The model will then be tested against the data of the economies under study and the results and implications are given in the last section of this chapter.

THE RELATIONS BETWEEN EXPORT EXPANSION AND ECONOMIC GROWTH: A REVIEW

The relations between foreign trade and economic growth have been much discussed in the post-war literature. Earlier attention on the effect of export expansion on income growth was confined to the simple Keynesian short-run multiplier analysis. On the other hand, much of the attention was directed to the effects of economic growth on the volume and terms of trade and the resulting adjustments required to maintain international equilibrium.[4] From the early sixties, attention has been increasingly diverted to new discussions on the role of foreign trade in promoting economic growth. The so-called export-led models of growth originated from attempts to explain the significant differences in the rate of growth of industrialised countries in the post-war period. Various hypotheses have been advanced; some stress such demand factors as the level or stability of aggregate demand, and international price competitivenesss; others emphasise such supply factors as the rate of capital formation and elasticity of the labour supply. The export-led models pick the rapid growth of exports as a necessary and perhaps sufficient condition for rapid growth of income. The study of export-led growth in the industrialised countries is soon extended to the economic growth in developing countries. This has raised various issues concerning the strategy of economic development, notably, the inward-looking strategy of import substitution versus the outward-looking strategy of export promotion.

A number of economists have provided theoretical links between export growth and income growth. An early attempt was made by Kindleberger (1962) to demonstrate how foreign trade may stimulate growth under some conditions and retard it in others. He argued that expanded exports offer investment opportunities and induce cost-reducing innovations and economies of large-scale production. Furthermore, he thought that expanded exports would lead to improved reallocation of resources though he did not explain the underlying mechanism and why such improvement has to come from exports. Beckerman (1962), in criticising a 'convergence' model of growth according to which there was some long run historical rate of growth from which substantial deviation must be of a temporary nature, maintained that a 'divergence' theory of the growth process seemed more appropriate in explaining the relative growth experience of countries in Europe in the fifties. According to Beckerman, rapid growth depended upon confident expectations concerning future demand prospects both domestically and in foreign markets. Entepreneurs are thus motivated to increase their investment rates and take other steps to increase productivity when exports perform well. A favourable initial position of international price competitiveness which permitted rapid growth would tend, consequently, to be perpetuated or maybe even accentuated by increases in investment and productivity. In Beckerman's model, labour productivity is assumed to be positively correlated with the rate of increase in output, which is in turn correlated with the rate of growth of exports. However, Beckerman did not make clear the mechanism through which output, exports, investment, and productivity were related. In addition, Beckerman did not mention the sources of a given country's initial export competitiveness and the conditions under which the rate of wage increases would be reduced relative to increases in productivity.[5] It can also be said that Beckerman's export-led model is over demand-oriented. There are certainly some important factors on the supply side that govern investment decisions. In particular, some reference could have been made to the investment and saving process in relation to the balance of payments position.

To establish some relationships between exports and income growth, it is necessary to link export growth to the rate of capital formation and/or productivity growth. We have seen that in Beckerman's model the linkage is provided by the 'animal spirits' of entrepreneurs in response to the prospects of expanded exports. On the other hand, Lamfalussy (1963), in comparing the growth experience of Britain and the six Common Market countries, stressed the importance of the balance of payments position. He maintained that the achievement of a surplus in the balance of payments as a result of expanded exports would enable the government to follow expansionist policies which encouraged domestic investment.[6] These increases in investment would expand productive capacity and productivity. Moreover, the resulting fast growth of income would raise both investment and saving. Assuming a balanced budget and the absence of international capital flows, the excess of exports over imports is equal to that of saving over investment *ex post*. If the growth of saving matches that of investment, then the induced increases in imports will not spoil the 'virtuous circle' of growth.

To understand the actual growth path of an economy governed by the various functional relationships proposed by Beckerman and Lamfalussy, it is useful to employ the framework of short-run income growth models along Harrod-Domar lines. An open Harrod-Domar model can be represented by the following equations (for simplicity, the time subscripts are omitted).

Production Equation:

$$dY = 1/v. I \tag{1}$$

Saving Equation:

$$S = s. Y \tag{2}$$

Import Equation:

$$M = m Y \tag{3}$$

Export Equation:

$$X = X_0 e^{xt} \tag{4}$$

Equilibrium condition:

$$I - S = M - X \tag{5}$$

where Y is output, I is investment, S is saving, M is import and X is export; v is the ICOR; and s and m are the marginal propensities; x is the exogenously given rate of export growth. Thus we postulate a fixed proportions production function, that saving and import are constant proportions of income, and that export grows at an exogenously given rate. Substituting equations (2), (3) and (4) into (5), we have

$$I = s.Y + m.Y - X \tag{6}$$

Substituting (6) into (1), and dividing through by Y, we obtain:

$$dY/Y = \frac{1}{v} \left(s + m - \frac{X}{Y} \right) \tag{7}$$

(7) states a negative relationship between the rate of growth of income and the proportion of export in income. This is the type of results obtained by some earlier attempts to extend the basic Harrod-Domar model to an open economy,[7] and it has led economists to cast doubts on

the role of exports in economic growth. The rather surprising results implied by equation (7) are mainly due to some unacceptable assumpitions included in it. Firstly, the above model assumes that investment has no imported component. This means that exports and domestic investment are essentially competitors for available saving. With the assumption that capital formation [from equation (1)] is the only source of growth, a rise in exports will give rise to a fall in the rate of income growth. Furthermore, the above model has no reference to the balance of payments position and in fact implies that there is a perfectly elastic supply of international credit, with balance of payments deficits or surpluses capable of being accumulated indefinitely.

In developing economies, a salient feature is the heavy reliance on imports, particualrly the imports of capital goods. The above-discussed framework based on an open Harrod-Domar Model can be used to derive more meaningful results when we assume that there is an imported component in investment. The system of equations then consists of:

$$\mathrm{d}Y = 1/v . I \qquad (1)$$
$$S = s . Y \qquad (2)$$
$$M = m . Y \qquad (3)$$
$$X = X_0 e^{xt} \qquad (4)$$
$$I = b . M' \qquad (12)$$
$$I - S = M - X \qquad (5)$$

Assuming balance of trade,[8] we have

$$X = M = M' + M'' \qquad (13)$$
or $\qquad M' = X - M'' \qquad (14)$

where M' is the imported capital goods and M'', the imported consumer goods. The most important feature of this model is the division of imported goods into capital goods and consumer goods and that part of the investment cost is for imported capital goods. To establish a relationship between the rate of growth and the behaviour of exports, we first substitute (14) into (12), and then substitute the resulting equation into (1). The reduced form of our model becomes:[9]

$$\mathrm{d}Y/Y = \frac{b}{v}\left(\frac{X}{Y} - \frac{M''}{Y}\right) \qquad (16)$$

Contrary to equation (7), equation (16) shows a positive relationship between the rate of growth and the proportion of exports in income. The intermediate links for such a positive relationship are as follows. An increase in exports helps to finance the import of capital goods, which in turn gives rise to a more rapid rate of capital formation and hence a higher rate of growth of output. Thus, this model postulates a link between exports and capital formation different from that suggested by Lamfalussy and Beckerman. This model does not rely on the 'animal spirits' of the entrepreneurs of the expansionist policies in response to expanded exports, but merely on the assumption that part of investment cost is for imported capital goods. This export-led model at first sight bears a close resemblance to the well-known 'two-gap' theory developed by Chenery and his associates.[10] This is however only partly true. The 'two-gap' theory in its simple form asserts that there is a minimum necessary additional amount of imports required to support a given increase in national output. At a certain projected level of output imports may exceed exports and very often the failure to achieve that level of output is not due to insufficient domestic saving but the lack of foreign exchange to finance the import-export gap which has then to be closed by foreign aid. It is true that our present model of export-led growth assigns an important role to imports (specifically capital goods imports) in the growth process. However we do not belive that a trade gap should exist and necessarily be dominant. The conventional 'two-gap' analysis has largely overlooked the export potential of developing countries, especially in the capability of developing countries in exporting manufactured products. If developing countries can expand their exports rapidly to generate sufficient earnings to finance imports, then there should not be any foreign exchange constraints on development. Thus in many of the cases where rapid development has failed to take place, one of the major reasons lies in their inward-looking policies based on their pessimistic view of export possibilities.[11] Thus, our model of export-led growth shares the view of the 'two-gap' analysis in that imports, particularly capital goods imports, play a crucial part in the process of rapid growth, but on the other hand our model stresses that such imports can be financed by expansion of exports, particularly manufacturing exports. This linking of exports to capital goods imports and the emphasis on the importance of the latter on output growth form the basis of our export-led model to be constructed and tested in the following sections.

A SIMULTANEOUS-EQUATION MODEL OF EXPORT-LED GROWTH

In the literature, the crucial role of exports in economic growth has as a rule been demonstrated by the close association between income growth and export expansion. Such an association is sometimes shown by presenting statistics on the two sets of data on income and exports and sometimes more explicitly by a simple regression of income on exports.[12] This approach of measurement without theory suffers, of course, from the drawbacks of missing the important and interesting intermediate links which explain the export-led mechanism. More recently an attempt has been made to ascertain the intermediate links (which are very similar to those proposed in our model here) by performing simple regression analysis with reference to each of the links.[13] In such an analysis income is first regressed on exports to establish their positive relationship. Then simple regressions of capital goods imports on exports, investment on capital goods imports, and finally income on investment are performed. It is argued that if positive regression coefficients are found in these simple regressions then the hypothesised model of export-led growth can be established. It cannot be denied that such an attempt is already a great improvement over the previous studies which focus simply on the simple correlation coefficients between exports and income. Unfortunately, this kind of study still can show only association and not causation. There are too many interdependencies involved for the casual links running from export expansion to income growth to be established by simple regression analysis. As a remedy to such defects, we propose a simple simultaneous-equation model encompassing the causal links of export-led growth described above.[14] Our simultaneous-equation model consists of the following three equations:

(1) The Income Equation

$$Y = a_0 + a_1 I + a_2 X + a_3 Y_{-1} \tag{17}$$

or
$$Y = a_0{}' + a_2{}' X + a_3{}' Y_{-1} \tag{17'}$$

where, Y, I, and X are GNP, gross investment and total exports respectively; the subscript -1 signifies a one-year time lag of the variable to which it is attached.

(2) The Capital Goods Import Equation

$$M' = b_0 + b_1 Y + b_2 X + b_3 M'_{-1} \tag{18}$$

or $\quad M' = b_0' + b_2' X + b_3' M'_{-1} \tag{18'}$

where M' is the import of capital goods.

(3) The Investment Equation

$$I = c_0 + c_1 M' + c_2 I_{-1} \tag{19}$$

In the above system of equations, Y, M', and I are endogenous variables and Y_{-1}, X, M'_{-1}, and I_{-1} are exogenous variables. All the equations satisfy the rank and order conditions for identifiability. Both income and capital goods import equations have an alternative form which includes only exogenous variables as explanatory variables. It can be seen that our simple model hypothesises that (1) income is related to both investment and exports or only to exports, (2) capital goods imports are related to both income and exports or only to exports, and (3) investment is related to capital goods imports. This model thus asserts that the role of export expansion in economic growth lies in its importance in financing capital goods imports which are necessary for rapid economic growth because of their significant effects on domestic investment. In view of the fact that the above hypothesised relationships must necessarily involve time lags, a specification of Nerlove's partial adjustment model of distributed lags is included in each of our equations.[15] In accordance with the Nerlove model, the time lag consideration is taken care of by the inclusion of the lagged dependent variable as an additional explanatory variable. In the Nerlove model, there is the advantage that all the lagged explanatory variables are substituted for a single variable, the lagged dependent variable.[16] In addition, it has the advantage that the disturbance term has no direct connection with its own previous values, so that we may assume that the new error term is not autocorrelated.[17]

The model of export-led growth as specified by equations (17) or (17'), (18) or (18'), and (19) is estimated with the data of the study's five economies by the two-stage least squares method. The choice between (17) and (17'), and between (18) and (18') is based on statistical criteria. It is thought that income may or may not have significant influence on the import of capital goods. Before we present and discuss our estimation results, we shall first make some comments on the question of testing goodness-of-fit in simultaneous-equation estimations.

For estimating the coefficients by the two-stage least squares method in an equation where endogenous variables also appear on the right-hand side of the equation

$$Y_1 = \beta_1 X_1 + \gamma_1 Y_2 + U \tag{20}$$

we first regress Y_2 on all exogenous variables (unrestricted and zero restricted) and find the fitted value $\hat{Y}_{2t}$. We then replace Y_{2t} by $\hat{Y}_{2t}$ in equation (20) and regress Y_1 on X_1 and $\hat{Y}_2$. However, it must be noted that in this second-stage estimation, the residuals $(\hat{U}_t)$ should be expressed as:

$$\hat{U}_t = Y_{1t} - \hat{\beta}_1 X_1 - \hat{\gamma}_1 Y_{2t} \tag{21}$$

i.e. $\hat{U}_t$ is calculated by using the second-stage estimates $\hat{\beta}_1$ and $\hat{\gamma}_1$, multiplied by the *original* observations of all the variables (even though $\hat{Y}_2$ instead of Y_2 is used in the second-stage estimation).[18] If we attempt to calculate an R^2 using these residuals, we have

$$R^2 = \frac{(\Sigma \hat{Y}_{1t}.Y_{1t})^2}{\Sigma \hat{Y}_{1t}^2.\Sigma Y_{1t}^2} \tag{22}$$

where $\hat{Y}_{1t} = \hat{\beta}_1 X_{1t} + \hat{\gamma}_1 Y_{2t}$.

We must note that the R^2 as defined in equation (22) is not equal to the 'explained' divided by the 'total' sum of squares. This is because on substituting $Y_{1t} = \hat{Y}_{1t} + \hat{U}_t$, the R^2 given in equation (22) becomes

$$R^2 = \frac{(\Sigma \hat{Y}_{1t}^2 + \Sigma \hat{Y}_{1t} \hat{U}_t)^2}{\Sigma \hat{Y}_{1t}^2.\Sigma Y_{1t}^2} \tag{23}$$

The R^2 given in equation (23) is equal to $\Sigma \hat{Y}_{1t}^2 / \Sigma Y_{1t}^2$ only if $\Sigma \hat{Y}_{1t} \hat{U}_t = 0$. This condition is satisfied automatically in the standard single-equation regression but not in the simultaneous-equation context. Thus there is no guarantee that the 'explained' over the 'total' is less than one, and hence one cannot claim that $\Sigma \hat{Y}_{1t}^2 / \Sigma Y_{1t}^2 = 1$ is a 'perfect fit' or even a good performance. We should further note that

$$\Sigma Y_{1t}^2 = \Sigma \hat{U}_t^2 + 2\Sigma \hat{U}_t \hat{Y}_{1t} + \Sigma \hat{Y}_{1t}^2$$

Since $2\Sigma \hat{U}_t \hat{Y}_{1t}$ may be negative it is quite possible that $\Sigma \hat{U}_t^2$ is larger than ΣY_{1t}^2. Hence we cannot argue that a 'low' $\Sigma \hat{U}_t^2$ (relative to ΣY_{1t}^2) is a good fit.[19] There may well be grounds for using R^2 as a measure of goodness of fit, but we are not aware of any statistical test (such as the standard F test in the single-equation context) that would tell us how to do it. Following this line of argument, we shall not present the R^2s in our regression results but just give the standard error of estimate defined as

$$\hat{\sigma}^2 = \frac{\Sigma \hat{U}_t^2}{N - K}$$

Where N is the number of observations and K is the total number of parameters estimated from the regression.

This standard error of estimation is of course used in computing the standard errors of the individual parameter estimates. T-tests can be carried out as usual but they are strictly valid for large samples only.

Lastly, we must also look at the use of Durbin-Watson statistic in models which include lagged dependent variables as explanatory variables. Although the Nerlove distributed lag model that we use would not induce serial correlation into the estimation equations (as would e.g. the Koyck model), we still have to test for the presence of serial correlation in our estimations as there is no reason to assume that serial correlation does not arise from other sources. Unfortunately, the use of the usual Durbin-Watson statistic is not appropriate in the present situations where the estimation equations contain lagged dependent variables among the explanatory variables.[20] It can be shown that the asymptotic values of the Durbin-Watson statistic are biased towards two and the bias can be quite substantial.[21] Thus, in the situations where lagged dependent variables are among the explanatory variables, the usual Durbin-Watson statistic could give very misleading information on the presence or absence of serial correlation. In the present estimations of our export-led growth model, we use Durbin's recently devised h-statistic to test for serial correlation.[22] This test is for models including lagged dependent variables in the set of explanatory variables and it has the great advantage of simplicity in calculating the statistic, h. The h-statistic is expressed as:

$$h = r \sqrt{\frac{n}{1 - n\hat{V}(b_1)}}$$

where r is the estimated first-order autocorrelation coefficient of the residuals, and it can be approximated by $1 - \frac{1}{2}d$ (d is the conventional Durbin-Watson statistic); n is the sample size; $\hat{V}(b_1)$ is the estimated variance of the regression coefficient of the lagged dependent variable. The h-statistic is then tested as a standard normal deviate; thus if $h > 1.645$ (using a one-tail test) one would reject the hypothesis of zero autocorrelation at the 5 per cent level. It should however be noted that Durbin's h-statistic is originally devised for single-equation estimations and as a matter of fact b_1 in the statistic refers to the OLS estimate. The validity of the h-statistic in the simultaneous-equation context has not been examined. We use it here as an approximate test because we are not aware of any statistical test which can test for serial correlation when lagged dependent variables are included in the regressors in the context of a simultaneous-equation system. It should also be noted that the h-statistic can be calculated only if $1 \geqslant n\hat{V}(b_1)$. In our estimations, the h-statistic can be calculated in all cases except four. The exceptions are the estimations of the capital goods import equation for Hong Kong, Singapore and Korea, and the estimation of the income equation for Taiwan. In all cases where h can be calculated, we find that $h < 1.645$, implying that we can accept the hypothesis of no serial correlation. In the other four cases where h cannot be calculated, we follow Durbin's suggestion of performing an asymptotically equivalent test of regressing U_t (the residual at time t) on U_{t-1} and the set of explanatory variables (including the lagged dependent variable) and then testing the significance of the coefficient of U_{t-1} by the conventional practice.[23] In all these four cases, we find that the coefficient of U_{t-1} is not statistically significant at the 5 per cent level. Hence, in all our estimations of the three equations in our export-led growth model for the five countries, we can accept the hypothesis of the absence of serial correlation.

EMPIRICAL RESULTS

Table 6.2 reports the regression results of our simultaneous-equation model of export-led growth in the five economies of this study. From the statistical point of view, the results are very satisfactory as the standard errors are relatively low and the presence of serial correlation can be rejected in all cases. From the economic point of view, the results are very informative and interesting. In three cases, viz. Hong Kong, Korea and Singapore, the empirical results lend strong support to our hypothesised intermediate links in the export-led process. In these economies, income is very much dependent on export performance for

TABLE 6.2 Regression Results of a Simultaneous-Equation Model of Export-Led Growth

Hong Kong

(1) $Y = 1022 + 0.575I + 0.378X + .651Y_{-1}$
$\qquad\qquad\quad (0.419) \quad (0.174)$
$\qquad$ S.E. $= 264 \qquad$ D$-$W $= 2.00$

(2) $M' = 169.4 - 0.0536Y + 0.160X + 0.698M'_{-1}$
$\qquad\qquad\quad (0.0460) \quad (0.042) \quad (0.323)$
$\qquad$ S.E. $= 87.4 \qquad$ D$-$W $= 1.51$

(3) $I = 254.5 + 0.444M' + 0.692I_{-1}$
$\qquad\qquad\quad (0.216) \quad (0.159)$
$\qquad$ S.E. $= 288 \qquad$ D$-$W $= 1.26$

Japan

(1) $Y = 236.8 + 0.515I + 0.969X + 0.845Y_{-1}$
$\qquad\qquad\quad (0.530) \quad (1.220) \quad (0.231)$
$\qquad$ S.E. $= 602 \qquad$ D$-$W $= 2.30$

(2′) $M' = 13.50 + 0.0517X + 0.589M'_{-1}$
$\qquad\qquad\quad\quad (0.022) \quad (0.232)$
$\qquad$ S.E. $= 42 \qquad$ D$-$W $= 1.57$

(3) $I = 291.8 - 1.729M' + 1.159I_{-1}$
$\qquad\qquad\quad (5.829) \quad (0.219)$
$\qquad$ S.E. $= 576 \qquad$ D$-$W $= 1.76$

Korea

(1′) $Y = 316.9 + 2.333X + 0.719Y_{-1}$
$\qquad\qquad\quad (0.994) \quad (0.195)$
$\qquad$ S.E. $= 39.8 \qquad$ D$-$W $= 2.05$

(2′) $M' = 7.766 + 0.512X + 0.502M'_{-1}$
$\qquad\qquad\quad (0.239) \quad (0.308)$
$\qquad$ S.E. $= 26.6 \qquad$ D$-$W $= 1.29$

(3) $I = 38.43 + 1.761M' + 0.375I_{-1}$
$\qquad\qquad\quad (0.330) \quad (0.154)$
$\qquad$ S.E. $= 42.8 \qquad$ D$-$W $= 2.29$

Singapore

(1) $Y = 1097 + 1.436I + 0.670X + 0.294Y_{-1}$
$\qquad\qquad\quad (0.768) \quad (0.374) \quad (0.152)$
$\qquad$ S.E. $= 66.3 \qquad$ D$-$W $= 2.11$

(2′) $M' = 179.7 + 0.337X + 0.682M'_{-1}$
$\qquad\qquad\quad (0.153) \quad (0.441)$
$\qquad$ S.E. $= 49.8 \qquad$ D$-$W $= 1.27$

(3) $I = 7.321 + 1.312M' + 0.279I_{-1}$
$\qquad\qquad\quad (0.398) \quad (0.254)$
$\qquad$ S.E. $= 45.4 \qquad$ D$-$W $= 1.69$

continued on p. 124

Table 6.2 *(Contd.)*

Taiwan

(1) $Y = 22.49 - 1.916I + 0.232X + 0.782Y_{-1}$
$\qquad\qquad (0.951)\quad (0.110)\quad (0.354)$
$\qquad$ S.E. $= 2.19 \qquad$ D $-$ W $= 2.38$

(2) $M' = 1.695 - 0.0468Y + 0.420X + 0.450M'_{-1}$
$\qquad\qquad (0.0240)\quad (0.089)\quad (0.199)$
$\qquad$ S.E. $= 0.79 \qquad$ D $-$ W $= 2.18$

(3) $I = 0.997 + 0.132M' + 0.735I_{-1}$
$\qquad\qquad (0.121)\quad (0.177)$
$\qquad$ S.E. $= 2.09 \qquad$ D $-$ W $= 2.18$

---

the period under study, but in no case was the regression coefficient of I statistically significant though its inclusion increases the goodness-of-fit in the income equation in the cases of Hong Kong and Singapore. In the case of Korea, the inclusion of the endogenous variable, I, actually decreases the goodness-of-fit and I is therefore omitted from the income equation. These three economies also indicate that the assumed to be exogenously determined X bear a very strong positive relationship with the import of capital goods. Only in the case of Hong Kong did the inclusion of Y in the capital goods imports equation improve the goodness-of-fit but in this case the regression coefficient bears a negative (though statistically insignificant) sign. The regression results of the investment function is of special interest to us as they should reflect whether domestic investment is constrained by the import of capital goods as hypothesised in the 'two-gap' theory.[24] The results suggest that such a hypothesised relationship is definitely found in the case of Korea and Singapore. It is less certain in the case of Hong Kong as the regression coefficient of M' is only marginally statistically significant.

Japan and Taiwan in one way or another show variance to our model. In the case of Japan, it is perhaps expected that our export-led model which is basically designed for semi-industrialised countries cannot be entirely applicable. In fact we do not find any significant positive relationship between export and income for Japan. In the literature of Japanese economic growth there have been debates on whether economic growth is export-led or rapid economic growth has led to fast expansion of exports. The general consensus tends to be that the pre-war (World War II) growth in Japan was definitely export-led while in the post-war period the phenomenon of growth-led exports was more likely to be true.[25] It seems it is most likely that exports and growth are mutually interdependent in the post-war growth of Japan and only a simultaneous-equation system spelling out such an interdependence can deal with the relathionship between export and income growth adequately. It is however not the intention of the present study to follow that up. Our results nonetheless further support the belief that the export-led mechanism may not be the sole or even an important factor in Japan's fast post-war growth. In addition, the 'two-gap' hypothesis that the import of capital goods imposes a constraint on domestic investment can be entirely rejected. This is again not a surprise to us considering the capability of the Japanese economy in supplying itself equipment and machinery tailored to its own needs. However, it is of interest to note that our results do suggest that the import of capital goods depends considerably on export performance. This could perhaps be explained by the fact that imports were indispensable to Japan's growth because of its lack of natural resources and hence rising imports in general and imports of capital goods in particular must be matched by equally rapid-rising exports. We should realise that Japan's borrowing, however large, could not have been sufficient to finance the increase in the import bill. This points to the interdependence between export expansion and economic growth and the conclusion that although export expansion might not have been a sufficient condition for Japan's rapid gorwth in the post-war period, it should have been a necessary one.

Somewhat to our surprise, the post-war growth of Taiwan also does not conform so well to our export-led model as Hong Kong, Korea and Singapore. Nevertheless, we do find a marginally statistically significant positive relationship between income and export, and that imports of capital goods are significantly dependent on export expansion. What we have failed to find support for is the 'two-gap' hypothesis that domestic investment depends on imports of capital goods. The clue to this can be found in the regression results of the income equation where it is shown that investment has no positive effects on income. The implication of this is that the effect of capital goods imports on income growth is not via investment but other determinants of growth such as technical progress and resources reallocation.[26]

To sum up, with the exception of Japan, we have been able to find support for our simultaneous-equation export-led growth model in the economies under study for the period 1955–70. The empirical support has been particularly strong in the cases of Korea and Singapore. For Hong Kong and especially Taiwan, some reservation should be given to the hypothesised 'two-gap' proposition that imports of capital goods impose a significant constraint on domestic investment. Our results tend to suggest that we should be more sceptical in accepting the assumption of imported capital goods being a fixed proportion of investment in the 'two-gap' analysis. It should, however, be pointed out that even if investment is not related to imported capital goods, it does not mean that the latter has lost its importance in the export-led mechanism. The importance of imported capital goods could be related to growth of income via other determinants of income growth.

PART III

The Effects of Growth

7 Capital Inflow, Saving, and Economic Growth

In Part II, we analysed the various factors explaining the fast rate of growth in the economies of this study. Specifically, we have examined such supply factors as technical progress, scale economies, factor inputs, capital-labour substitution, and such demand factors as the growth in exports. In Part III, we will examine some other elements of economic growth. In this chapter, we shall look at the relationships between savings and growth, in the following the relationship between income distribution and growth. The part played by saving and income distribution poses an identification problem when their relationships with growth are being studied. This is because it is often difficult, if not impossible, to ascertain the direction of causation when relating growth to such economic variables. It can be argued, on the one hand, that saving and the pattern of income distribution are crucial factors affecting the rate of growth. On the other hand, it is equally plausible that the rate of growth to a greater or lesser extent affects the rate of saving and the pattern of income distribution.

THE ROLE OF SAVING IN ECONOMIC GROWTH

In the last chapter, we argued that capital inflow or export growth promotes economic growth through the linkage of imported capital goods. In brief, we maintained that capital inflow or export expansion helps to finance the import of capital goods which form a substantial proportion of investment in developing economies. With an increase in investment made possible by increased import of capital goods, the rate of growth will be enhanced. There is however another possible linkage through which export growth or capital inflow can affect the rate of growth. Such a linkage works through the rate of savings. There are some good reasons to believe that increased export earnings will lead to higher domestic savings. The first reason is that the propensity to save out of the export sector is as a rule higher than other sectors because export earnings are often concentrated on incomes of which a higher proportion is saved. Secondly, export earnings are administratively easier to tax than more diffused wage and profit incomes and hence very often constitute a major source of government saving. Thirdly, countries with higher rates of export growth may face less of a foreign exchange constraint on investment; because of this domestic saving is encouraged. A rise in export earnings causes other sectors of the economy to save more in order to take advantage of profitable investment opportunities. There is also a great deal of empirical evidence to support a strong correlation between the growth of export earnings and the level of savings. In a study covering eight out of eleven Sterling area countries during the period 1950–62, Maizels (1968) finds that export earnings contribute significantly to saving. Lee (1971) has extended Maizels' analysis by taking 28 countries for a longer time period and found export earnings to be a significant determinant of domestic saving. In a cross-country study of LDC's, Papanek (1973) comes to similar conclusions.

It is however much more difficult to see how foreign capital inflows can raise the level of domestic saving. As a matter of fact, the literature is replete with both theoretical arguments and empirical evidence of a negative relationship between capital inflows and saving. Such a negative relationship was first put forth by Haavelmo (1965), and later tested by Rahman (1968), Griffin (1970), Griffin and Enos (1970), and Weisskopf (1972), among others, on the basis of cross-country studies. Time-series studies have been undertaken by Chenery and Eckstein (1970), Suckling (1975), and Bose (1976). All these studies, time-series and cross-country, invariably arrive at a negative relationship between foreign capital inflow and saving. Nevertheless, great caution should be taken in interpreting the negative correlation between saving and capital inflows based on *ex post* observations of saving. The negative relationship is in fact predictable from the national accounting identities. Given that $I - S = M - X = F$, and that not all F are invested, i.e. investment rises by less than the increase in capital inflow and saving, saving therefore necessarily falls for the identity to hold. However, this *ex post* behaviour is not necessarily related to the *ex ante* saving behaviour of the economy. This means that no necessary causal relation is implied between large capital inflows and low saving in the sense that a decision has been taken by the people to save less. In other words, the regression of saving on capital inflows cannot distinguish between changes in the decision to save on the one hand and consumption out of capital inflows on the other. A further difficulty arises in cross-section studies. A negative relationship between saving and capital inflow may not imply that capital inflow lowers the rate of saving, but is simply the result that the poorer the country, and the lower the saving ratio, the more foreign capital the country is likely to attract.

It is however possible to argue that the effects of increased capital inflow are similar to increases in export earnings, and thus capital inflows can raise the level of domestic saving instead of reducing it. When an economy is largely subject to a foreign resources constraint, investment will be dependent on capital imports and so investment opportunities will increase with more capital inflow which helps to finance imports. Domestic saving will increase with increases in investment opportunities if the economy is not constrained by domestic resources. Thus, when the foreign resources constraint is in operation, higher capital inflows will on the one hand substitute for domestic saving in financing investment and on the other hand increase investment opportunities for a higher level of domestic saving. If the latter effect is stronger than the former, we expect a positive relationship between capital inflows and saving. In fact, Gupta (1970) in commenting on Rahman's (1968) cross-section results, finds a positive, though statistically insignificant relationship between capital inflows and saving based on a regrouping of countries. It remains to be seen whether a positive relationship can also be obtained from time-series studies of individual countries.

Our arguments have so far concentrated on a one-way causation running from saving to growth. It is true that a good deal of cross-country evidence suggests that a high proportion of the variance in the rates of growth is explained by the variation in the saving ratio.[1] There is however always the identification problem which is inherent in such regression analysis. As a matter of fact, there are also theoretical grounds and empirical evidence for the dependence of saving on the rate of growth. The dependence of the saving ratio on the growth of income can be derived from the life-cycle hypothesis of saving.[2] The basis of the hypothesis is that individuals and households attempt to distribute consumption evenly over their life-time so that decisions to save are not a function of current income but of total life-time earnings and the stage reached in that pattern of earnings. A typical pattern envisaged by the life-cycle hypothesis is dissaving in youth in anticipation of future earnings, and positive saving in middle age in anticipation of a lower income after retirement. If there is no income growth (together with no population and productivity growth), positive saving and dissaving would exactly offset each other, and the aggregate saving ratio would be zero. On the other hand, if income rises over time as a result of productivity growth, the life earnings and consumption of each successive age group will be higher than the preceding one. On the assumption that each successive age group aims at a higher level of consumption in retirement, the volume of saving of the active group of the population will exceed the dissaving of the currently retired population with a lower level of lifetime consumption. The saving ratio will tend to rise with the rate of growth of income because the higher the growth rate the greater will the gap tend to be between the dissaving of the currently retired people and the consumption standard aimed at by the currently active group. Income growth is of course also influenced by population growth. Income growth due to population growth affects the saving ratio according to how that growth changes the age structure of the population. In general, an increase in the rate of population growth will increase the ratio of active to retired households, and as a result the saving ratio will tend to rise. The life-cycle hypothesis has been tested empirically by Modigliani (1970) and others on a cross-sectional basis by taking a mixed sample of developed and developing countries. All these studies give strong support to the hypothesis.

Thus, there is an interdependence between saving and growth. Growth determines saving according to the life-cycle hypothesis, and growth partly depends on saving as a determinant of the rate of capital accumulation. In empirical testing, this interdependent relationship gives rise to an identification problem, which can only be solved by simultaneous-equation techniques of estimation. From the practical point of view, the interdependence between growth and the saving ratio is a blessing. Such interdependence implies a 'virtuous circle' of growth. Higher saving ratios give rise to higher growth rates and higher per capita income; higher growth rates and higher per capita income in turn lead to higher saving ratios which will then give rise to even higher rates of growth. This means that once growth is initiated, the process will pick up its own momentum.

The present chapter attempts to study the relationships between domestic saving and economic growth in three innovative ways. First, we shall conduct time-series studies of the economies. In the development literature, almost all studies on the relationships between saving and growth are conducted on the basis of cross-section analysis. Very often, the sample under consideration is a mixture of developed and developing countries. Besides the econometric problems associated with the regression analysis of a diversified group of countries, there is also the problem of the usefulness of applying cross-section results to policy formulation in individual countries. Thus, time-series studies of individual countries on the relationships between saving and growth are badly needed. There are of course good reasons for the lack of time-series studies in the literature. For developed countries, growth rates and saving ratios show very little variation over the period covered by the available data. For developing countries, the limiting factor is the lack of reliable data covering a sufficiently long period of time. Fortunately, in the post-war period of rapid growth the five economies have experienced considerable variations in their growth rates and saving ratios. In addition, reasonably reliable data are available for analysis.

Second, we shall construct some simple simultaneous-equation models to study the saving-growth relationships so that the interdependent characteristics of saving and growth can be taken into account. Conventional single-equation methods will also be used. Despite the fact that single-equation estimates are subject to bias, the results are still presented and discussed in this chapter. There are two reasons for doing so. In the first place, the findings on the relationships between domestic saving and growth in the literature are mainly based on single-equation methods; our single-equation estimates are thus presented for the purpose of making comparisons with the existing findings.In the second place, we would like to find out the extent to which the single-equation estimates depart from the corresponding simultaneous-equation estimates when the same sets of data for our economies are used.

The third innovative attempt of this chapter is that capital inflows instead of being treated as a single homogeneous element are separated into official and private inflows. It is rather remarkable that for a long time in the literature capital inflows are treated in this way despite the fact that available data normally enable us to distinguish official capital inflow from private capital inflow. Official capital inflow (F_g) is defined in the present study to include official aid and loans, while private capital inflow (F_p) is defined to include private loans and direct investment. Total capital inflow (F) is

$$F = F_p + F_g \tag{1}$$

There are good reasons for distinguishing official inflow from private inflow as official and private capital inflows are often of a different nature and used in different ways. Official inflow in the form of aid or loans is more often associated with particular large projects and social overheads. Sometimes, foreign aid is in the form of commodities which are solely for consumption purposes. On the other hand, private inflow in the form of direct investment is more often allocated to the manufacturing sector and projects which are directly related to industrial activities. For example in Korea, 60 per cent of private capital inflow as opposed to 25–30 per cent of official inflow is allocated to the manufacturing sector.

SAVING AND ECONOMIC GROWTH: THEORETICAL MODELS AND EMPIRICAL EVIDENCE

In the last section, we discussed how capital inflow and export expansion can promote growth through raising the level of domestic saving, and how growth itself can have further impacts on saving forming a virtuous circle of growth. We shall in this section examine empirically the relationship between saving and growth.

(1) *Saving and Growth: Single-Equation Estimation*

In the 'virtuous circle' of growth discussed in the last section, domestic saving must increase with the rise of either the rate of growth or the level of income, or both. A positive relationship between saving and the level of income is of course the essence of the Keynesian income hypothesis that

$$S = S(Y) \tag{2}$$

In empirical studies, the usual practice is to assume that the saving function is linear and saving and income are expressed in per capita forms.[3] In so doing, the saving function takes into account the size of the population, and can be expressed as

$$S/N = a + b(Y/N) \tag{3}$$

where N is the size of the population.

Equation (3) implies a saving function of the following form

$$S = aN + bY \tag{4}$$

Thus the level of national saving is dependent on both the population level and the income level. It is generally believed the intercept, a, in equation (3) is negative. A negative intercept implies that the saving ratio(S/Y) rises with the level of income, but less than proportionately. From equation (3), an expression can be derived relating the saving ratio to per capita income. Multiplying equation (3) by N and then dividing it by Y, we have

$$S/Y = a(N/Y) + b \tag{5}$$
or $$S/Y = b + a(Y/N)^{-1} \tag{6}$$

and we expect a to be negative. Thus, the saving ratio will rise with the level of development, as measured by per capita income. In addition, as Y/N approaches infinity, S/Y approaches a constant, b. This means that S/Y increases with per capita income at a decreasing rate, and the asymptotic value of it is b. To test the validity of the Keynesian absolute income hypothesis, time-series data of the five economies under study are fitted to equations (3) and (6). In addition, the following two forms are also tried.

$$S/Y = a + b(Y/N) \tag{7}$$
$$S/Y = a + b(Y/N) + c(Y/N)^2 \tag{8}$$

Equation (7) specifies a linear relationship between the saving ratio and per capita income instead of a hyperbolic form as specified by (6). Equation (8), on the other hand, specifies a parabolic relationship. Equation (8) in fact enables us to find the level of per capita income at which the saving ratio is maximised. Differentiating S/Y with respect to Y/N in equation (8) and setting the result equal to zero, we have

$$Y/N = -b/2c \tag{9}$$

Provided c is negative (for the fulfilment of the second-order condition), (9) gives the level of per capita income which maximises the saving ratio.

The regression results are reported in Table 7.1. In relating saving per capita to income per capita, the intercept and the regression coefficient for all the economies have the expected signs, i.e the former is negative and the latter positive. Furthermore, all the intercepts and coefficients are highly statistically significant. The regression coefficient, which is the marginal propensity to save (MPS), ranges from 0.221 in Hong Kong to 0.41 in Taiwan and 0.45 in Japan. Singapore has an MPS of 0.263 which

TABLE 7.1 Regression Results of the Relation between Saving and Income

Economy	D.V.	Intercept	Regression Coefficient of			R^2	$D-W$
			Y/N	$(Y/N)^2$	$(Y/N)^{-1}$		
Hong Kong	S/N	−0.295 (0.060)	0.221 (0.023)			0.867	1.22
	S/Y	−0.0185 (0.0156)	0.0452 (0.0060)			0.803	1.73
	S/Y	0.125 (0.060)	−0.0754 (0.0497)	0.0234 (0.0096)		0.865	2.32
	S/Y	0.200 (0.019)			−0.244 (0.042)	0.701	1.25
Japan	S/N	−0.0092 (0.0022)	0.450 (0.017)			0.981	1.52*
	S/Y	0.161 (0.012)	0.306 (0.074)			0.566	1.76*
	S/Y	0.191 (0.035)	0.976 (0.305)	−1.155 (0.578)		0.806	1.00
	S/Y	0.439 (0.011)			−0.0184 (0.0020)	0.852	1.18
Korea	S/N	−0.0143 (0.0010)	0.352 (0.018)			0.962	2.44
	S/Y	−0.153 (0.024)	4.220 (0.430)			0.873	2.18
	S/Y	−0.427 (0.133)	13.71 (4.56)	−78.05 (37.36)		0.905	2.54
	S/Y	0.354 (0.025)			−0.0144 (0.0013)	0.902	2.44
Singapore	S/N	−0.264 (0.058)	0.263 (0.032)			0.882	1.74
	S/Y	−0.0185 (0.0335)	0.0725 (0.0184)			0.632	1.57
	S/Y	−0.129 (0.201)	0.189 (0.209)	−0.0295 (0.0529)		0.646	1.61
	S/Y	0.263 (0.037)			−0.263 (0.063)	0.659	1.67
Taiwan	S/N	−1.903 (0.062)	0.410 (0.007)			0.995	1.51
	S/Y	−0.0652 (0.0119)	0.0278 (0.0014)			0.965	1.04
	S/Y	−0.242 (0.044)	0.0713 (0.0107)	−0.0025 (0.0006)		0.985	1.63
	S/Y	0.406 (0.009)			−1.873 (0.070)	0.981	1.32

D.V., dependent variable
* Results obtained after correcting for 1st-order serial correlation.

is quite close to that of Hong Kong. Korea falls in the middle of the group with an MPS of 0.352. The MPSs obtained for our group of economies must be considered as extremely high by any standard. Houthakker's cross-section study of both developed and developing countries yields an MPS of 0.081; Williamson's study of eight Asian countries over the period 1950–64 yields an MPS of 0.20 by pooling cross-section and time-series data together. Thus, inasmuch as our group of economies is distinguished from most of the other developing economies by their high growth rates, it seems that the marginal propensity to save may be an important factor affecting the rate of growth. Furthermore, as the estimated MPSs of our economies spread over a considerable range, another inference seems to be that for a country to achieve a high rate of growth a certain high value of MPS, say around 0.20, is helpful and very often essential. However, further increases above this may not have significant effects on the rate of growth. One very interesting observation emerging from our estimates of the MPSs is on the relationship between the value of MPS and the size of a country. Our results indicate a very neat positive relationship between MPS and country size. The two city economies have the lowest MPSs, and Japan, Korea, and Taiwan have MPSs related to their relative size as measured by the size of population. In the absence of other time-series studies of individual countries, it is difficult to tell whether this is a coincidence or country size does matter in determining the value of marginal propensity to save.

In relating S/Y to Y/N, all three functional forms, linear, parabolic, and hyperbolic, give reasonably good fit to our data. In the case of Hong Kong, the best fit is obtained when the linear form {equation (7)} is used. In fitting a hyperbola {equation (6)}, the regression coefficient is statistically significant and bears the expected sign. However, in fitting a parabola {equation (8)}, the regression coefficients are not of the expected sign, the coefficient of Y/N is negative instead of positive and that of $(Y/N)^2$ is positive instead of negative. This result implies that the saving ratio decreases at a decreasing rate as per capita income rises. But such a negative relationship between the saving ratio and per capita income cannot be taken seriously as the regression coefficient of per capita income is statistically insignificant. In the case of Japan, the hyperbolic form of equation (6) gives the best fit. Moreover, the regression coefficients of the two other functional forms are statistically significant and bear the expected sign. The estimates for the parabolic form suggest that the saving ratio reaches a maximum of 40 per cent at a per capita income level of 422,511 ¥ or US $1170 (at 1965 prices). Japan passed this level of per capita income in 1968, and theoretically Japan's saving ratio should now be declining. In the case of Korea, like Japan it is the hyperbolic form which gives the best fit. The asymptotic value for the saving ratio is 35 per cent. Again, the regression coefficients of the two other functional forms are statistically significant and bear the expected sign. The estimates for the parabolic form suggest a maximum saving ratio of 17 per cent at a per capita income level of 87,823 won or US $281 (at 1970 prices). The actual per capita income in Korea in 1970 is US $259, and so the saving ratio should continue to show a rising trend. As the hyperbolic form gives better fit than the parabolic form, it is more likely that the saving ratio in Korea will move above 17 per cent towards the asymptotic value of 35 per cent after the per capita income of US $281 has been attained. In the case of Singapore, the hyperbolic form again gives the best fit. The saving ratio will move towards the limit of 26 per cent when per capita income increases. The fitting of a parabola is unsatisfactory as both of the regression coefficients are statistically insignificant. The statistical fit of the linear form on the other hand is only slightly worse than the hyperbola case. In the case of Taiwan, it is again the hyperbola that gives the best fit. The statistical fit of the two other forms is also good; the regression coefficients are significant and bear the expected sign. The estimates for the parabolic form suggest that the saving ratio reaches a maximum of 27 per cent at a per capita income level of NT $14260 or US $356 (at 1964 prices). On the other hand, the hyperbolic functional form suggests that the asymptotic value of the saving ratio is 41 per cent. Inasmuch as the hyperbola gives better fit than the parabola, it seems that the saving ratio in Taiwan will move above 27 per cent even after attaining the per capita income level of US $356. In 1970, the actual per capita income level in Taiwan is US $304. Thus, with the exception of the case of Hong Kong, the hyperbolic form of the saving ratio function invariably gives better fit than the linear or the parabolic form. These results give strong support to the Keynesian income hypothesis that the saving ratio will rise with per capita income, but at a decreasing rate, i.e. the saving ratio will move towards an asymptote as per capita income moves towards infinity.

In contrast to the absolute income hypothesis, the life-cycle hypothesis states that it is the rate of income growth and not the level of income that determines the saving ratio. This means that

$$S/Y = a + b\dot{Y} \tag{10}$$

where $\dot{Y}$ is the rate of growth of income. Equation (10) has however neglected the part played by population growth. Besides increasing income, population growth also changes the age structure of population which is a factor affecting saving in the life-cycle hypothesis. The age structure of the population is uniquely related to population growth only if population is in balanced growth, i.e. stabilised at a particular level. Thus if population is not in balanced growth, population growth should enter the saving ratio function as a separate variable, and this means that equation (10) may give rise to misleading results. A simple way to overcome this problem is to relate the saving ratio to the rate of growth of per capita income (Y/N) instead of the rate of growth of income. In so doing, we have

$$S/Y = a + b \ Y/N \tag{11}$$

In order to test whether the level of per capita income exerts an independent influence on the saving ratio or its relationship with it is simply as a proxy for the rate of growth of income, the level of per capita income as well as the rate of growth of income are included as independent determinants of the saving ratio.

$$S/Y = a + b \ \dot{Y} + c Y/N \tag{12}$$
$$S/Y = a + b \ \dot{Y}/N + c \ Y/N \tag{13}$$

Equations (10) to (13) are applied to the time-series data of the five economies under consideration.[4] The regression results are shown in Table 7.2. The first observation is that the use of $\dot{Y}$ as the independent variable generates very similar results to the use of $\dot{Y}/N$. This suggests that population growth in the economies under study is fairly stable. The second observation is that the five economies under study can be divided into two groups insofar as the relationship between the saving ratio and the rate of income growth in concerned. For the city economies of Hong Kong and Singapore, the relationship between the saving ratio and the rate of income growth is positive but weak. Japan, Korea, and Taiwan form the group in which the relationship between the saving ratio and the rate of income growth is positive and very strong. The third observation is that when the level of per capita income is considered alongside the rate of growth of income, its regression coefficient is statistically significant in all cases, even in Japan, Korea, and Taiwan. These results indicate that the level of per capita income is not simply a proxy for the rate of income growth, but exerts independent influence on the saving ratio. This conclusion contrasts with that of Modigliani

TABLE 7.2 Regression Results of the Relation between Saving and Income Growth (equation (10) to (13))

Economy	Intercept	Regression Coefficient of			R^2	D−W
		$\dot{Y}$	Y/N	Y/N		
Hong Kong	0.0317 (0.0073)	0.0477 (0.1366)			0.010	1.89*
	0.0325 (0.0068)		0.0178 (0.1156)		0.002	1.93*
	−0.0172 (0.0210)	0.0121 (0.1168)		0.0445 (0.0067)	0.784	1.74
	−0.0158 (0.0178)		−0.0264 (0.0983)	0.0449 (0.0069)	0.785	1.74
Japan	0.0800 (0.0051)	0.334 (0.112)			0.425	1.69*
	0.0808 (0.0050)		0.326 (0.111)		0.418	1.70*
	0.239 (0.016)	0.401 (0.144)		0.303 (0.046)	0.846	1.14
	0.242 (0.150)		0.396 (0.142)	0.306 (0.045)	0.846	1.15
Korea	−0.0167 (0.0154)	1.428 (0.210)			0.781	1.49
	0.0205 (0.0103)		1.357 (0.186)		0.803	1.38
	−0.127 (0.015)	0.688 (0.125)		2.898 (0.356)	0.966	2.00
	−0.104 (0.019)		0.652 (0.138)	2.814 (0.419)	0.959	1.76
Singapore	0.0993 (0.0176)	0.213 (0.190)			0.135	1.44
	0.104 (0.014)		0.213 (0.183)		0.144	1.48
	−0.0172 (0.0386)	−0.222 (0.189)		0.0832 (0.0262)	0.645	1.65
	−0.0292 (0.0417)		−0.250 (0.188)	0.0879 (0.0269)	0.661	1.70
Taiwan	0.0289 (0.0053)	1.734 (0.650)			0.354	0.88
	0.0896 (0.0300)		1.557 (0.558)		0.374	0.92
	−0.0632 (0.0107)		0.359 (0.133)	0.0253 (0.0015)	0.976	1.66
	−0.0785 (0.0122)	0.406 (0.150)		0.0256 (0.0014)	0.976	1.51

* Results obtained after correcting for first-order serial correlation.

whose work dismisses the level of per capita income as an independent explanatory variable determining the saving ratio, but confirms the results obtained by Thirlwall (1974) in a cross-country study. In summary, in the case of Hong Kong and Singapore, the saving ratio is largely determined by the level of per capita income, while in Japan, Korea, and Taiwan, both the level of per capita income and the rate of income growth exert important influence on the saving ratio. Inasmuch as the saving ratio is related to the level of per capita income and/or the rate of income growth, a 'virtuous circle' of growth is likely to exist once a breakthrough is made. The dependence of the saving ratio on the level of per capita income seems to be a less imposing condition than the dependence on the rate of income growth, as it is certainly less difficult to raise just the level of income than the rate of growth of income.

(2) *Saving and Growth: Simultaneous-Equation Estimations*

In the above section, we assumed that income growth and the level of per capita income are exogenously determined. However in practice, it is more likely that saving and income are interdependent. Specifically, we envisage that the saving ratio itself might have an effect on income growth and the level of per capita income. If this is in fact the case, the single-equation estimation results obtained above contain simultaneous-equation bias. To remove the bias, we can specify the following equation system which employs the capital inflow ratio (F/Y) as the exogenous variable.

$$S/Y = a_1 + b_1(\dot{Y}) \tag{14}$$
$$\dot{Y} = a_2 + b_2(I/Y) \tag{15}$$
and $$I/Y = S/Y + F/Y \tag{16}$$

Thus our model specifies that the saving ratio is a linear function of the rate of income growth, and the latter is itself a function of the investment ratio (I/Y) which is composed of the saving ratio plus the deficit on the balance of payments. The deficit is by definition equal to capital inflow (F/Y). Substituting (16) into (15), we have

$$\dot{Y} = a_3 + b_3(S/Y) + c_3(F/Y) \tag{17}$$

Our model therefore consists of equations (14) and (17), in which the endogenous variables are $\dot{Y}$ and S/Y, and the pre-determined variable is F/Y. Equation (14) in the model is estimated by the two-stage least squares method and the results are given in Table 7.3.[5] As data on capital inflow are not available for Hong Kong, the simultaneous-equation model is applied to Japan, Korea, Singapore, and Taiwan only.

TABLE 7.3 The Relationship Between Saving and Income: Simultaneous-Equation Estimation

Country	Intercept	Regression Coefficient of		S.E.	D−W
		$\dot{Y}$	Y/N		
Japan	0.0660	0.249 (0.180)		0.0163	1.79*
	0.0522		0.237 (0.689)	0.0621	2.15*
Korea	−0.0403	1.604 (0.402)		0.0383	2.40
	0.189		4.821 (0.578)	0.0207	1.31
Singapore	0.0928	0.262 (0.245)		0.0264	1.71
	0.0308		0.0450 (0.0245)	0.0224	1.30
Taiwan	−0.209	4.352 (1.950)		0.0887	1.14
	−0.073		0.0286 (0.002)	0.0139	1.68

* Results obtained after correcting for first-order serial correlation.

In fitting equation (17) and other equations involving capital inflows, it is to be noted that we use long-term capital inflow data (see the Appendix on the sources and derivation of data, p. 192) for F and not F as defined in equation (16). This implies that the difference between these two concepts of F (which in the first instance is equal to the net short-term capital inflows, reserve movements, etc.) must be included in the error term. The use of long-term capital inflow data can be justified on the grounds that net short-term capital inflows are unstable, and that the long-term inflows may provide a more stable relationship with the growth of real income.

If we think that it is the level of per capita income rather than the rate of income growth that affects the saving ratio, then we have the following system of equations:

$$S/Y = a_1 + b_1(Y/N) \tag{18}$$
$$Y/N = a_2 + b_2(S/Y) + c_2(F/Y) \tag{19}$$

Of course, the reasoning underlying equations (18) and (19) is exactly the same as equations (14) and (17); the only difference is that now Y/N replaces $\dot{Y}$ as the endogenous variable in the system. The results of estimating (18) by the two-stage least squares method are also given in Table 7.3. Alternatively, we can break up F/Y into private inflow (F_p/Y) and official inflow (F_g/Y) to take into account the possible differences between these kinds of inflows. In so doing, we have the following two systems of equations:

$$S/Y = a_1 + b_1(\dot{Y}) \tag{14}$$
$$\dot{Y} = a_3 + b_3(S/Y) + c_3(F_p/Y) + d_3(F_g/Y) \tag{17a}$$

and

$$S/Y = a_1 + b_1(Y/N) \tag{18}$$
$$Y/N = a_2 + b_2(S/Y) + c_2(F_p/Y) + d_2(F_g/Y) \tag{19a}$$

However, the use of private and official capital inflows as exogenous variables does not give any significantly different interpretations of results, although in the cases of Singapore and Taiwan the statistical fit has become improved.[6]

A comparison of the results in Table 7.3 with those in Tables 7.1 and 7.2 suggests that in the cases of Korea, Singapore, and Taiwan, the single-equation estimates are very similar to those derived from the simultaneous-equation system. For Korea, the two sets of results are almost identical; the saving ratio always bears significant positive relationships with income growth or per capita income. For Singapore, the relationship is always positive but not statistically significant, and higher statistical significance is obtained when the simultaneous-equation method with capital inflow separated into private and official sources is employed. In the case of Taiwan, the regression coefficients are positive and highly statistically significant in both methods of estimation; in the simultaneous-equation method, the value of the regression coefficients is large. It is in the case of Japan that we find some differences between the single-equation estimation and the simultaneous-equation estimation. In the single-equation method, we find that there is a highly significant positive relationship between the saving ratio and income growth and between the saving ratio and per capita income. However, in the simultaneous-equation estimation, the regression coefficient of income growth is positive but only statistically significant at the 25 per cent level, and the regression coefficient of per capita income is totally statistically insignificant. Although these results could mean that the single-equation estimates have overstated the relationship between income and saving, it is more likely that our simultaneous-equation model is not so applicable to Japan as to the other economies under study. The reason for inapplicability of the simultaneous-equation model must lie in the inappropriate use of F/Y as the exogenous variable in the model. While it is largely true that the rate of income growth is related to F/Y in the cases of Korea, Singapore and Taiwan, this is evidently a wrong choice of variable in the case of Japan.[7]

It is unfortunate that we do not have data to estimate the simultaneous-equation model for Hong Kong, and that the model we have established is not applicable to Japan. Nevertheless, we have found that saving and growth are positively related and largely mutually interdependent in the cases of Korea, Singapore, and Taiwan.

(3) Exports, Capital Inflow, and Saving

We now turn our attention to some additional factors affecting domestic saving in the context of an open economy. Earlier in this chapter, we argued that for several reasons we expect the export sector to contribute more to domestic saving than other sectors do. Regarding the influence of foreign capital inflow on domestic saving, we have argued that although most empirical evidence and theoretical analysis is in favour of a negative relationship between capital inflow and domestic saving, there are good reasons for a positive relationship. We shall now perform some simple tests on these alternative propositions in the light of the experience of the economies in this study. To test whether the export sector affects saving more than the other sectors do, we use the following estimation equation:[8]

$$S = a_1 + b_1(Y - X) + c_1(X) \qquad (20)$$

where S is the level of domestic saving; Y, GDP; and X, exports. Moreover, in view of the fact that economic growth in the economies under study is very much associated with the growth in the export of manufactured products, we try to break down total exports into export of manufactured goods (X_m) and exports of non-manufactured goods $(X - X_m)$, and see whether they have different effects on the level of domestic saving. Thus, instead of equation (20), we have

$$S = a_2 + b_2(Y - X) + c_2(X - X_m) + d_2(X_m) \tag{21}$$

Regression results of equations (20) and (21) are reported in Table 7.4. In three cases, Hong Kong, Korea, and Taiwan, the regression coefficient of X is positive and statistically significant.[9] However, while the coefficient of $(Y - X)$ is statistically insignificant in the cases of Hong Kong and Korea, it is positive and highly significant in the case of Taiwan. This means that for Taiwan the export sector and the non-export sector are equally important in generating domestic saving; the effect of export earnings may be more important as the magnitude of the coefficient of $(Y - X)$ is considerably smaller than that of (X). When exports are divided into the manufactured and non-manufactured categories, we find significant differences between Hong Kong and

TABLE 7.4 Saving and Export Earnings

Country	\multicolumn{4}{c}{Regression Coefficient of}	R^2	$D - W$
	$Y - X$	X	$X - X_m$	X_m		
Hong Kong	−0.0150 (0.0594)	0.275 (0.028)			0.938	2.08
	0.0023 (0.062)		−0.613 (0.942)	0.302 (0.040)	0.942	2.17
Japan	0.534 (0.064)	−0.352 (0.566)			0.984	1.22*
	0.498 (0.069)		0.888 (1.097)	−7.562 (5.449)	0.985	1.36*
Korea	0.0893 (0.1207)	1.182 (0.616)			0.962	2.16
	0.157 (0.111)		−1.125 (1.222)	1.414 (0.559)	0.972	2.72
Singapore	0.344 (0.157)	0.0120 (0.2708)			0.908	1.66
	0.140 (0.178)		−0.983 (0.598)	2.371 (1.321)	0.937	1.40
Taiwan	0.255 (0.025)	0.464 (0.045)			0.996	1.02
	0.205 (0.036)		0.858 (0.218)	0.447 (0.043)	0.997	1.46

* Results obtained after correcting for first-order serial correlation.

Korea on the one hand and Taiwan on the other. In the cases of Hong Kong and Korea, the results clearly indicate that it is earnings from exports of manufactured goods that have positive effects on saving inasmuch as the coefficient of X_m is highly statistically significant and X_m constitutes a significant proportion of total exports. On the other hand, the coefficient of $(X - X_m)$ bears a negative sign though it is statistically insignificant. In contrast the results for Taiwan indicate that exports both of manufactured and non-manufactured goods are important factors. This is however not surprising as the composition of the exports of Taiwan is considerably different from the other economies. Even in the latter part of the sixties a significant proportion of Taiwan's exports was composed of primary products, notably sugar.

In the cases of Singapore and Japan, it seems that it is the non-export sector that contributes more to domestic saving. Indeed in Japan the level of domestic saving bears a negative (though statistically insignificant) relationship with the level of export earnings. The results remain the same in the case of Japan when export earnings are separated into the manufactured and non-manufactured components. In the case of Singapore, the results are however considerably modified. With the separation of exports into two categories, the regression coefficient of non-export earnings becomes statistically insignificant and that of X_m positive and statistically significant at the 10 per cent level. This shows that the effect of export earnings from manufactured goods on domestic savings cannot altogether be ignored in Singapore. In Japan, it is likely that the increased extent of import-substitution and the expanded domestic market caused a higher percentage of production oriented to the home market, and thus less dependence of domestic saving on the export sector.

Next, we shall discuss the controversial issue of the relationship between capital inflow and domestic saving. We shall begin with Haavelmo's hypothesis that saving is a function of income and capital inflow; his original specification is

$$S = g(Y + F) \tag{22}$$

where S is domestic saving; Y, GDP, and F, capital inflow; and g, a constant.

Assuming that the marginal change in S with respect to Y is different from that with respect to F, we have

$$S = aY + bF \tag{22'}$$

Dividing through by Y, we obtain

$$S/Y = a + b(F/Y) \tag{23}$$

Equation (23) is the most often used estimating equation in the existing literature on saving-inflow relationships.[10] It is also one of the estimating equations in this study.

Alternatively, we can bring in income growth to take care of the life-cycle hypothesis by specifying the following relationship:

$$S = aY + bF + e(dY) \tag{24}$$

where dY is the change of income over the previous year.
Dividing through by Y, we obtain:

$$S/Y = a' + b'(F/Y) + e'(\dot{Y}) \tag{25}$$

where $\dot{Y}$ is the proportional rate of income growth.

Data of the five economies are fitted to equations (23) and (25), and the results are given in Table 7.5. The statistical fit is good only in the cases of Korea and Taiwan. In Korea, the regression coefficient of F/Y is highly significant whether income growth is included in the equation or not. In the case of Taiwan, there is on the other hand a significant negative relationship between saving and capital inflow. Indeed, such a negative relationship is hardly affected by the inclusion of the income growth variable. In the case of Japan, the statistical fit is very bad for equation (23); when the income growth variable is included, the fit greatly improves and the regression coefficient of (F/Y) is negative, though statistically insignificant. From every indication, it can be concluded that there does not exist any significant relationship between saving and capital inflow in the case of Japan. The statistical fit of the Singapore data to equations (23) and (25) is also bad. In fact, the fit worsens when income growth is included in the estimation. In the case of equation (23), the regression coefficient of (F/Y) is positive and statistically significant at the 25 per cent level. In brief, using the conventional single-equation method of estimation, we can find a significant negative relationship between saving and capital inflow only in the case of Taiwan. Our results though cannot overthrow the existing findings (which are mostly derived from cross-section studies) yet suggest that it is dangerous to apply the conclusions drawn from cross-section studies to individual countries. The negative relationship

TABLE 7.5 Saving and Capital Inflow: Single-Equation Estimation

Country	F/Y	Regression Coefficient of F_p/Y	F_g/Y	$\dot{Y}$	R^2	$D-W$
Japan	0.404 (0.454)				0.057	1.66*
	−0.104 (0.476)			0.367 (0.152)	0.387	1.30*
Korea	1.306 (0.148)				0.847	2.44
		1.136 (0.263)	1.696 (0.517)		0.854	2.39
	0.882 (0.242)			0.607 (0.271)	0.896	1.76
		0.710 (0.307)	1.285 (0.501)	0.605 (0.273)	0.903	1.73
Singapore	0.492 (0.361)				0.171	1.40
		1.409 (0.545)	−0.942 (0.767)		0.455	1.13
	0.193 (0.445)			0.141 (0.259)	0.157	1.60
		1.084 (0.684)	−0.830 (0.752)	0.0335 (0.244)	0.411	1.07
Taiwan	−1.768 (0.243)				0.790	1.36
		2.899 (0.828)	−1.023 (0.187)		0.940	1.92
	−1.746 (0.312)			0.556 (0.414)	0.821	1.36
		2.925 (0.662)	−0.889 (0.181)	0.599 (0.180)	0.969	2.63

* Results obtained after correcting for first-order serial correction.

between saving and capital inflow obtained from cross-country studies largely reflects the fact that the poorer, more slowly-growing countries are likely to be those with low saving ratios. Thus, it is highly possible that cross-country results indicate a causal relationship running from lower saving ratios to higher levels of aid instead of from higher capital inflows to changes in saving behaviour. It is therefore more useful and meaningful to investigate the relationship between saving and capital inflow by time-series studies of individual countries.

As we argued earlier in this chapter, foreign capital inflows are often highly heterogeneous; they consist of grants, aid, official and private long-term capital, etc. The effects of each kind of capital inflow on domestic saving and growth may be quite different from the others. We accordingly divide capital inflow into private capital inflow (F_p) and official capital inflow (F_g) which consists of grants, aids, and direct investment. In so doing, equations (23) and (25) can be written as:

$$S/Y = a' + b_1(F_p/Y) + b_2(F_g/Y) \qquad (23a)$$

and

$$S/Y = a' + b_1(F_p/Y) + b_2(F_g/Y) + c'(\dot{Y}) \qquad (25a)$$

The regression results of equations (23a) and (25a) are also given in Table 7.5.[11] Our results indicate that the effects of capital inflow on saving can be very different for different types of inflow. In the cases of Korea, Singapore, and Taiwan, the regression coefficient of (F_p/Y) is highly positive and statistically significant. The statistical fit of the equations becomes very much improved in the cases of Singapore and Taiwan. The result is particularly worth noting in the case of Taiwan where we find a negative relationship between S/Y and F/Y, and now we find a significant positive relationship between S/Y and F_p/Y. In Korea, the regression coefficient of (F_g/Y) is also positive and statistically significant, implying that both private and official capital inflows have important positive effects on the saving ratio. It is of interest to note that in both Singapore and Taiwan, the regression coefficient of (F_g/Y) bears a negative sign. While it is statistically significant in the case of Taiwan, it is not in the case of Singapore. Thus, in Taiwan the negative effect of capital inflow on the saving ratio is entirely due to the official inflow. Thus our results show that in analysing the relationship between capital inflow and the saving ratio, we have to divide total capital inflow into its various sources and consider each by itself. In considering the different effects of private and official capital inflow on saving, we find that it is very often true that private inflow tends to have a positive effect on saving while the effect of official inflow on saving is a negative one.[12] These findings of course have great appeal to common sense. This is because the availability of capital inflow, especially that in the form of official inflow associated with specific projects and social overheads, has the effect of reducing the need for, and thus the level of, domestic saving. On the other hand, although private capital inflow may compete with domestic capital for best opportunities of investment, it tends to create more new investment opportunities through linkage effects,[13] and therefore give greater stimulus to domestic saving. Thus, many of the seemingly contradictory results obtained in the empirical literature concerning the relationship between saving and capital inflow can in fact be sorted out by a more disaggregative definition of foreign resources inflows.

The above estimation equations are subject to the possibility of simultaneous-equation bias as both saving and income enter the equations, and as we have discussed earlier, they are likely to be interdependent.[14] To remove such a bias, we may specify the following system of equations:

$$S/Y = a_1 + b_1(F/Y) + c_1(\dot{Y}) \tag{26}$$
$$\dot{Y} = a_2 + b_2(S/Y) + c_2(X/Y) + d_2(\dot{I}) \tag{27}$$

where X/Y is export ratio and I is the proportionate growth rate of investment. Thus, besides the saving ratio equation, we specify another equation relating income growth to the saving ratio, the export ratio and the growth rate of investment. Furthermore, equation (26) can also be specified as:

$$S/Y = a_1' + b_{11}(F_p/Y) + b_{12}(F_g/Y) + c_1(\dot{Y}) \tag{26a}$$

TABLE 7.6 Saving and Capital Inflow: Simultaneous-Equation Estimation

Country	Intercept	F_p/Y	F_g/Y	F/Y	$\dot{Y}$	S.E.	$D-W$
			Regression Coefficient of				
Japan	0.064			−0.126 (0.431)	0.315 (0.123)	0.0170	1.83*
Korea	0.057			1.950 (0.771)	−0.733 (0.871)	0.0294	2.77
	0.051	1.711 (0.763)	2.339 (0.990)		−0.631 (0.811)	0.0293	2.54
Singapore	0.098			1.145 (0.480)	0.153 (0.255)	0.0276	1.63
	0.090	1.109 (0.754)	−0.825 (0.750)		0.015 (0.249)	0.0251	1.06
Taiwan	0.035			1.012 (0.822)	2.109 (1.510)	0.0464	1.04
	0.109	3.073 (0.703)	−0.809 (0.209)		0.659 (0.242)	0.0124	2.55

* Results obtained after correcting for first-order serial correlation

i.e. we try to distinguish the effects of the different types of capital inflows on saving. Using the two-stage least squares method, we arrive at the results shown in Table 7.6. The results for all the four economies under study (Japan, Korea, Singapore and Taiwan) are surprisingly close to those obtained from the single-equation estimations. This is particularly true for Japan, Singapore, and Taiwan. In the case of Korea, the sign of the regression coefficients of income growth changes from positive in the single-equation estimations to negative in the simultaneous-equation estimations, and as a result the magnitudes of the regression coefficients of capital inflows become greater in the simultaneous-equation estimations. Nonetheless, the implications of the results on the relationships between saving and capital inflows are the same in all cases. Thus, it seems that while there is every justification for us to direct our attention to simultaneous-equation systems in the study of the relationships between saving and growth, the use of single-equation methods in such studies is not as disastrous as one would at first think.

8 Economic Growth and Income Distribution

THE RELATIONSHIP BETWEEN GROWTH AND INCOME DISTRIBUTION

The recent surge of interest of economists in the distribution of income in the developing countries during their process of growth has produced considerable work on the subject.[1] For instance, there are many concepts of income distribution: functional distribution by factor services, regional and geographical distribution, and size distribution by person or household. It is size distribution in which most development economists are interested and that is also the concept studied here. Of the various concepts of distribution, size distribution is perhaps the most satisfactory indicator of how increases in welfare are distributed among the people. The relationship between changes in income distribution by size and economic growth is of special interest to development economists as after a decade or more of rapid growth in some developing countries, they begin to worry not so much about the rate of increase in output but more about to whom these increases in output go.[2] It is clear that economic growth can do more harm than good if the benefits of growth are confined to a small group of people. Since the 1960s, some economists have become dissatisfied with using the criterion of growth of national income as the only indicator of economic development.[3] More equal income distribution in the process of development has been increasingly regarded as highly desirable even if this means a reduction in the rate of output growth.

Although the discussion of distribution in a dynamic context goes back to the classical economists, the first systematic work on the changes of income distribution in the process of development was that of Kuznets (1955). Kuznets hypothesised that distribution is likely to become more unequal in the early stage of development and later begin to equalise. This is his famous 'inverted-U' hypothesis which has received so much attention in the literature. He argued that in the early

152

stages of development the greater proportional accumulation of assets by the rich tends to widen inequality. In the process of development, there will be legislative interference, demographic changes, technical changes, and a greater proportional increase in service incomes (professional and entrepreneurial earnings and the like) received by the lower income group. These forces counteract the concentration of property assets. Also, at the early stage of development the shift of labour away from agriculture tends to widen inequality. This is because the average income of the rural population is usually lower than that of the urban and inequality within the urban population is usually greater than that of rural. Assuming intersectoral difference in average income and the intrasectoral inequality do not change, it can be shown that an intersectoral shift of resources and urbanisation in a later stage of development will narrow inequality. Thus, the 'inverted-U' relationship between inequality and development can be generated from the phenomenon of intersectoral shift of resources alone. Kuznets (1955) tried to show this by rather cumbersome numerical examples while more recently Robinson (1976b) and Knight (1976) show this by simple mathematical models. Thus, the 'inverted-U' relationship is an automatic result of the structural change associated with development. It is meant to describe the long-run development process rather than the short-run growth phenomenon.

Later on, further explanations have been formulated to account for the pattern of distribution in the process of development. Kravis (1960) brought out the importance of differentiation in labour skill and Becker and Chiswick (1966) emphasised human capital and education. These explanations fit well into the Kuznets' type of structuralist point of view. It is generally the case that economic development is accompanied by increases in the provision of labour training and education, and a more-educated and better-trained population usually means a greater equality in income distribution. The qualification that needs to be made is that the increasing supply of skilled and educated workers does not lead to a significant fall in their factor prices. This can normally be guaranteed by the rapid technical progress taking place in the urban sector of the economy.

To summarise, the structuralist with the 'inverted-U' hypothesis believes that in the process of development, the following changes will take place:[4] First, there will be changes in the structure of production. Specifically, the share of agriculture in total output will decline and the share of urban population will rise. Second, there will be increases in school enrolment and labour training. Third, there will be decreases in the rate of population growth. As a rule, such decreases in natural growth rates of population are greater for the lower income groups and as a result the growth of their average income is higher than that of the rich. Thus, development is associated with these changes in structure and these changes will give rise to the 'inverted-U' relationship between development and income inequality. There is also some empirical support for such a hypothesis; e.g. the cross-section studies of Kravis (1960), Oshima (1962), Adelman and Morris (1971, 1973), Paukert (1973), Chenery, *et. al.* (1974), Ahluwalia (1976b), and the time-series studies of Kuznets (1963), Soltow (1968, 1969). Most of the time-series studies deal however with developed countries. Only very recently do studies on developing countries appear,[5] and in most cases the analysis has been inconclusive.

Despite the theorization and some empirical support mentioned above, the 'inverted-U' hypothesis is subject to serious doubts. It must be noted that the structuralist arguments are not that convincing. First, the changes in the structure of production will give rise to the 'inverted-U' relationship only if it is assumed that the intrasectoral inequality and intersectoral differences in average income remain unchanged in the process of development. These assumptions are clearly highly unrealistic. Worse still, there can be no generalisation concerning the changes in intrasectoral inequality and intersectoral differences in average income. Such changes depend on a complex set of technological, social, historical and institutional factors. We are going to see how these factors have operated differently in the economies of the study. Second, increased education and training may not always help to narrow income inequality. Some groups of people may be able to benefit from increased education and training more than others, and if this does happen the intrasectoral inequality will be increased. Furthermore, the increased supply of skilled labour will raise the average income of the lower income groups permanently only if substitution of skilled for unskilled labour is always possible and the rate of return to skilled labour will not fall because of, for example, high rates of technological change. Third, the structuralist often neglects the importance of changes in economic-demographic structure in the process of development. Very often, it is not the differential rate of population growth of different income groups that is important, but such changes as household size, female labour participation rates, and age and sex composition. These changes will certainly not invariably give rise to an 'inverted-U' relationship between development and inequality.

Moreover, the structuralist has neglected changes other than structural changes. The most important is price changes which can be induced by structural changes and can occur independently. Knight (1976) has raised some interesting points concerning the relationship between price changes and income distribution. He argues that it is implausible for any single distribution theory to be applied to the economy as a whole. The economy should be divided into the modern and traditional sectors (or the industrial and agricultural sectors) and the tradable and non-tradable sectors. Relative prices in the contrasting sectors bear an important relation to income distribution. For instance, population growth and rural-urban migration associated with development have important effects on food prices and, therefore, on the average income of farmers and finally intersectoral inequality. Furthermore, when a country is dependent on foreign trade, changes in world prices of exports and imports and exchange rates will have uneven effects on different sectors of the economy and will therefore disturb the initial pattern of income distribution. These price changes are entirely independent of structural change. In a study on income distribution in Malaysia, Lee (1977) points out that the declining trend in the export price of rubber was a major factor causing the increase in inequality because the decline in export prices has the effect to widen the intersectoral difference in income.[6] Since there are no general rules governing price changes in different economies, it cannot be expected that changes in income distribution in the process of development would follow the 'inverted-U' path.

Although the structuralists place some emphasis on the changes of wealth distribution in the process of development, they tend to neglect the role of the initial distribution of income-generating assets. In developing countries, this initial distribution of assets very often governs the distribution-development relationship and the actual level of inequality in income distribution. To a large extent, the initial distribution of income-generating assets is governed by the specific social, historical, and institutional factors of individual countries. Similarly, the structuralists tend to overstate the importance of the 'automatic' forces of structural change in development and neglect the role of government policy. It is evident that the changes in relative prices, intrasectoral inequality, intersectoral shift of resources, and distribution of property assets, etc. brought about by structural change can be modified or even reverted by government policies. In the next section we will illustrate the importance of the initial distribution of assets and government policies in income distribution in some of the economies under study.

To sum up, there cannot be an inexorable law describing the changes in income distribution in the process of development. There must be more factors than just structural change which govern the pattern of income distribution in individual economies. In view of the heterogeneous situations in different countries, cross-country studies are at best informative, and very often give rise to misleading results concerning the relationship between development and income distribution. From this point of view, time-series studies should shed more light on the evolution of income distribution in the course of development. It is the purpose of this chapter to present and analyse the evolution of income distribution by size in the economies under study and hence to see in what ways the experience of these economies can shed light on the current discussion of this issue.

CHANGES IN INDIVIDUAL ECONOMIES

The lack of income distribution data in the developing countries is well known. Very seldom is a continuous time-series on income distribution available for a considerable time period so that we can trace the pattern of changes in inequality. Of the five economies under study, one might expect Japan to have good data on income distribution. It is perhaps a little surprising that Taiwan also has reasonably good data on income distribution, especially for the period since the early 1960s. There are many estimates on personal distribution of income in Korea. But they are mostly based on small samples and contain considerable biases, and since they are based on different methodology their degree of comparability is rather low. It is therefore difficult to trace the change over time in income distribution in Korea. For the two city economies, data on income distribution are very limited. In Hong Kong, data are available only for those years, 1966, 1971, and 1976 in which censuses took place. In Singapore, some data can be made available from the household surveys in 1966 and 1972 and the labour force surveys in 1973–5.

In discussions of income distribution by size, a number of measures of inequality have been used. The most popular is undoubtedly the Gini coefficient which is a ratio showing the degree of inequality by expressing the area between the Lorenz curve and the diagonal as a proportion of the total area under the diagonal.[7] The Gini coefficient is zero when incomes are exactly equally distributed, and one when all incomes are received by only one income unit (person or household). This coefficient has a number of drawbacks; for example, it treats absolute differences as equal wherever they may occur in the income range, and it is insensitive to small changes in income dispersion.[8] However, the Gini coefficient is preferred and will be used here as the measure of inequality because it is a summary measure in the sense that it incorporates all income differences in a simple way and because it is the most widely available data.

(1) *Hong Kong*

Owing to lack of data, changes in income distribution in Hong Kong can only be examined with reference to the period 1966–76. With the information for 1966, 1971, and 1976 obtained from censuses, we compiled Table 8.1. The data for the three years are largely comparable as they are based on a system of classification common to the various censuses. From Table 7.1, it can be seen that there was a move towards greater income equality in Hong Kong in the latter half of the 1960s, but there was little change in inequality for the period 1971–6. For 1966–71, the income share of the lowest two deciles increases from 4.7 per cent to 5.7 per cent but that of the richest 20 per cent decreases from 58 per cent to 51 per cent. This results in a fall of the Gini coefficient from 0.487 to 0.439. For 1971–6, there is almost no change in the Gini coefficient. However, both the share of the lowest two deciles and that of the highest two deciles decline; the Gini coefficient has no noticeable change because

TABLE 8.1 Income Distribution by Size in Hong Kong, 1966–76*

Year	Share of Lowest 20%	Share of Middle 40–60%	Share of Highest 20%	Gini coefficient
	%	%	%	
1966	4.7	12.3	58.0	0.487
1971	5.7	13.7	51.1	0.439
1976	5.3	14.2	50.1	0.435

* This table refers to land households only. The marine population has a higher Gini coefficient but it constitutes only about 1.5 % of the total population.

Sources: Census and Statistics Department, *Census Circular, No. 5/71*, Hong Kong Government, October 1971, (mimeographed). Census and Statistics Department. *Hong Kong Population and Housing Census: 1971 Main Report*, Hong Kong Government, 1972.
Census and Statistics Department, *Hong Kong By-Census 1976, Basic Tables*, Hong Kong Government, 1977.

of the rise in the share of the middle 40–60 per cent. One might argue that these findings lend support to the Kuznets 'inverted-U' hypothesis in the sense that by the mid-sixties Hong Kong had passed the early phase of industrialisation and thus we observe a decrease and then a levelling off in income inequality. However, there are no data for us to test the assertion of an increasing inequality in the early phase of Hong Kong's industrialisation, and it is doubtful whether the turning point of income inequality should occur as early as the mid-sixties. To obtain some idea of changes in inequality in the period 1960–6, we can identify the various probable sources of declining inequality during 1966–71 and then examine the extent to which these factors also operated in the earlier period.

The factors contributing to a decrease in inequality during 1966–71 can largely be identified by examining the breakdown of income distribution by industry and by occupation. This is because it is mainly the intersectoral shift of resources between different industrial sectors and occupational groups that has caused the decreasing inequality in income distribution. Inasmuch as such an intersectoral shift of resources represents structural change in the process of development, the structuralist arguments about decreasing inequality and development can largely be applied to the case of Hong Kong. We observe that the primary factor contributing to greater equality is structural change in the form of changes in the sectoral distribution of employment and output. The Hong Kong experience shows that over time increasingly larger proportions of the labour force belong to those sectors which have relatively lower income inequality. Data on the income distribution by sector in 1971 show that the manufacturing sector had the lowest Gini coefficient among the one-digit industries.[9] As we showed in Chapter 3, there were significant increases in the manufacturing sector's share in output and employment during the period 1966–71 in Hong Kong. In fact almost invariably those sectors with a lower-than-average concentration ratio aimed at employment and output shares during the period 1966–71. Thus the structural changes associated with economic development have produced an automatic mechanism for improvement in income distribution by size. However, we must be cautious in extending this result to other developing economies. This is because while it is true that the manufacturing sector almost invariably gains in employment and output share in the process of development, it is not always the case that the manufacturing sector has a higher-than-average equality in income distribution. Whether the manufacturing sector has a relatively lower Gini coefficient is of course related to the social and economic structure of the country and the deliberate policies pursued by the authorities concerned.

Changes in the occupational structure also have important effects on income distribution in Hong Kong as over time increasingly larger proportions of the working population belong to those occupations which have relatively lower income inequality. There are two important changes in occupational structure leading to greater income equality. First, industrial labour with the lowest inequality in income distribution among all occupational groups had the greatest gain in its employment share during the period 1966–71. Second, the administrative, executive and managerial occupations with the highest inequality in income distribution experienced a sharp decline in their employment share. These two factors contributing to greater equality are however to some extent offset by the decline in the employment share of services and clerical and sales occupations which have relatively low inequality in income distribution. Nevertheless, on the whole there is little doubt that the changes in occupational structure during the period 1966–71 have contributed significantly to greater overall income equality.

The other important factor contributing to greater equality in Hong Kong during the period 1966–71 is a decline in intersectoral inequality, i.e. a reduction in the differences of the average income received by different industrial sectors. From the wage-rate statistics published by the Labour Department, we find that within the broad sectors of the economy, those industries with above-average wage rates such as utilities experienced the slowest rate of increase in wages, and those industries with much below-average wage rates such as textiles and garments had the fastest rate of increase in wages. These differential changes in wage rates among the broader industry groups are largely the result of differential growth in productivity and output associated with rapid economic growth. Unlike many other developing countries, changes in educational status and household size have contributed very little to greater equality during the period 1966–71 in Hong Kong. This is because there has been virtually no change in the share of university graduates (the group with the highest inequality) and the share of those with primary education (the group with the lowest inequality) in the total working population. With regard to changes in household size, we find that between 1966 and 1971 the share of small households (one to four members) slightly increased. From the 1971 census results that small households as a group had higher-than-average inequality in income distribution, we can deduce that the changes in household size during the period were towards greater inequality. However as the

changes were small, the effect on the overall distribution should not have
been significant.

The intersectoral shift of workers from those industries and occupations with greater income inequality to those with smaller inequality
which occurred during 1966–71 cannot be found in 1971–6. The 1976
by-census results show that the share of manufacturing workers in total
employment declined from 47.4 per cent to 45 per cent, that of financial
and business increased from 2.5 per cent to 3.3 per cent, and that of
community, social and personal services increased from 14 per cent to 15
per cent. In view of the fact that income inequality in finance and
business (with a Gini coefficient of 0.57) and that in services (0.50) are
much higher than that in manufacturing (0.36), the overall Gini
coefficient could have increased during the period 1971–6 if not for the
increase in average income of many during the same period. The
increase in education and training received by many has resulted in a
considerable increase in the share of the middle 40–60 per cent. It seems
that the adverse effect of intersectoral shift of resources during 1971–6
on income distribution has been more or less exactly balanced by a
narrowing down of intersectoral and intrasectoral inequality in income
distribution.

What are the implications of the above analysis on changes in income
inequality during the period 1960–6? Inasmuch as structural change in
the period 1960–6 was in the same direction and even more rapid than
the period 1966–71, the same favourable effect on income distribution
that occurred during 1966–71 should have also operated over the period
1960–6. This means that there are reasons for us to believe that income
inequality also decreased during the earlier phase of industrialisation in
Hong Kong. The only factor worth noting is perhaps the changes in
educational status. The increase in the proportion of university
graduates was quite marked during the earlier period of development,
and as we have noted this group has a much above-average inequality in
income distribution. Thus changes in educational status might have
considerable effect in counteracting the factors contributing to greater
equality during the earlier period. However, there is no reason for us to
believe that such a force was significant enough to bring forth a
decreasing equality in Hong Kong during its early period of industrialisation. Thus, the Kuznets 'inverted-U' hypothesis of income
distribution in the process of development cannot exactly be established
in the case of Hong Kong. Instead of an 'inverted-U' relationship,
structural change in Hong Kong has produced a continuous decline and
then a levelling off in income inequality.

(2) *Japan*

Japan has among the economies under study the most reliable and elaborate data on income distribution. There are three main sources of distribution data. The first is the Employment Status Survey which surveys the total population. The second and third are the Family Income and Expenditure Survey which is based on samples from the non-agricultural population, and the Survey of Taxes and Public Levies of Farm Households which is based on samples from the agricultural population. As the information given by the Employment Status Survey is usually more comprehensive, we used it for our present analysis. Table 8.2 shows the pattern of income distribution in Japan during the period 1956–71.

TABLE 8.2 Distribution of Income by Size in Japan, 1956–71

Year	Share of Lowest 20%	Share of Middle 40–60%	Share of Highest 20%	Gini coefficient
	%	%	%	
1956	7.2	14.7	39.6	0.313
1959	6.1	14.1	42.5	0.357
1962	5.5	13.8	44.6	0.382
1965	5.4	13.9	44.2	0.377
1968	4.6	14.0	43.8	0.380
1971	3.8	13.6	46.2	0.407

Source: Office of the Prime Minister, Japan, *Employment Status Survey*, 1956–1971, Tokyo: Bureau of Statistics.

There are a few observations worth noting in Table 8.2. First, the overall income distribution as measured by the Gini coefficient became more unequal over time during the period 1956–62. Though there was a sign of increasing equality in distribution during the period 1962–5, there was again a definite trend of decreasing equality during the period 1968–71. Second, the income share of the households in the lowest two deciles had a marked decline throughout the period 1956–71. There was at the same time a rise in the income share of the households in the highest two deciles. These observations unmistakably indicate widening inequality in Japan during the period 1956–71. How can we account for this widening inequality over time? The explanations can be found by considering the complex interaction of social, demographic and economic factors in the process of rapid growth. The two most important explanations are discussed below. To a large extent, they are related to structural change in the process of growth and development. However, they are not usually emphasised by the structuralists.

1. An Increase in One-Person Households.

One-person households increased not only in number but also as a proportion of all households. During the period 1956–71, the number increased rapidly from 2.8 million representing 13.7 per cent of all households in 1956 to 6.7 million representing 21.3 per cent of all households in 1971. Data on the changes in the number of one-person households by age groups show that the largest increases in proportions are the young (less than 30) and the very old (over 65). This rapid increase in one-person households is partly due to changes in employment structure accompanying the rapid growth in Japan. The drastic reduction in non-agricultural employment and the migration of the non-agricultural population to urban areas means that there is a drastic increase in the number of new entrants in the urban labour force residing in company dormitories, in boarding houses, or establishing separate households in cities. Since these new entrants belong to single-earner households and because they have recently been employed, their incomes are low. This is why a high percentage of one-person households tend to be in the lowest income groups. Another cause of increases in one-person households is the economic, political, and social changes in Japan, which have generated a general change in attitude towards the size of family.[10] One result of such a change is that both young adults and retired and semi-retired persons prefer to have their own home if they can afford it. Thus, with rapid growth in income, there is an increase in the propensity of unmarried adults to form separate household units.[11] Moreover, economic development and rising per capita income has also provided the means for retirement and early retirement. Thus, the one-person households in Japan consist mainly of young and aged persons who largely fall into the low income brackets. The statistics below would illustrate this point: in 1956 about 30 per cent of all one-person households were in the lowest decile and 2/3 in the lowest three deciles. Another way of looking at this is that 40 per cent of the households in the lowest decile in 1956 were one-person households. Over time, as we have seen, the proportion of one-person households increased markedly from 13. 7 per cent in 1956 to 17. 9 per cent in 1962 to 21.3 per cent in 1971. However, such increases in proportion are mainly in the lower deciles. In 1971, 33.4 per cent of all one-person households were in the lowest decile and 71.7 per cent of all households in the lowest decile and about one half in the second decile consisted of one-person households. From these statistics and our analysis, we can deduce that the increasing proportion of one-person households in Japan means an increasing proportion of households in the lowest income groups and is therefore an important contributing factor to the increasing inequality of overall income distribution during the period 1956–71.

2. An Increase in the Share of Property Income.
Property Income refers to rent, interest, and dividends received by households, excluding returns on the equity of unincorporated entrepreneurs. Property income typically has the highest inequality among the various types of income.[12] In fact Kuznets tried to account for the greater equality in developed countries in recent times by the observed declining share of property income in total income.[13] Comparing the last columns of Tables 8.2 and 8.3, we observe that it is also true in Japan that the distribution of property income is always more unequal than the overall income distribution as the Gini coefficients of property income are always greater than those of overall income. However, we do not observe a declining trend in the share of property income. As can be seen from Table 8.3, we find that there was instead a significant increase in the share of property income over the period 1956–71: from 7.6 per cent in 1956 to 11.5 per cent in 1962 and to 13.2 per cent in 1971. It is not our purpose here to investigate the causes of the increase in the share of property income, but this has had definite effect in making the

TABLE 8.3 Distribution of Property Income in Japan, 1956–71

Year	Share of Property Income	Distribution by Ordinary Households		Gini Coefficent
		Lowest 20%	Highest 20%	
	%	%	%	
1956	7.6	8.4	49.4	0.384
1959	10.3	7.0	53.0	0.427
1962	11.5	6.7	56.7	0.467
1965	12.2	6.8	57.0	0.465
1968	12.4	7.0	56.5	0.465
1971	13.2	6.7	57.4	0.469

Source: See Table 2.

distribution of income less equal over time. Furthermore, there is also an increasing inequality in the distribution of property income during the period 1956–62. It can be seen from Table 8.3 that the Gini coefficient increased from 0.384 in 1956 to 0.427 in 1962; the property income share of the lowest two deciles decreased from 8.4 per cent to 6.7 per cent, and that of the top two deciles increased from 49. 4 per cent to 56.7 per cent. Thus during the period 1956–62, there are two forces within the distribution of property income contributing to greater inequality over time. The first is that even assuming a constant Gini coefficient of property income the rising property income share in total income will give rise to greater overall inequality. Secondly, the widening of inequality in the distribution of property income itself gives further impetus to greater overall inequality. After 1962, it seems that the Gini coefficient of property income changed only slightly and hence the rising share of property income in total income became the principal force for increasing inequality in income distribution.

(3) *Korea*

Until very recently, there were no reasonably acceptable data for the size distribution of income in Korea. However, there were two sets of data which had been used widely in the English-speaking world. The first is the result of a study by the Chung Ann University for the year 1966, based on a rather small sample.[14] The report on this study did not give a Gini coefficient for the entire sample. Chae (1972), using the generalised Pareto model,[15] estimates the Gini coefficient to be equal to 0.335. On the other hand, using the conventional method of approximate triangles,[16] Paukert (1973) estimates it to be equal to 0.26. Paukert's estimation was based on quintiles, a method in which the margin of error can be large and the estimate bound to be understated. In view of this fact, Chae's estimate of 0.335 is perhaps nearer to the 'true' coefficient for the entire sample of the Chung Ann study. Even if we take the Gini coefficient of 0.335, it is very low by all standards. The second source of income distribution data is family income and expenditure surveys.[17] In Korea, these surveys are divided into cities and farm household surveys conducted by the Economic Planning Board and the Ministry of Agriculture and Forestry respectively. This was the source used and made known internationally by the World Bank – Sussex study.[18] The Gini coefficient according to this study is 0.36 for the year 1970. Thus, if we accept both sets of data, we find an increase in income inequality in Korea for the period 1966–70.

Very recently, Renaud (1976) has brought up some of the neglected estimates on income inequality in Korea, notably those estimates made by Chae (1972) based on tax data for the years 1958, 1960, 1961, and 1970. Also, Mizoguchi, Kim, and Chung (1976) have made estimates for the overtime change in income distribution in Korea for the period 1965–71. Their estimates (hereafter MKC estimates) are based on family income and expenditure surveys together with census and tax statistics. With these recent estimates, we can now have a clearer picture of the overtime changes in inequality in Korea.

Table 8.4 shows the various sets of income distribution data for different time periods. Owing to the different methodology used in arriving at the data, the different sets of data are not comparable. This means that we do not have continuous and comparable data for the entire period, 1958–71. Yet from these sets of data we can deduce at least to some extent the direction of change in inequality over this period. In Table 8.4, Column (1) shows Chae's estimates based on tax data. This set of estimates together with the Chung Ann estimate for 1966 and the MKC estimate for 1965 tends to suggest that there was a decline in income inequality in Korea in the period 1958–1964. On the other hand, in the period 1964–8 there appeared to be an increase in

TABLE 8.4 Various Estimates of Gini Coefficient for Korea,
1958–71

Year	(1)	(2)	(3)	(4)
1958	0.464			
1960	0.448			
1961	0.438			
1965				0.343
1966			0.335	
1967				0.396
1968		0.305		0.425
1969		0.298		0.425
1970	0.375		0.372	0.355
1971		0.272	0.360	0.365

Source: (1) Chae (1972).
  (2) Economic Planning Board, *Korean Statistics Yearbook, 1970 and 1971*.
  (3) 1966, from Chung Ann Study, quoted in Renaud (1976). 1970 and 1971 estimated from family and expenditure surveys. The Chung Ann estimate and the family and expenditure surveys estimates are grouped together because of their largely similar concepts and methodology.
  (4) Mizoguchi, Kim, and Chung (1976).

inequality according to the MKC estimates. Finally, in the period 1968–71, there seemed to be a decline in income inequality again. This is the indication of all sets of data shown in Table 8.4. Thus, it is of interest to note that instead of an 'inverted-U' relationship between inequality and development, there is a wave-like relationship in Korea. Income inequality first declines, then increases and then declines again. It is difficult to predict the path of changes in the future. However, if we consider the period 1964–71 alone and expect inequality to fall or level off after 1971, then the 'inverted-U' hypothesis describes very nicely the experience of Korea.

Let us now try to see whether explanations can be offered to account for such observations of wave-like changes in inequality in Korea. It seems that the answer is yes and the explanations are largely related to historical and institutional factors and discretionary government policies and are not an automatic mechanism resulting from structural change. Both the low level of inequality in Korea and the decline of inequality in 1958–64 can largely be attributed to the rather even distribution of property assets in Korea at the time when industrialisation and modernisation took place. In developing countries, an important source of income inequality is very often the concentration of returns from income-generating assets to the upper-income groups. In this regard, we find many historical reasons for a relatively even distribution of assets and thus of income in Korea. Firstly, at the end of World War Two, the major portion of non-agricultural assets previously owned by the Japanese were gradually disposed of and sold to the private sector over a period of more than a decade. Secondly, there were two land reforms which proceeded in two stages. In 1947 land once held by Japan was redistributed, reducing the full-time tenancy rate from 70 per cent to 33 per cent within one year. A second land reform in 1950 redistributed Korean landlord holdings, with nominal compensation, and virtually eliminated tenancy. Furthermore, the damage and destruction of the Korean War had the effect of flattening wealth distribution. This is because firstly the properties of upper income classes were lost and/or damaged because of the war, and secondly because during the years of war and the years immediately after the truce, the terms of trade between agricultural and non-agricultural products were in favour of the former thus leading to an urban to rural redistribution of wealth. Also, a policy of the government in the early sixties to confiscate the illegally accumulated wealth obtained from profiteering during and immediately after the Korean War had further effects in reducing the concentration of income-generating wealth. All these historical reasons affected the distribution of assets, reduced the relative share of income generated from them, and thus increased the relative equity in income distribution. This is supported by the distribution of national income statistics. The share of property income in Korea was consistently lower than in most other developing countries during the period 1955–70. Some economic measures primarily for the promotion of economic growth such as monetary reforms also had some side-effects on income distribution. There have been three monetary reforms in Korea, 1950, 1953, and 1962. To curb inflation, the cash holdings of the wealthy class above a certain limit were put into restricted accounts, resulting in a freeze of the cash holdings of the rich. These monetary reforms of course only had the effect of producing a temporarily more equal distribution of income as the freezing was temporary. But they should have played some part in promoting a more equal distribution of income at least up to the year 1962 when the freeze of cash holdings was partly lifted. Thus it is the historical past coupled with policy measures that have contributed to the prevention of concentration of income-generating wealth in Korea and therefore the decline in inequality in the period 1958–64.

During the period 1964–8, we witness the Korean government's strong emphasis on industrialisation and the adoption of a low agricultural price policy. Such a policy changes the relative prices in favour of the industrial sector and as a result the rural-urban inequality is widened. This is well supported by statistics on household income derived from family income and expenditure surveys and farm household surveys. We observe that the farm household income was nearly equal to that of non-agricultural employees in the early sixties, but there was an increasing tendency toward disparity during the period 1964–8. Renaud (1976) also shows that the rural-urban gap in terms of consumption expenditures widened during the period 1964–8 and the farm price parity ratio (which measures the relative movements of prices received and prices paid by farmers) dropped by 15 per cent during the same period. Another explanation for the increasing inequality during 1964–8 was a considerable increase in inequality of business income. According to the MKC estimates, the Gini coefficient of business income increased from around 0.4 in 1964 to around 0.5 in 1968. This means in this period of rapid growth, relatively large amounts of profits are distributed to a relatively small number of entrepreneurs. The reason for this is not at all clear and further research into this phenomenon is evidently needed. The growing importance of the big business in the latter half of the sixties could have been an important reason.

All available data suggest that income inequality declined in the period 1968–72. One of the important factors must be the change in government policy towards agricultural production in the late sixties. Agricultural production was encouraged and for that purpose the government had to raise agricultural prices. From the year 1968, the difference between non-agricultural income and farm income began to decrease and the farm price parity ratio began to rise.[19] The narrowing down of the intersectoral inequality must have contributed greatly to the decline in overall income inequality after the year 1968. Furthermore, inequality of business income also showed signs of decline, especially after 1970. This is perhaps due to the fact that the extremely rapid growth of the economy in the early 1970s gave considerable opportunities to the relatively smaller entrepreneurs, and the rapid technological change has reduced the profitability of many entrepreneurs in the older industries. In addition, many of the new industries have been closely controlled by the government, directly and indirectly. At the same time, the spread of education services and the fall in population growth rate should also have some effect on the decline in inequality in the period after 1968. However, these factors representing structural change in the process of development could not have played a very important part.

(4) *Singapore*

The growth experience of Singapore should provide an interesting case study of inequality and development in terms of the Kuznets hypothesis. This is because the development strategy of Singapore is a single-minded devotion to growth.[20] In the absence of income distribution policies, it is of interest to observe how the pattern of inequality changes in the course of rapid growth. However, there have been extremely few studies on the issue of income distribution in Singapore.[21] Undoubtedly, the problem lies with the availability of data. Using the basic data in the reports of different sample surveys, some attempts have been made to measure the change over time in income distribution in Singapore. Two sets of Gini coefficient estimates are given in Table 8.5. The first set is estimated by Pang (1975); it is based on sample surveys undertaken by the Economic Research Centre in the University of Singapore. The second set is estimated by Rao and Ramakrishnan (1976); the estimate for 1966 is from the same source,[22] but the estimates for 1972–5 are based on household expenditure and labour force surveys conducted by the Singapore government. Both sets of data unambiguously indicate that there was a substantial decline in income inequality during the period of

TABLE 8.5 Gini Coefficient of Personal Income Distribution in Singapore, 1966–75

Year	(1)	(2)
1966	0.457	0.498
1972		0.443
1973	0.415	0.457
1974		0.434
1975		0.448

Source:
- (1) Pang (1975, Table 2)
    For 1966: Sample Household Survey conducted by the Ministry of National Development and Economic Research Centre.
    For 1973: Labour Force Participation Survey conducted by the Economic Research Centre.
- (2) Rao and Ramakrishnan (1976, Table 8)
    For 1966: same as (1)
    For 1972: Preparatory Survey for the Household Expenditure Survey, 1972/73.
    For 1973–75: Labour Force Survey.

rapid growth 1966–73. Pang's set of Gini coefficients indicates a lower level of inequality. But, in relative terms, the percentage decline in the Gini coefficients is not very much different for the two sets of estimates. Pang's estimates give a 9.1 per cent decline for the period 1966–73, while Rao and Ramakrishnan's estimates give a 8.2 per cent decline for 1966–73, and 11 per cent decline for 1966–72. There is no clear trend we can detect for the period 1973–5. In any case, such a period of rapid inflation and slow growth should not be taken into account when we are looking at a longer term process of growth and development.

What are then the explanations for declining inequality and rapid growth in Singapore? It seems that to a large extent the automatic forces of structural change have an important role. The rapid growth of the economy has led to both a shift of resources from the more unequal sectors to the more equal sector and a decline in the inequality within the different sectors of the economy. Pang (1975) emphasises the importance of intersectoral shift of workers. He points out the rise in the share of manufacturing in total working population and the fall in the share of services in the period 1966–73. Indeed, the share of manufacturing in total working population increased from 19.4 per cent in 1966 to 24.1 per cent in 1973 while the share of services decreased from 36.6 per cent to 26.3 per cent. Such a change has the effect of lowering the overall income inequality because the Gini coefficient of the manufacturing sector (0.482 in 1966) is considerably lower than that of the service sector (0.521 in 1966). However, this argument of intersectoral shift of workers has overlooked the counter-balancing effect of an increase in the share of commerce in total working population. This share increased from 22.8 per cent in 1966 to 27.1 per cent in 1973, and the Gini coefficient of the commerce sector is rather high, being equal to 0.521 in 1966. As a matter of fact, according to the decomposition analysis performed by Rao and Ramakrishnan (1976), it is shown that the decline in the Gini coefficient over the 1966–75 period is due largely to the decline in intra-sectoral inequality and only marginally to the changes in the sectoral composition of employment and output. The importance of the decline in intra-sectoral inequality is illustrated by Table 8.6 which shows the Gini coefficient. by sector of economic activity. The decline in the inequality of the commerce and services sectors is very notable. There is also a considerable decline in inequality in the manufacturing sector.

TABLE 8.6 Gini Coefficient by Sector of Economic Activity in Singapore 1966–75

Sector of Activity	Gini Coefficients		
	1966	1974	1975
Agriculture & Fishing	0.447	0.333	0.436
Quarrying	0.521	0.543	0.544
Manufacturing	0.482	0.433	0.446
Construction	0.351	0.402	0.372
Utilities	0.315	0.392	0.486
Commerce	0.523	0.457	0.461
Transport & Communication	0.399	0.321	0.341
Services	0.521	0.439	0.469

Source: Rao and Ramakrishnan (1976, p. 109).

According to the analysis of Rao and Ramakrishnan (1976), the most important reason for the decline in intra-sectoral inequality in the major sectors of the economy is the high rate of increase in employment over the period 1966–72 during which employment increased by 40 per cent. This rapid growth in employment is only partly the result of the rapid growth of income but largely related to the wage restraints and labour-intensive development strategy of the Singapore government. Data from the labour force surveys reveal some significant changes in the characteristics of the working population over the period 1966–75.

Specifically, there were changes in the age, sex and employment status of the working population. Over the 1966–75 period, an increasing proportion of young workers (aged 10–29) is found in all sectors of the economy, notably in the manufacturing, utilities, transport and communications, and services sectors.[23] The labour participation rate of females increased significantly resulting in a great increase in the percentage of female workers in the manufacturing and commerce sectors. As most of all females joining the labour force are young, the increased labour participation of females is an important factor to account for the increase in the proportion of young people in the working population. These changes in the age and sex composition of the working population also imply that the proportion of employees in the working population would increase. It can be argued that the increase in the proportion of young people in the labour force will reduce overall inequality because the income received by the lower income groups will be increased. Similarly, the increase in the share of employees tends to increase the share of employee income in total income and it is well known that employee income has a much lower Gini coefficient than proprietors or business income. It is however of interest to note that unlike the case of Japan, the increase in the proportion of young workers does not seem to have increased the number of one-person households and produce an adverse effect on overall income inequality. This can perhaps be explained by the geographical fact that in Singapore, increases in employment do not involve the rural to urban movement of workers and the setting up of new households in the urban district. At the same time, the public housing scheme in Singapore provides accommodation for the workers and family (including parents) and the separation propensity is thus smaller than in the case of Japan.

(5) Taiwan

There have been a number of studies on income distribution by size in Taiwan resulting in some fairly reliable estimates even for the earlier period of industrialisation. Since 1964, the government has been collecting data on income distribution making available continuous time-series data. Table 8.7 gives a summary of the changes in income distribution in Taiwan over the two decades 1953–72. The Table shows that from 1953 to 1964, there was a very drastic improvement in income distribution, the income share of the lowest 20 per cent increased from 3.0 per cent to 7.7 per cent, that of the highest 20 per cent dropped from

61.4 per cent to 41.0 per cent and the Gini coefficient fell from 0.558 to 0.328. There was however very little change in distribution during the period 1964–8, but after 1968 we again witness a considerable improvement in distribution over time. In 1970, the Gini coefficient for Taiwan was 0.307 which is the lowest among the five economies we study here. Over the two decades 1953–72 there was a fall of 46 per cent in the Gini coefficient. Our next question is of course how we could explain this drastic reduction in inequality over the period of rapid growth and industrialisation in Taiwan. The Kuznets hypothesis of increasing inequality at the initial stage does not seem to apply. To a large extent, it is the peculiar economic, social, and political conditions in Taiwan that have contributed to the reduction in inequality.

TABLE 8.7 Distribution of Income in Taiwan, 1953–72

Year	Income share of Lowest 20%	Income share of Middle 40–60%	Income share of Highest 20%	Gini-Coefficient
	%	%	%	
1953	3.0	9.1	61.4	0.558
1959/60	5.7	13.9	51.0	0.440
1961	4.5	14.0	52.0	0.461
1964	7.7	16.6	41.0	0.328
1966	7.9	16.2	41.4	0.330
1968	7.8	16.3	41.4	0.335
1970	8.3	16.9	39.4	0.307
1971	8.3	17.0	39.4	0.306
1972	8.6	17.0	39.1	0.301

Sources: For 1953: Kowie Chang, "An Estimate of Taiwan Personal Income Distribution in 1953 – Pareto's Formula Discussed and Applied," *Journal of Social Science*, August 1956. (in Chinese)
For 1959/60: Kowie Chang. "Report on Pilot Study of Personal Income and Consumption in Taiwan," paper prepared under the sponsorship of working group of National Income Statistics Directorate-General of Budget, Taipei: the Executive Yuen, 1960.
For 1961–72: Directorate-General of Budget, Account and Statistics, *Report on the Survey of Family Income and Expenditure and Study of Personal Income Distribution in Taiwan*, various years.
The 1970–72 data have been adjusted by Kuo (1975) by also taking the tax levy data of the Ministry of Finance into account.

The primary factor contributing to a reduction in inequality over time in Taiwan is very probably the fairly even initial distribution of income-generating assets in both the agricultural and non-agricultural sectors. In the agricultural sector, such a fairly even initial distribution has been due to the land reforms started in 1949. The land reforms limited the amount of farm rent on private tenanted land to 37.5 per cent of the annual main crop yield and this used to be over 50 per cent before the reforms. Also land reforms drastically reduced the number of tenant farmers through the sale of public land and the 'land-to-the-tiller' programmes. With the continuous redistribution of land during the early period of growth, overall income distribution became more equal over time. In the non-agricultural sector initial asset distribution was also fairly equal because there had been no major industrial concentration and most of the assets were in the hands of relatively small- and medium-scale entrepreneurs, mainly migrants from the mainland during 1948/49. Over time, this industrial structure was maintained and in fact there was a decline in the degree of oligopoly.[24]

The second factor contributing to reduced inequality is that throughout the period of industrialisation in Taiwan the income differential between the agricultural and non-agricultural sectors was unusually small, and furthermore there was a tendency for it to narrow down over time. In 1964, the average industrial family had an income only 15 per cent above that of the average agricultural family. The upward 'pull' on wages of such exogenous forces as multinational corporations and union pressure, reinforced by government salary increases, was apparently much weaker in Taiwan than in most contemporary less developed countries.[25] At the same time, the situation of the agricultural population was improved as a result of a rapid reduction in the collection of 'hidden rice tax' by the government. The hidden rice tax takes the form of the government asking the farmers of paddy land to pay taxes and to exchange rice for chemical fertilisers[26] at a government price which is substantially below the wholesale market price. Over time the government has gradually increased its purchasing price bringing it more in line with the market price. This has had the effect of improving the average income of the agricultural population over time and it has thus contributed to a more even income distribution.

The third factor contributing to reduced inequality is that within both the industrial sector and the agricultural sector, there was no increase in the share of those categories of income (e.g. property income) which have been found to have higher-than-average income inequality. In fact the national income data show that the income share of the compensation of employees (which had lower-than-average income inequality) increased from 45.6 per cent in 1965 to 54.8 per cent in 1972, while there was little change in the share of property income which was 22.4 per cent in 1955 and 23.5 per cent in 1972. In the agricultural sector, land reforms had provided the farmers with a higher incentive to work and therefore higher productivity and higher returns. As a result, increases in agricultural earnings were able to keep pace with increases in farm rent. In the industrial sector, although increases in the wage rate in general lagged behind productivity changes, there was an increase in the proportion of the overall wage bill as the rapid growth in the industrial sector (especially during the export-oriented phase) had been able to generate very large increases in employment. In addition, there had been marked social mobility in Taiwan which enabled substantial numbers of both industrial and agricultural workers to emerge as small entrepreneurs.

SUMMARY AND CONCLUDING REMARKS

We find that of the five economies under study, Japan has shown an increase in inequality over time while there was a definite trend of decreasing inequality in Hong Kong, Singapore and Taiwan. In Korea, the trend of changes in income inequality is difficult to generalise as it consists of both rises and falls. In general, with the information available for the five fast-growing Asian economies, there is no indication of an 'inverted-U' relationship between inequality and growth. Furthermore, in all cases, the factors affecting the change in income inequality are not purely those suggested by the structuralists, viz., the intersectoral shift of resources, increase in education and training, and changes in the rate of population growth. Almost invariably government policies and the social and institutional peculiarities have played the dominant part either in affecting income distribution directly or in reshaping the influence of structural change on inequality.

Our study suggests that in Hong Kong, Singapore, and Japan, rapid growth has produced some automatic mechanisms to affect changes in income distribution to a greater or lesser extent. In Hong Kong structural change accompanying rapid economic growth led to changes in the shares of employment and output in different industrial and occupational groups. Such changes were in the direction of increasing (decreasing) the proportion of households in the group with lower (higher) inequality in income distribution. In consequence, Hong Kong has experienced an increase in equality in income distribution. In addition, there was a decline in intersectoral inequality resulting from the faster increases of wage rates in those industries which used to offer below-average wage rates. Thus, it is in the case of Hong Kong that we find that structural change alone has played the dominant role in affecting the change of income distribution over time. In the case of Singapore, structural change did occur in the form of intersectoral shift of resources. However, the net result of such a shift tends to have a rather neutral effect on income distribution. This is because while some resources moved to the sectors with a lower inequality there were also resources moving to the sectors with a higher inequality. The major factor explaining the decline in overall inequality appears to be the reduction in intra-sectoral inequality resulting from a massive increase in employment and changes in the characteristics of the working population. These changes are however more related to the wage restraints and labour-intensive development strategies of the government than structural change alone. In the case of Japan, on the other hand, rapid economic growth gave rise to higher levels of per capita income, and this, coupled with changes in social values gave rise to increases in one-person households, a high proportion of which were in the low income groups. Furthermore, in Japan, the long history of monopolistic and oligopolistic controls in industry and agriculture has produced a fairly uneven distribution of income-generating assets at the beginning of Japan's postwar growth. Hence, the share of property income increased over time and the degree of concentration in property income (which was already much above-average in concentration) also increased over time. Consequently rapid economic growth in Japan was accompanied by increasing inequality. However, structural change has played only a minor part. The social and institutional factors have been more important.

In Korea and Taiwan, in addition to the historical, social and institutional factors, the role of government policies has been very important. The economic forces of rapid growth and structural change in themselves are relatively insignificant. In both Korea and Taiwan, the fairly even initial distribution of income-generating assets to a large extent accounted for the rapid decrease in income inequality in the process of rapid growth. In both cases, land reform constituted an important factor in effecting asset redistribution. In Korea, there were also important historical factors such as the transfer of most of the country's industrial assets to the government after independence for gradual resale, and the impact of the Korean War on the assets of the high-income groups. In Taiwan, the historical factor of migration of medium- and small-scale entrepreneurs from the Mainland during 1948/49 made for a fairly even-initial distribution of income-generating assets in the industrial sector. In addition, the increase in income equality in Korea and Taiwan was also due to the implementation of certain public policies such as the agricultural prices policies and monetary reforms in Korea, the reduction of the 'hidden rice tax' in Taiwan.

In sum, the study of the changes in income distribution in five Asian economies in the process of growth indicates that there is no inexorable law governing the pattern of income distribution at different levels of development. The changes in distribution are mainly related to the historical past, the dynamic aspects of the social and political system, and changes in economic policies. It is therefore unrealistic and misleading to formulate hypotheses of income distribution and the stage of development on the basis of cross-section evidence. Our results therefore throw serious doubts on the Kuznets 'inverted-U' hypothesis of changing inequality in the process of economic development. In view of the multi-dimensional aspects of income distribution and its relation to economic development, more fruitful conclusions can only be obtained from detailed studies of individual countries or a group of fairly homogeneous economies.

PART IV

Conclusion

9 Summary and Implications

SUMMARY OF FINDINGS

The focus of the present study has been on the morphology, causes, and effects of economic growth in the five fast-growing Asian economies. We began with a presentation of the contours of economic growth so that we could establish some bases for our later empirical analysis. Then we examined the trends of growth in output and factor inputs. We observed that during the period 1955–74, all of the selected economies experienced exceptionally high growth rates of 7.8 per cent to 9.5 per cent in real output and above 5 per cent in real income per capita. Indeed, in the late sixties and early seventies, growth rates had been above 10 per cent in most cases. Population growth in Japan was stable at the 1 per cent level throughout the period under study. On the other hand, population growth in the four other economies was at first relatively fast but slowed down in the later sub-periods. At the same time, the growth of the labour force in these four economies was also very rapid, due largely to the rapid increases in the labour participation rate. Generally speaking, during the period 1955–60, population grew faster than the labour force but the trend was generally reversed for the period 1960–74. This rapid increase in manpower resources played an important part in supporting the growth of the industrial sector. There was also a rapid growth in investment resulting in rapid growth in capital input for the economy. The high rates of growth in investment in these economies were due to the massive foreign capital inflows and/or high saving rates.

The rapid growth in output and factor inputs in these economies was accompanied by equally rapid structural changes in the sectoral shares of total product and employment. In general, we witness a drastic shift of resources from the primary sector to the secondary and the tertiary sectors. For the five economies as a group, our results indicate that the per capita income level of US$1100 (at 1970 prices) is a dividing line between two different phases or levels of growth and development. Before such a per capita income level is attained, our results suggest drastic declines in the share of the primary sector and

179

significant increases in the share of the secondary and tertiary sectors. Beyond the US $1100 level, the rate of changes in sectoral shares slows down and the share of the secondary sector shows signs of slow decline.

Next our study tried to identify the various possible sources of economic growth and examine their relative importance. Specifically, we tried to identify such sources of growth as scale economies, factor substitution elasticities, rate of technical progress, and growth in factor inputs. For this task, we used the aggregate production function approach. We admit that there are various estimation and aggregation problems associated with this approach but we would like to use it in a constructive manner to generate useful empirical results. In view of the fact that the economic characteristics of different sectors in these economies (notably the agricultural and the non-agricultural sectors) can be very different, we estimated the production function of the agricultural and the manufacturing sectors separately in addition to the estimation of the whole economy. Specifying the Cobb-Douglas and CES production functions and using alternative estimation methods, we found that economies of scale were relatively unimportant in explaining growth in the economies under study, while technical progress was found to be a crucial factor. However, in the cases of Hong Kong, Singapore, and Korea, the estimated rates of technical progress (2–3 per cent per annum) are relatively low, implying that there were other equally important factors contributing to growth. This result is in some ways different from the Solow-Denison findings for developed nations which indicated that technical progress was the single important factor contributing to growth. The part played by the growth in capital per worker in explaining productivity growth is less clear, as the regression coefficients are statistically significant in some cases but not in others. The estimated elasticities of substitution take a wide range of values. In many cases, the estimates are high and statistically significant indicating the importance of the ease of factor substitution in productivity growth.

Using an alternative approach of the national income accounting method, we analysed the contribution to economic growth of factor inputs relative to total factor productivity (which is a somewhat broader term than technical progress). We found that changes in factor inputs accounted for about one-half of income growth in our group of economies for the period under study. It is of interest to note that this result lies somewhat between the existing findings for developed nations on the one hand and developing countries on the other. When we confined ourselves to the contribution of factor inputs to growth, we found that for the economy as a whole the contribution of capital to growth is generally greater than labour. We also attempted to quantify the contribution to growth of reallocating resources from the agricultural to the non-agricultural sector. We found that the gains from reallocation were substantial in the cases of Japan, Korea, and Taiwan where the agricultural sector is relatively large.

To take a more realistic view of technical progress, we assumed that technical progress is partly endogenously determined and constructed some testable hypotheses of endogenous technical progress. Our estimation results show that learning by doing was an important determinant of technical progress in Japan, and it also had some effects on technical progress in Singapore but relatively little effect in the cases of Hong Kong, Korea and Taiwan. It seems that the importance of learning by doing has something to do with the level of technology already attained. Furthermore, investment activities were found to be an important determinant of technical progress in Japan but not in the four other economies under study. Further investigations revealed that in the cases of Hong Kong, Singapore and Taiwan, it is the importation of foreign technology that has been the principal determinant of technical progress. In the case of Korea, technical progress was largely related to foreign aid directed to the manufacturing sector, which is surely just another form of importation of foreign technology.

From the supply side of the production structure, we turned to the foreign demand for products produced by the economies under study. In this connection, we examined the role of foreign trade and export expansion as causes of rapid economic growth. A simultaneous-equation model relating exports to income growth through their effects on capital goods imports was formulated. We were able to show that in three economies, viz. Hong Kong, Korea and Singapore, all our hypothesized relationships in the model can be established. The results for Taiwan are not completely satisfactory as our hypothesis of a close link between investment and capital goods import does not seem to be valid. However in view of the high explanatory power of exports on income in the case of Taiwan, we should perhaps take the view that capital goods import in Taiwan affects income growth via some determinants other than investment. Our export-led model largely fails to account for the growth experience of Japan for the period under study. Evidently, our model, which assumes a foreign-resources constraint, is not very suitable for Japan considering its capability of financing growth by its own capital good supply.

From the causes of growth we turned to the possible effects of growth on the economic system. We built up simultaneous-equation models to investigate the interdependent relationships between income growth, saving, and capital inflow. Capital inflow is separated into private and official inflows, an attempt which turned out to be highly important as their effects on saving and growth can be quite different from each other. We find that both saving and income, and saving and capital inflow (particularly private inflow) are positively related to each other. Our results on the relationship between saving and capital inflow are contrary to other similar studies which however almost invariably used the single-equation estimation methods. We also investigated the relationship between export earnings and domestic saving. It was found that in the cases of Hong Kong, Korea and Singapore, export earnings, especially earnings from manufacturing exports, constitute the major source of domestic saving. In the case of Taiwan, both the foreign-trade and domestic sectors are important in generating saving. For Japan, saving is mainly generated from earnings in the domestic sector.

Lastly, we focused on a more recently raised issue in development economics: the relationship between economic growth and income distribution. We found that with the exception of Japan, rapid economic growth was compatible with increases in income equality. In the case of Korea, however, the trend of declining inequality is not a straightforward one as there were both increases and decreases in inequality over the period 1958–71. There is therefore no evidence as far as the economies under study are concerned to support the established 'inverted-U' hypotheses concerning the relationship between income inequality and stages of economic development. We find that a set of very complicated historical, social, economic, and political factors affected the determination of income distribution in the process of economic development. For instance, in our group of economies, changes in income distribution in Hong Kong and Japan was to a greater or lesser extent related to the economic forces of structural change while historical factors and particularly government policies were crucial in the cases of Korea and Taiwan. To sum up, there cannot be any inexorable laws governing the relationships between equality and economic development. Cross-section studies made in the hope of generating universal laws of changing distribution over time should be replaced by the more fruitful studies of individual countries.

SOME IMPLICATIONS: ECONOMIC GROWTH AND THE PRICE MECHANISM

Our remaining task is to make some remarks on the policy implications of the present study. It is of course always a dangerous matter to arrive at some general policy recommendations based merely on the study of a few selected countries. Nevertheless, it is thought that the growth experience of the five fast-growing Asian economies under study throws some light on the possibility of achieving rapid economic growth through the smooth working of the market mechanism. This of course does not imply that rapid growth under central planning is not possible or that it is less likely to be achieved. There are in fact many successful cases of economic growth through central planning; notable examples include the growth of China, some Eastern European countries, and North Korea. However, the present study suggests that the price mechanism can certainly work in some cases and rapid growth can thus be achieved with less detailed direction and control. Let us very briefly summarise how the smooth working of the price mechanism in our group of economies has produced favourable effects to stimulate rapid growth.

First, we found that substantial increases in factor inputs are required for rapid economic growth. Technical progress has been important but generally can only account for about one-half of the growth of output in the economies under study. With the need of large increases in factor inputs in the process of growth, there arises the question of how to make factor inputs available to production. It seems that in the economies under study, this problem was handled very well by the smooth working of the price mechanism. There was no need to mobilise resources (like the Great Leap Forward Movement in China in the late fifties) and/or to direct resources to the desired channels by state intervention. It seems that in relying on the price mechanism, the process of mobilising resources is less painful and yet not necessarily less speedy than through direct governmental control.

Second, in connection with the capability of the economies under study to allocate resources efficiently, mention must be made of the role of entrepreneurs, though it has not been discussed explicitly in this study. In the situation where state intervention is largely absent, entrepreneurs play the most important part in mobilising and directing resources for both production and research and development activities. The supply of entrepreneurs was exceptionally plentiful in the economies under study. What the state has provided is simply a suitable environment for the entrepreneurs to perform their functions. In Hong Kong, Japan, and Singapore, institutional and historical factors have resulted in a free-enterprise environment in which entrepreneurs can work with maximum flexibility. In Korea and Taiwan, the 'correct' environment for entrepreneurs has developed as a result of various changes in the monetary system, the correction of the over-valued foreign exchange rate, and the relaxation of restrictions on foreign trade. These measures had the effect of removing impediments to the working of the price mechanism.

Third, the large amount of capital required for investment was made possible by the high rates of domestic savings in these economies. These high saving rates were achieved without direct government intervention, and were due largely to the thriftiness of the people and partly to the abundant supply of entrepreneurs who are normally the important savers. Moreover, there have been no conceivable adverse effects of foreign capital inflow on domestic saving.

Fourth, besides the fact that a large amount of capital was necessary for rapid growth, an adequate supply of labour was also important in supporting the process of industrialisation in the economies of the study. Rapid growth in the industrial sector can be checked if there are shortages of labour which will then push up wages and reduce the resources for capital formation and the competitiveness of exports in overseas markets. In all the economies under study, a continuous supply of labour was somehow available to the industrial sector. In Japan, Korea, and Taiwan, this was made possible by the rural-urban migration of workers and in Hong Kong and Singapore by the influx of a working population from the neighbouring territories. We have not in the present study explicitly employed any dualistic or surplus-labour models to study the economies under consideration. But, it is apparent that certain aspects of such models are useful in explaining the rapid growth in our economies irrespective of whether the classical or the neoclassical version of the model is used. However, it should be noted that the realisation of rapid growth based on surplus labour is not an 'automatic' or 'painless' process. There are prerequisites for the effective use of surplus labour. There must be measures to remove distortions in both the traditional and the modern sectors so that the modern sector is capable of effective utilisation of the abundant supply and the traditional sector can increase its productivity. One way of accomplishing this is to allow the price mechanism to work smoothly in the different sectors of the economy. It seems that the price mechanism was able to perform such functions well in the economies under study. As a matter of fact, even in the cases of Korea and Taiwan, unemployment and underemployment existed only at the early stage of industrialisation. Very soon, surplus labour released from the traditional sector was almost simultaneously absorbed by the rapidly growing modern or industrial sector.

Fifth, from our particular model of export-led growth, we note that for countries subject to foreign resources constraints, export growth is the necessary and sometimes the sufficient condition for rapid growth. Without exception, all the economies under study export light and labour-intensive manufactured goods, though in the case of Japan the export of heavy industrial products is even more significant. Viewed from this angle, the production of labour-intensive products for exports is an important policy recommendation for rapid growth in many less developed countries. However, we must again realise that the movement of an economy to a position where it is capable of exporting labour-intensive manufactures at competitive world prices is not an effortless endeavour. The movement of an economy to its potential production possibility frontier where it finds its comparative advantage in the export of labour-intensive manufactures requires a set of reforms to remove impediments to the functioning of free markets unless the economy is strictly under central planning. So far as the growth experience of our economies is concerned, it seems that the free market environment provided the necessary mechanism to gear the economies towards their optimal points on the production possibility frontier. Recent world development has made an export-oriented type of growth become more difficult than before. This is the result of the increasing popularity of protectionist policies among developed countries which are the major markets for the exports of developing countries. Thus, while many developing countries are themselves trying to remove their internal impediments to a free market, there are growing external impediments which are largely outside their control. These difficulties on the part of developing countries can only be removed and reduced by working towards international cooperation and economic integration.

Lastly, we note that with the exception of Japan, rapid growth in our economies was generally accompanied by increasing equality in income distribution. Thus, growth under the working of the free forces of demand and supply is not necessarily associated with increasing inequality, as many critics of the market economy would assert. There is however no strong evidence to support the view that growth under the working of the price mechanism will necessarily increase equality in income distribution, as to a large extent historical and institutional factors coupled with appropriate government policies are important in determining income distribution in the economies under study. But it seems to make good sense that under a free-market system, we shall have less market imperfection and greater social mobility resulting in a more even distribution of income-generating wealth. These are important contributing factors to a more equal distribution of income and at the same time cause no impediments to rapid economic growth.

Appendix A: Data and their Sources

The detailed sources of data on individual economies are given together with the statistical tables in this appendix. However, in view of the fact that much of the analyses in this study depends crucially on the reliability of the data used, some comments on the sources and derivation of data are given first. Much of our attention is directed to explaining the Hong Kong and Taiwan data. In the case of Hong Kong, the general lack of data means that much of that used are based on private or government estimates and so greater attention has to be directed to explaining their sources. In the case of Taiwan, the problems are that: (1) there is often more than one source for the data on the same economic variable, e.g. the labour force and population, and (2) the same series of an economic variable is often revised very substantially and in a non-proportional manner in the newer editions of the same statistical source, e.g. the national income statistics.

Y – refers to GDP in the case of the economy as a whole. With the exception of Hong Kong, national income data are taken from official national income statistics collected by government agencies along the United Nations guidelines on national accounts. In the case of Hong Kong, the national income data before 1961 are based on private estimates and those after 1961 on government estimates. As there was no special body responsible for national income statistics in Hong Kong before 1971, even the government estimates of GDP 1961–70 are based simply on the information that was readily available and not on special surveys. However, to our comfort, it is found that estimates derived from other sources and the government estimates are well within the margin of difference thought to be acceptable. Despite the recognised deficiencies, the GDP series for Hong Kong we have used in this study is the best available to date and should reflect a reasonably accurate picture of the economic growth in Hong Kong during the period under study. There is little doubt that Japan has produced very reliable national accounts due to its long history of data collecting at the national level. Korea, Singapore, and Taiwan have also produced reasonably reliable national accounts relative to other developing economies; this is due to their special effort in collecting basic economic data since the early post-war period. Output (Y) of individual sectors in the basic statistical tables refers to value added statistics. With the exception of Hong Kong, such value added data are taken from the data on national income by industrial origin. In the case of Hong Kong, the value added series of the manufacturing sector is based on a private estimate. The methodology of such an estimate is to use the 1960 and 1961 GDP data by industrial origin as a starting point and proceed to estimate the annual growth rates of each sector for the period 1960–1970. The 1960 and 1961 base year data were made available by a work on national income statistics commissioned by the Hong Kong government (E. R. Chang, *Report on the National Income Survey of Hong Kong*, Hong Kong: Government Printer, 1969).

It should however be noted that in the case of Taiwan, the national income statistics published in the earlier years are very often subject to substantial revisions in the later published statistics. This is an especially serious problem when we notice that the revisions are usually confined to the last few years of the new series. This often makes the revised series exhibit entirely different characteristics when compared with the earlier published series. In addition, as the revision always occurs every year, we have no choice but to take the most up-to-date series available to us at the time of taking up the research. To illustrate this problem, let us take the 1974 and 1975 editions of the national income statistics published by the Director-General of Budget, Accounting and Statistics. It can be seen that for the national income statistics relating to the period 1952–66, both editions report the same figures, while for those relating to the period 1967–73, the editions give different figures. In the present study, the national income statistics for Taiwan together with other statistics derived from them are based on the 1972 publication for the period 1955–70 and on the 1975 publications for the period 1970–74.

K – Gross capital stock. Gross capital stock refers to that stock of capital in which obsolescence has been allowed for but not depreciation. Reasonably reliable estimates for K are available for Taiwan and Japan. These estimates are mainly based on the perpetual inventory method and are reconciled with some census data. For the manufacturing sector of Singapore, K data are made available by the regularly conducted censuses on industrial production. In the case of Hong Kong manufacturing we use a privately estimated capital series based on the perpetual inventory method. The annual gross fixed capital formation data in this case are estimated on the basis of capital invested in industrial structures, plant machinery and equipment and vehicles. For Korea and the whole economy of Hong Kong and Singapore, we have no choice but to estimate the K data by a rather crude method. We assume that the capital-output ratio in the mid-period is equal to the average ICOR over the entire period under study. We then apply the perpetual inventory method to calculate the gross capital stock for the other years, using the obsolescence rates of capital goods reported in the capital formation statistics.

$L -$ In the case of Japan (all sectors) and the case of the manufacturing sector of Singapore and Taiwan, L is number of workers adjusted by indices of hours of work. In other cases, L is simply the number of persons employed. A continuous L series is not available for the whole economy of Hong Kong and Singapore as no labour force survey for the economy was conducted until recently. But the changes in the labour force over a five-year period in these two cases can be obtained from the population censuses results. Thus, while it is not possible to carry out regression analyses which require a continuous L series in the cases of the whole economy of Hong Kong and Singapore, it is nonetheless possible to know the changes in the labour force over the sub-periods. In the case of Taiwan, the most reliable series of labour force statistics should be that compiled by the Taiwan Provincial Labour Force Survey and Research Institute. Unfortunately, this series is available for the years after 1965 only. Consequently, the labour force data of Taiwan is taken from those compiled by the Department of Civil Affairs, Taiwan Provincial Government which produced a labour series covering the entire period of our study.

$N -$ Mid-year estimates of population. As a rule, government authorities revise their population estimates from time to time in accordance with the census and by-census results. The population statistics used in this study are generally based on the official data published during the 1972–3 period. In the case of Taiwan, there has been a change in the population covered in the statistics published by the Ministry of Interior since 1969. As from 1969, population includes servicemen. To correct this upward bias in the official population data of Taiwan for the years 1969 and 1970, we use the 1968/69 and 1969/70 population growth rates (excluding servicemen) reported by the Taiwan Provincial Labour Force Survey and Research Institute (*Report on the Labour Force Survey in Taiwan*, Taipei, 1975). Generally speaking, in the economies under study regular censuses and by-censuses are conducted and in addition periodical sample surveys are undertaken. Thus, the population estimates reported by the official agencies in the economies under study should be quite reliable.

w – This refers to the average earnings per month. The only exception is the agricultural sector of Taiwan where w refers to the index of real earnings per worker. Wage data for the economy as a whole are available in some of the economies under study. However, in view of the serious aggregation problems inherent in such aggregative wage data, it is decided that such data are not to be used in hypothesis testings in the present study. Wage data for the agricultural sector are available in the cases of Japan, Korea, and Taiwan. In the case of Taiwan, a privately estimated wage series based on data for production costs of paddy rice is used and the official agricultural wage data are available only after 1963. The agricultural wage data employed in the present study generally refer to the earnings of general farm labourers and they represent weighted averages of permanent workers, seasonal workers and day workers. It should be pointed out that it may be permissible to use the estimated agricultural wage data in time-series studies of an individual country as long as the same concepts and methods of calculating agricultural wages has been used throughout the period under study. On the other hand, great caution must be taken in making comparisons between countries. In all our three cases, Japan, Korea, and Taiwan, payments in kind are to a greater or lesser extent included in the wage data. But there are significant differences in coverage and methods of estimating the money value of the payments in kind. For the manufacturing sector, official annual wage data are available for all the economies under study. Generally speaking, wage data of the manufacturing sector are more reliable than agricultural wage data as the former are as a rule based on clearer concepts and wider samples. Of the five economies only Hong Kong and Japan publish separate data wages excluding and including fringe benefits; in other economies, wages are defined to include remunerations of all kinds related to work performed. For the purpose of uniformity, all manufacturing wage data used in this study include fringe benefits though different countries may define and calculate the money value of fringe benefits in different ways.

I – Gross domestic capital formation, i.e. fixed capital formation plus increases in stocks. In all the economies under study, the method of measuring *I* is generally the expenditure approach. The estimates are based on the production and foreign trade data, supplemented by other relevant information based on special studies, censuses and surveys.

S – Gross domestic saving which is equal to net national saving plus provision for capital consumption. The estimates used include both the public and private sectors, and represent the balancing item on the income and outlay account of resident institutional units after all current receipts and disimbursements have been accounted for. Note that in all the economies under study (even including Japan) unincorporated business units are dominant in many sectors of the economy, and it is generally true that unincorporated business units do not provide very reliable information on fixed capital expenditure as they are usually small and find it difficult to maintain the needed accounts and information. Thus, the investment and saving data of the economies under study tend to be subject to a considerable margin of error. In Japan, Taiwan, and Korea, this problem has been remedied to some extent by information collected from special studies and surveys.

X, *X_m*, *M*, and *M'* – They are total exports of all goods, exports of manufactured goods, total imports of all goods, and imports of capital goods respectively. Manufactured goods refer to categories 6, 7, and 8 of the Standard International Trade Classification. Capital goods refer to machinery and transport equipment under the same classification. Exports and imports of services have not been included in our trade statistics. In Japan, Korea, and Taiwan, exports and imports of services are relatively insignificant while they are quite important in the cases of Hong Kong and Singapore where *entrepôt* trade and the supporting services were once the major sources of income. The imports and exports of services are excluded in our analysis for two reasons. First, the estimates of service exports and imports are typically subject to a wide margin of error. Second, such exports and imports do not show significant changes over the period under study in all economies and on *a priori* grounds the rapid growth of the economies under study should be related to foreign trade in goods rather than services. In the cases of Hong Kong and Singapore where *entrepôt* trade is important, export and import data used in our analysis refer to domestic exports and retained imports. Trade statistics are generally very reliable in all the economies as the governments of these economies have great interests in ensuring accurate trade returns for the supervision and promotion of trade. As a result of our omitting the exports and imports of services in our X and M series, I minus S is no longer equal to M minus X in the basic statistical tables given below.

F, F_p, and F_g – They are total capital inflow, private capital inflow, and official capital inflow respectively with $F = F_p + F_g$. It should be noted that the capital inflow data we use in the present study are not obtained by simply substracting S from I. The F_p and F_g data are taken from independent sources such as the balance of payments account, and statistics on aid, loans, transfers, and direct investment. F is obtained by adding F_p to F_g Thus, our data only include long-term capital movements. Monetary movements (which usually fluctuated greatly from year to year in these economies), net factor income from abroad, and errors and ommissions in the balance of payments account are excluded. As a result of our special choice of data for capital inflow, $(I-S)$ is not necessarily equal to F (or $F_p + F_g$) in our basic statistical tables Owing to the fact that different economies under study have different capital inflow data available, the F, F_p, and F_g series used in the present study are not directly comparable across countries. This problem should not be serious as the major purpose of our study is to compare the time-series results of individual countries. Furthermore, we think that our method of extracting capital inflow data from available statistics is better than the crude method of obtaining F by substracting S from I. While constant price series of the various components of GDP deflated by their own price index are generally available for the economies under study, it is not true for capital inflow data. Theoretically, if one defines capital inflow as the difference between exports and imports, then one should deflate exports and imports separately by the export and import price indices respectively. A terms of trade effect will be produced if one simply deflates the export-import differences by an export or by an import price index. (See Ady (1976)) In the present case, capital inflow is not defined as the export-import difference and the capital inflow data have been deflated by the import price index. In the case of Singapore where the export and import price indices are not available, the GDP implicit deflator has been used. Capital inflow data of Hong Kong are not available in any form and in consequence Hong Kong cannot be included in the discussion of issues related to capital inflow.

TABLE A.1 Hong Kong: The Economy as a Whole (1958 prices)

Year	Y HK$m.	K HK$m.	I HK$m.	S HK$m.	N '000	X HK$m.	X_m HK$m.	M HK$m.	M' HK$m.
1955	3962	6994	483	204	2340	1021	894	2243	187
1956	4227	7013	576	243	2440	1103	985	2443	248
1957	4490	7300	707	299	2736	1175	1032	3278	331
1958	4861	7789	708	300	2854	1260	1109	2865	304
1959	5105	7763	871	363	2967	2088	1808	3167	335
1960	6202	9009	1334	557	3064	2728	2398	4561	544
1961	6870	9642	1170	470	3175	2674	2348	4530	562
1962	7830	10763	1509	609	3805	3083	2770	5192	660
1963	8740	12010	1989	835	3421	3614	3259	5898	800
1964	9558	13308	2338	981	3504	3936	3587	6406	915
1965	11004	15480	2725	1144	3598	4558	4206	6766	1085
1966	11373	16812	2676	1124	3630	5062	4728	7300	1160
1967	11520	17156	2206	1577	3723	5574	5245	6962	1082
1968	12279	17520	1818	1237	3803	6841	6466	8385	1282
1969	13576	18164	2253	2032	3804	8243	7813	9572	1694
1970	14793	18769	2904	2737	3959	9311	8849	11097	2063
1971	15266	20007	3115	1812	4045	9888	9424	12540	2350
1972	16366	21290	3284	2563	4077	10484	10044	13006	2537
1973	18689	22931	3770	2538	4160	11788	11256	14360	2678
1974	19101	24390	3752	2057	4249	10773	10238	12928	2428

Sources: Y – Census and Statistics Department, *Estimates of Gross Domestic Product*, Hong Kong: Government Printer, various years; K. R. Chou, *The Hong Kong Economy: A Miracle of Growth*, Hong Kong: Academic publications, 1966.

K – Estimated by assuming that the capital-output ratio in the medium year of the period under study is equal to the average ICOR over the entire period. (See the text of this Appendix)

I and S – Sources as for Y.

N – Hong Kong Government, *Hong Kong Annual Report*, Hong Kong: Government Printer, various issues.

X, X_m, M, and M' – Hong Kong Government, *Hong Kong Trade Statistics*, Hong Kong: Government Printer, various issues.

TABLE A.2 Japan: The Economy as a Whole (1960 prices)

Year	Y billion ¥	K billion ¥	L '000	I billion ¥	S billion ¥	N million	X billion ¥	X_m billion ¥	M billion ¥	M+ billion ¥	F ¥ million
1955	9723	25773	41190	1678	2488	89.3	822	672	837	64	−82
1956	10641	27151	41970	2290	3047	90.2	980	819	1030	79	12
1957	11614	28990	43030	2721	3629	90.9	1079	910	1229	183	−224
1958	12218	30925	43240	2704	3486	91.8	1099	906	955	153	−96
1959	13395	33129	43680	3327	4127	92.6	1289	1069	1139	155	−131
1960	15499	36279	44610	4342	5285	93.4	1460	1236	1336	172	−52
1961	18181	40395	45180	5515	7032	94.3	1450	1223	1611	234	353
1962	19289	45225	45740	5666	6894	95.2	1611	1339	1460	275	18
1963	21163	50096	46130	6009	7335	96.2	1698	1434	1730	275	280
1964	24274	56176	46730	6680	8681	97.2	2022	1723	1911	276	173
1965	25268	62004	47480	6275	8647	98.3	2419	2069	1841	224	−335
1966	27770	66829	48470	7305	9751	99.0	2675	2292	2014	232	−449
1967	31419	72811	49200	8655	11802	100.2	2740	2381	2380	288	72
1968	35919	79971	50020	10073	14095	101.3	3279	2877	2584	353	−377
1969	40271	88656	50400	11914	16136	102.5	3881	3388	2908	407	−764
1970	44913	98115	50940	12976	18193	103.7	4398	3844	3417	540	−709
1971	48192	105430	51140	14183	18889	105.1	5287	4654	3412	543	−525
1972	52577	113740	51090	15686	20567	107.6	5648	4999	3857	547	−1172
1973	57782	128050	52330	17725	22916	109.1	5934	5262	4938	568	−2834
1974	57089	135070	52010	15988	18846	110.4	6949	6054	4825	467	−1066

Sources: K –From K. Ohkawa (ed), *Studies on Long-Term Economic Statistics*, Tokyo: Statistical Research Association, Volume 3, 1971.
S and F – Economic Planning Agency, *Annual Report on National Income Statistics*, Tokyo: Government of Japan, various years.
All other data – Bureau of Statistics, *Statistical Yearbook*, Tokyo: Prime Minister's Office, various years.

TABLE A.3 Korea: The Economy as a Whole (1970 prices)

Year	Y b.Won	K b.Won	L '000	I b.Won	S b.Won	N '000	X b.Won	X_m b.Won	M b.Won	M' b.Won	F_p b.Won	F_g b.Won
1955	929	2844	6384	112	46	21526	7.3	0.8	139	30.8	—	—
1956	934	2876	6484	89	−13	21982	7.4	1.1	119	21.6	—	—
1957	1006	2974	6713	155	56	22677	5.6	1.0	113	16.4	—	—
1958	1058	3052	7269	138	53	23331	4.1	0.7	97	14.9	1.8	—
1959	1099	3110	7290	119	44	24003	4.5	0.6	76	13.0	0.2	—
1960	1121	3145	7082	97	16	24695	9.6	1.2	102	16.3	0.8	4.0
1961	1178	3203	7328	121	46	25402	21.2	3.0	164	26.8	0.1	8.7
1962	1213	3259	7461	120	19	26125	24.9	4.4	192	45.0	1.3	2.6
1963	1302	3321	7947	225	82	26868	30.4	13.5	196	52.9	20.8	3.2
1964	1434	3343	8210	188	108	27248	63.1	30.5	214	43.8	33.3	19.3
1965	1521	3373	8522	197	115	28002	90.5	54.9	239	44.8	52.0	39.4
1966	1704	3522	8659	318	205	29160	113.1	69.1	323	95.7	49.2	69.0
1967	1828	3714	8914	368	227	29541	131.3	87.3	409	156.5	72.1	32.5
1968	2061	4038	9261	509	290	30171	169.9	125	546	228.4	193.6	19.0
1969	2374	4550	9347	714	429	30738	221.9	168	651	246.5	174.1	92.0
1970	2577	5027	9574	705	423	31435	264.0	201	627	217.4	113.5	90.2
1971	2827	5474	9889	749	422	31828	356	287	798	2б6.3		
1972	3024	5814	10373	668	466	32360	512	419	796	280.2		
1973	3523	6387	10943	922	823	32906	842	697	1055	335.7		
1974	3826	6696	11396	1102	692	33460	1054	873	1275	401.1		

Sources: K – See text and the method of estimating K for the Hong Kong economy (Table A.1).
F_p and F_g – Economic Planning Board, *Korea Statistical Yearbook*, 1971; capital inflow data from this source are also given in Brown (1973).
All other data – Bank of Korea, *Economic Statistical Yearbook*, various years; and Bank of Korea, *Monthly Statistics*, various issue.

TABLE A.4 Singapore: The Economy as a Whole (1963 prices)

Year	Y	K	I	S	N	X	X_m	M	M'	F_p	F_g
	S$m.	S$m.	S$m.	S$m.	'000	S$m.	S$m.	S$m.	S$m.	S$m.	S$m.
1957	2133	3672	258		1446	617	69	1421			
1958	2235	3849	260		1514	620	72	1272			
1959	2156	3814	157		1580	656	68	1342			
1960	2252	3771	148	125	1634	664	85	1504	90	19	4
1961	2544	3788	242	228	1687	625	96	1456	116	40	-26
1962	2630	3837	268	241	1723	711	105	1474	183	24	2
1963	2906	3892	327	286	1775	774	121	1801	209	16	25
1964	2954	4054	414	393	1820	711	135	1629	242	32	-11
1965	3177	4311	468	382	1865	840	179	1835	270	55	28
1966	3330	4468	455	406	1914	924	212	2069	267	88	-40
1967	3530	4593	483	361	1956	986	230	2171	269	109	9
1968	3920	4967	681	359	1988	1166	279	2727	346	180	133
1969	4416	5567	885	676	2017	1374	375	3300	505	176	26
1970	5327	6491	1273	876	2074	1690	516	5095	796	314	71
1971	5998	7600	1563	1018	2110	1828	671	5612	980	372	68
1972	6798	8862	1794	1117	2147	1984	912	5858	1114	584	164
1973	7585	10187	1945	1435	2185	2554	1282	6829	1308	722	24
1974	8070	11673	2199	1686	2219	3517	1450	9649	1752	1548	-4

Sources: Y, I, S, and N–Department of Statistics, *Yearbook of Statistics*, Singapore: Government Printer, 1967–1976.

K–See text and the method of estimation for the Hong Kong economy.

X, X_m, M and M'–Department of Statistics, *Singapore External Trade Statistics*, Singapore: Government Printer, various years.

F_p and F_g–Ministry of Finance, *Singapore Trade and Industry Yearbook*, 1972, 1975. Private capital inflow refers to private long-term capital and official capital inflow refers to official long-term capital as they appear in the balance of payments account.

TABLE A.5 Taiwan: The Economy as a Whole (1964 prices)

Year	Y NT$b.	K NT$b.	L '000	I NT$b.	S NT$b.	N '000	X NT$b.	X_m NT$b.	M NT$b.	M' NT$b.	F_p NT$b.	F_g NT$b.
1955	42.2	133	3026	6.1	4.5	9078	5.1	0.4	6.4	1.5	0.20	5.66
1956	43.8	136	3015	7.3	5.0	9390	5.4	0.6	8.0	2.1	0.15	4.33
1957	46.8	139	3110	7.5	5.8	9690	5.9	0.5	8.5	2.4	0.06	4.21
1958	49.2	144	3178	8.8	6.0	10039	7.1	1.1	9.8	2.4	0.13	4.28
1959	53.0	149	3272	10.4	6.5	10431	7.8	2.0	10.2	3.8	0.05	6.53
1960	56.1	155	3344	12.6	8.6	10792	8.8	2.6	10.9	4.4	0.73	4.76
1961	60.8	162	3429	14.2	9.9	11149	9.9	4.0	12.5	4.8	0.65	4.29
1962	64.2	169	3504	14.9	10.7	11512	10.9	5.2	13.8	4.0	0.23	2.90
1963	72.8	177	3617	15.8	14.9	11884	14.2	6.5	14.1	4.3	0.78	4.94
1964	84.6	185	3710	19.2	19.6	12257	17.9	8.3	16.9	5.1	0.83	3.49
1965	90.3	196	3755	25.5	22.6	12628	21.6	9.0	21.5	8.3	1.67	2.27
1966	97.5	213	3870	28.5	27.3	12993	24.7	12.4	22.6	9.6	1.20	0.17
1967	106.8	232	4130	34.2	31.3	13297	29.3	14.9	27.9	12.8	2.30	0.18
1968	115.4	246	4337	40.6	33.5	13650	32.1	20.0	34.4	13.4	3.49	0.38
1969	124.2	286	4624	40.7	38.4	13982	41.4	27.2	41.0	18.3	3.68	0.38
1970	140.8	297	4741	47.0	45.8	14306	55.8	40.2	49.3	24.7	4.54	0.38
1971	156.9	331	4909	55.4	57.4	14617	76.0	56.2	65.0	28.0		
1972	175.2	373	5114	65.3	68.5	14904	102.8	77.9	80.2	34.5		
1973	196.5	419	5476	71.8	76.9	15173	126.5	97.1	93.0	43.4		
1974	197.2	469	5664	78.9	69.8	15453	116.2	89.1	121.2	57.5		

Sources: Y, I, and S–Director-General of Budgets, Accounts and Statistics, *National Income of the Republic of China,* 1972, 1975.
K–For 1955–65, from S. W. Kuo, "The Economic Development of Taiwan: an Overall Analysis," in K. Chang (ed.), *Economic Development in Taiwan,* Taipei: Cheng Chung, 1968, p. 90. For 1966–1974, estimated by adding I_t to K_{t-1} after allowance for obsolescence.

Table A. 5 *(Contd.)*

X, X_m, M and M'—Foreign Exchange and Trade Commission, *Taiwan Import and Export Statistics*, , various issues.

F_g—This refers to the arrival amount of U.S. aid estimated by the Executive Yuan; see Economic Planning Council, Executive Yuan, *Taiwan Statistical Data Book*, Taipei, 1972, Table 11–3. The last arrival of U.S. aid was in 1968 and it was meant for the three-year period 1968–70; hence the arrival amount in 1968 is spread over 1968–70 in the F_g data we have used.

F_p – This refers to private foreign investment estimated by the Ministry of Economic Affairs, see Economic Planning Council, Executive Yuan, *Taiwan Statistical Data Book*, Taipei, 1972, Table 12–2.

L–Department of Civil Affairs, *Household Registration Statistics of Taiwan*, various issues.

N–For 1955–68, from Ministry of Interior, *The Statistical Report of Household Registration*, see Economic Planning Council, *op.cit.* Table 2–2. For 1969–74, from Taiwan Provincial Labour Force Survey and Research Institute, *Report on the Labour Force Survey in Taiwan*, Taipei, 1974, 1976.

TABLE A.6 Hong Kong: Manufacturing Sector (1958) prices)

Year	Y HK $m.	K HK $m.	L '000	W HK$	I HK $m.
1960	1945	1806	495	217	244
1961	1970	2152	475	230	299
1962	2264	2587	510	246	387
1963	2471	3007	513	253	575
1964	2691	3472	551	277	373
1965	3059	4273	548	306	1150
1966	3392	4886	551	318	788
1967	3506	5258	606	330	1055
1968	4131	5712	684	340	1440
1969	4672	6121	728	353	1136
1970	5015	6347	742	382	1624

Sources: Y – L. C. Chau, "Estimates of Hong Kong's Gross Domestic Product," *Hong Kong Economic Papers*, September 1972.

K and I – Based on N. C. Owen, "The Decline of Competition with Industrial Maturity: the Implication for Income Distribution in Hong Kong," Working Paper, Centre of Asian Studies, University of Hong Kong, 1971. The present estimates also include industrial constructions.

L – Based on Hong Kong Government, *Labour Department Annual Report*, various years. Adjustment has been made to allow for employment in unregistered undertakings.

W – Hong Kong Government, *Labour Department Annual Report*, various years.

TABLE A.7 Japan: Agricultural Sector (1960 prices)

Year	Y billion ¥	K billion ¥	L '000	W hundred ¥	I billion ¥
1955	1866	6253	16540	63	213
1956	1749	6586	16150	63	235
1957	1770	6779	15800	63	245
1958	1822	6959	15200	67	236
1959	1836	7258	14620	68	291
1960	1941	7615	14490	70	299
1961	2028	7969	14090	79	372
1962	2087	8486	13690	95	350
1963	2099	8891	12960	106	389
1964	2209	9448	12510	118	396
1965	2324	9999	12120	124	432
1966	2520	10481	11730	130	482
1967	2953	11144	10360	138	663
1963	2950	11893	9880	160	749
1969	2924	12744	9460	170	851
1970	2816	13617	8860	179	873

Sources: K – K. Ohkawa (ed.), *Studies on Long-Term Economic Statistics*, Tokyo: Statistical Research Association, Vol. 3, 1971, p. 167.
All other data – Bureau of Statistics, *Statistical Yearbook*, Tokyo: Prime Minister's Office, various years.

TABLE A.8 Japan: Manufacturing Sector (1960 prices)

Year	Y billion ¥	K billion ¥	L '000	W hundred ¥	I billion ¥
1955	1867	4824	7560	183	378
1956	2216	5288	8292	201	681
1957	2634	5908	8786	202	838
1958	2590	6629	9180	203	708
1959	3142	7358	9370	215	1047
1960	3891	8644	9986	226	1679
1961	4544	10138	10465	236	2087
1962	4712	11805	10720	248	1691
1963	5292	13448	11120	261	1803
1964	5731	15518	11256	279	1953
1965	5808	17069	11223	287	1536
1966	6484	18484	11633	308	1756
1967	7671	20735	12270	332	2621
1968	9019	23490	12789	370	3170
1969	10224	26924	12912	416	3904
1970	11167	30546	13082	452	4160

Sources: The Same as Table A.7.

TABLE A.9 Korea: Agricultural Sector (1970 prices)

Year	Y billion Won	K billion Won	L '000	W Won	I billion Won
1960	417	330	4670	7326	15.6
1961	481	333	4775	6811	19.2
1962	450	330	4800	6498	14.0
1963	554	331	5021	6289	18.8
1964	666	334	5084	6700	20.1
1965	589	343	5000	6897	26.1
1966	610	368	5013	7041	41.5
1967	598	385	4924	7698	34.9
1968	604	406	4863	8510	40.8
1969	701	427	4798	8557	41.1
1970	725	452	4834	9710	45.8

Sources: K–See explanation on gross capital stock on p. 188–9. All other data: Bank of Korea, *Economic Statistical Yearbook*, various years.

TABLE A.10 Korea: Manufacturing Sector (1970 prices)

Year	Y billion Won	K billion Won	L '000	W hundred Won	I billion Won
1960	156	398	487	119	23.4
1961	160	405	513	113	28.0
1962	179	422	560	105	35.1
1963	196	441	631	89	40.8
1964	230	458	746	83	39.8
1965	274	493	906	88	58.1
1966	320	577	978	91	108.5
1967	358	652	1116	99	102.7
1968	434	746	1352	112	126.8
1969	506	841	1367	132	131.6
1970	560	926	1353	142	127.4

Sources: The same as Table A.9.

TABLE A.11 Singapore: Manufacturing Sector (1963 prices)

Year	Y S$m.	K S$m.	L '000	W S$	I S$m.
1960	191	457	27.4	167	71
1961	221	523	27.6	163	135
1962	247	580	29.5	176	130
1963	289	648	37.7	176	162
1964	317	754	42.3	175	224
1965	400	883	48.2	174	243
1966	462	992	53.9	166	239
1967	564	1102	59.5	170	268
1968	654	1296	77.8	171	345
1969	821	1594	106.8	168	389
1970	1048	1900	126.5	162	417

Sources: Department of Statistics, *Report on the Census of Industrial Production*, Singapore: Government Printer, various years.

TABLE A.12 Taiwan: Agricultural Sector (1964 prices)

Year	Y NT$m.	K NT$m.	L '000	W Indices	I NT$m.
1955	17174	24714	1812	119	1141
1956	17383	25491	1806	120	1487
1957	18203	26101	1810	129	1320
1958	19861	27040	1813	138	1513
1959	20329	28193	1853	139	1997
1960	19139	29386	1877	136	1817
1961	20045	30897	1912	139	2167
1962	21068	32314	1936	140	1969
1963	20721	33848	1972	141	2218
1964	24465	35500	2010	170	2696
1965	26096	37749	2017	178	3535
1966	27117	39429	2050	–	3630
1967	28518	41042	2043	–	3488
1968	30459	43319	2144	–	4198
1969	26882	46259	2056	–	4305
1970	26905	48530	2099	–	3767

Sources: Y, L, and I – Provincial Department of Agriculture and Forestry, *Taiwan Agricultural Yearbook*, Taipei, 1972.

K – See the source and method of estimating K as stated in Table A.5.

w – T. H. Lee, 'The Problem and Solutions for Unbalanced Growth between Agriculture and Industry,' *Thought and World*, January 1969.

TABLE A.13 Taiwan: Manufacturing Sector (1964 prices)

Year	Y NT$m.	K NT$m.	L '000	W NT$	I NT$m.
1955	6176	17028	332	1005	1808
1956	6380	18050	336	1033	2191
1957	7032	19079	367	1044	2207
1958	7868	20567	395	1057	2666
1959	9825	21788	414	1056	2276
1960	10638	24151	433	1074	3895
1961	12372	26928	444	1267	4340
1962	12406	29406	463	1308	3950
1963	15060	32376	487	1339	4056
1964	17277	37102	531	1326	6189
1965	18466	43966	570	1413	8798
1966	19789	51221	568	1471	9033
1967	24071	61362	649	1618	12732
1968	30103	73328	645	1691	14708
1969	36483	82787	730	1669	11893
1970	43980	93384	812	1721	13430

Sources: Y and I – Directorate-General of Budgets, Accounts and Statistics, *National Income of the Republic of China*, 1972.

K – K for the year 1964, from Council for International Economic Co-operation and Development, *Census of Commmerce and Industry 1964*, Taipei, 1966. K after 1964 is derived by adding gross investment to K of the previous year after allowance for obsolescence. K before 1964 is derived by subtracting gross investment from K of the same year after allowance for obsolescence.

L – Department of Civil Affairs, *Household Registration Statistics of Taiwan*, various issues. Allowance has been made for changes in the hours of work per week.

w – Directorate-General of Budgets, Accounts, and Statistics, *Statistical Abstract of the Republic of China*, 1972.

Appendix B: Method of Calculating the Contribution of Resources Reallocation to Growth (Chapter 4)

Denison has proposed a method to quantify the contribution of reallocation of labour between the A and non-A sectors by estimating the amount by which the initial year national income would have been higher if the final year employment pattern had prevailed during a given period of study. The amount is calculated as (1) the gain in non-A national income from reducing the percentage of resources devoted to agriculture minus (2) the offsetting loss in agricultural national income resulting from the same cause. The detailed procedure in arriving at the results given in Table 4.4, Chapter 4 is shown in Table A.14.

1. Line 1 is the decline in percentage of agricultural employment.

2. Line 2 is the percentage decline in agriculture employment as percentage of non-agricultural percentage in total employment; it gives the percentage by which the non-A employment in the initial year would have been higher if the non-A percentage of total employment in the initial year is the same as the final year of the period under study.

3. As it is generally true that the decline in capital input in the A sector is less than labour and that the reallocated non-A workers are usually less efficient than the existing non-A workers, we assume that the percentage increase in total non-A inputs resulting from the shift out of agriculture was 0.6 of the percentage increase in non-A employment. Denison assumes 4/5 for Northwest Europe and 3/4 for the US and Italy. We further assume that constant returns prevails, i.e. a given percentage increase in non-A input would raise non-A output proportionately. Thus, Line 3 is obtained by multiplying Line 2 by 0.6 and it is the estimated percentage increase in non-A national income due to reallocation.

4. Line 4 is equal to Line 3 times non-A percentage of national income

TABLE A.14 Method of Calculating the Contribution of Reallocation of Labour to Growth

		Hong Kong	Japan	Korea	Singapore	Taiwan
1955–60	1		7.70	1.74		5.50
	2		12.88	8.58		14.32
	3		7.73	5.15		8.59
	4		5.97	2.73		5.10
	5		19.15	17.31		8.93
	6		3.83	2.16		1.79
	7		0.87	1.02		0.72
	8		5.10	3.64		4.38
	9		1.00	1.71		0.86
	10		9.14	4.22		5.24
	11		10.90	40.50		16.4
1960–6	1	2.60	8.30	8.00	3.58	11.00
	2	2.83	12.30	23.46	3.86	25.06
	3	1.70	7.38	14.08	2.32	15.03
	4	1.64	6.30	8.84	2.18	9.91
	5	32.10	25.54	12.14	49.45	19.61
	6	6.42	5.11	2.43	9.89	3.92
	7	0.22	0.75	0.90	0.60	1.34
	8	1.42	5.55	7.94	1.58	8.57
	9	0.24	0.90	1.28	0.17	1.38
	10	10.57	8.94	6.91	5.36	9.28
	11	2.30	10.10	18.50	3.20	14.9
1966–70	1	1.20	6.80	7.40	3.16	6.20
	2	1.27	8.97	17.58	3.28	11.29
	3	0.76	5.38	10.55	1.97	6.78
	4	0.74	4.79	6.77	1.88	4.89
	5	21.82	28.10	12.78	86.34	13.75
	6	4.36	5.62	2.56	17.27	2.75
	7	0.09	0.61	0.92	0.78	0.76
	8	0.65	4.18	5.85	1.10	4.13
	9	0.16	1.03	1.43	0.27	1.02
	10	6.90	12.04	10.11	11.64	8.07
	11	2.30	8.60	14.10	2.30	12.6

and is equal to the gain of total national income due to reallocation.
5. Line 5 is the percentage decline in agricultural employment as percentage of agricultural percentage in total employment.
6. It is usually true that the reduction in agricultural employment has relatively little effect on agricultural output, especially in economies with substantial surplus labour in the A sector. We therefore assume

that in the cases of Japan, Singapore, and Hong Kong, a 1 per cent fall in agricultural employment would reduce agricultural output by 0.2 per cent, and in Korea and Taiwan by 0.125 per cent, taking into account the different degree of underemployment in the A sector. Line 6 is equal to Line 5 times 0.2 or 0.125, and is also the estimated percentage reduction in agricultural national income due to reallocation of labour.

7. Line 7 is Line 6 times the agricultural percentage of national income and is therefore equal to the percentage loss of total national income due to reallocation of labour.

8. Line 8 is Line 4 minus Line 7, giving the net gain of percentage points in national income due to reallocation.

9. Line 9 is the gain due to reallocation per annum during the period under consideration, calculated on the basis of compound rates.

10. Line 10 is the growth rate of national income per annum.

11. Line 11 is Line 9 divided by Line 10 and is therefore the percentage contribution of reallocation of labour to income growth.

Appendix C: Some Additional Results of Production Function Estimations (Chapter 4)

TABLE A.15 CES Production Function with Constant Returns: *regression results of equation (18)*

| | | Regression Coefficient of | | | | | |
		K/L	$(K/L)^2$	t	R^2	$D-W$	σ
Hong Kong	M	0.323 (0.088)	0.157 (0.130)	0.0293 (0.0071)	0.977	2.13	−2.29
Japan	E	0.392 (0.278)	0.0408 (0.0826)	0.0575 (0.0218)	0.995	1.27	1.52
	A	2.842 (0.663)	−0.621 (0.236)	−0.176 (0.059)	0.987	1.27	1.31
	M	0.470 (0.839)	−0.112 (0.159)	0.0319 (0.0685)	0.954	1.16	0.527
	N	0.0422 (0.3727)	−0.106 (0.149)	0.0698 (0.0237)	0.987	1.05	0.160
Korea	E	0.735 (0.128)	−1.188 (1.229)	0.0485 (0.0029)	0.984	1.36	0.076
	A	−0.651 (0.288)	3.805 (2.647)	0.0554 (0.0101)	0.885	2.77	0.124
	M	0.672 (0.286)	−3.434 (4.651)	0.0464 (0.0050)	0.899	1.08	0.031
	N	0.816 (0.209)	7.659 (1.540)	0.0720 (0.0072)	0.927	2.29	−0.010
Singapore	M	0.598 (0.213)	3.447 (2.581)	0.0408 (0.0045)	0.885	1.80	−0.036
Taiwan	E	1.743 (0.420)	−3.792 (2.048)	0.0205 (0.0085)	0.991	1.31	−0.206
	A	−0.316 (1.811)	−0.195 (1.564)	0.0366 (0.0603)	0.779	1.02	0.516
	M	0.284 (0.158)	0.469 (0.251)	0.0704 (0.0139)	0.977	1.51	−0.277
	N	1.375 (0.469)	−17.52 (13.64)	0.0499 (0.0001)	0.961	1.08	−0.015

TABLE A.16 CES with Distributed Lag
regression results of equation (26a)

		Regression Coefficient of				
		lnw	*t*	$ln(Y/L)_{-1}$	R^2	$D-W$
Hong Kong	M	1.120 (0.556)	−0.0097 (0.0291)	0.0107 (0.3320)	0.945	2.20
Japan	A	−0.153 (0.270)	0.0482 (0.0232)	0.220 (0.176)	0.977	1.62
	M	0.288 (0.253)	0.0408 (0.0253)	0.292 (0.278)	0.980	1.80
Korea	A	−0.160 (0.482)	0.0498 (0.0311)	0.0027 (0.4003)	0.668	1.92
	M	0.234 (0.125)	0.0105 (0.0061)	0.559 (0.414)	0.786	2.16
Singapore	M	−0.857 (0.666)	0.0063 (0.0113)	0.360 (0.325)	0.729	2.52
Taiwan	A	0.895 (0.131)	−0.0093 (0.0052)	0.956 (0.1603)	0.960	2.38
	M	−0.0132 (0.439)	0.0580 (0.0275)	0.301 (0.271)	0.969	2.15

TABLE A.17 VES Production Function
regression results of equation (28)

		a_1	a_2	a_3	R^2	$D-W$
Hong Kong	M	0.397 (0.574)	0.204 (0.113)	0.0140 (0.0260)	0.974	2.55
Japan	A	−0.211 (0.321)	0.838 (0.399)	0.0236 (0.0507)	0.948	1.49*
	M	0.0886 (0.344)	0.675 (0.326)	0.0103 (0.0729)	0.952	1.29
Korea	A	0.499 (0.689)	−0.974 (0.848)	0.0600 (0.0129)	0.811	2.30
	M	−0.264 (0.089)	1.231 (0.644)	0.0541 (0.0041)	0.951	2.04
Singapore	M	−0.338 (0.574)	0.456 (0.323)	0.0308 (0.0129)	0.559	1.50*
Taiwan	A[a]	0.867 (0.187)	0.558 (0.841)	−0.0225 (0.0234)	0.951	2.11
	M	−0.258 (0.482)	0.408 (0.207)	0.0601 (0.0169)	0.956	1.35

* Results obtained after correcting for first-order serial correlation.
[a] 1955–65
For explanations of a_1, a_2, and a_3, see Chapter 4.

Notes

Chapter 1
1. The most elaborate study is undoubtedly that undertaken by Simon Kuznets who published a series of articles in *Economic Development and Cultural Change* from 1956 to 1965.
2. Such studies include Denison (1962, 1967, 1974), Kendrick (1961, 1973), and Carre, Dubois & Malinvaud (1976).
3. Among the few studies are Paauw and Fei (1973) and Kelley, Williamson and Cheetham (1972).
4. The rapid growth of Singapore began a little later, in the late fifties.

Chapter 2
1. United Nations, *Statistical Yearbook of National Accounts*, 1976.
2. The influx of population was especially large during 1958−60 when the Mainland suffered from both the collapse of the Great Leap and natural disasters.
3. These refer to the bank run on most of the local banks in 1965, and the anti-British riots in mid-1967.
4. The major exports of all the five economies are light industrial products such as textiles and electronic goods. Of course, Japan also exports certain 'heavy' industrial products such as machinery and transport equipment while the others do not. For all the economies, the United States constitutes the most important market for exports.
5. For a recent challenge of this view, see Tobin and Nordhause (1972).
6. For a review of and some new contributions to this issue, see I. B. Kravis, *et. al.* (1975).
7. For the discussion of a classical model of growth with the inclusion of the female labour participation rates, see Chen (1976a).
8. Gross capital stock is defined as that stock which includes allowances for obsolescence but not for depreciation.
9. From 1969 onward, the rate of investment has started to pick up again in Hong Kong as a result of the restoration of confidence by potential investors.
10. If the sub-period 1971−4 is also included, the statistical significance is greatly reduced. In view of the fluctuation of the level of economic activities during 1971−4, such a sub-period is dropped from our regression analysis.
11. Phelps Brown and Weber (1953).
12. Cairncross (1962).
13. Bicanie (1962), and Khan (1965).
14. Domar (1961), and Mayor (1968).
15. Kim and Winston (1974).

16. Another method of finding the ICOR for a certain period is to find the average of each year's ICOR during that period. Owing to the year to year fluctuations in the ICOR, this method is less satisfactory than the method of regressing capital on output.
17. Beckerman, *et. al.* (1965).
18. See Chapter 4.

Chapter 3

1. Fisher (1939), Clark (1957), and Kuznets' studies of the quantitative aspects of the economic growth of nations appeared in *Economic Development and Cultural Change* 1956–65.
2. Chenery (1960), Chenery and Taylor (1968), Chenery (1962).
3. See references quoted in Note 1 above.
4. Mining and quarrying are sometimes placed under the primary sector and at other times under the secondary sector. Similarly, transport and communication, and utility are sometimes classified as secondary and sometimes tertiary.
5. They are calculated on the basis of totals in current prices. It is assumed that the error implicit in the neglecting of possible differences in the trend of relative prices does not loom too large.
6. Hong Kong has also been an *entrepôt* economy. But the importance of *entrepôt* trade has become small by the late fifties.
7. Kaldor (1968).
8. Chenery (1960), and Chenery and Taylor (1968).
9. Chenery (1960), and Temin (1967).
10. Chenery and Taylor (1968).
11. There are broadly speaking two versions of growth models with unlimited supplies of labour: the classical view as held by Lewis (1954) and Fei and Ranis (1964), and the neoclassical view most often associated with the name of Jorgenson (1961).
12. Thirty million is the approximate average population of the five economies. The choice of this size does not affect the general pattern revealed, but of course will affect the absolute magnitude of the sectoral shares associated with each level of per capita income.

Chapter 4

1. The Cambridge (England) objections to the notion of aggregate production functions hinge on the measurability of capital. However, as pointed out by Blaug (1975), such a criticism if not irrelevant to the issue is relatively much less important than the problems of aggregation.
2. By 'neoclassical' economic environment, we refer to the prevalence of competitive markets as a result of which products are largely charged the competitive price and the factors are largely paid according to their marginal products.
3. The 'entrepreneurial' disturbance is attributable to human inertia, mistakes in judgment, etc.
4. This becomes clear if we consider what could happen if we deflated our data for size of firm so that each firm had the same production function, with the same prices. In that case they would all be at the same point (ignoring

random variation) on the same isoquant, and a line cannot be estimated from a single point.

5. See Zellner, Kmenta and Dreze (1966).
6. For an elaboration, see Hodges (1969).
7. Liu and Hildebrand (1965).
8. Fisher (1969, pp. 571–2).
9. D. Ricardo, *The Principles of Political Economy and Taxation*, London: Dent and Son, 1911 (p. 55).
10. Lewis maintained that the central problem in the theory of economic growth is to understand the process by which a community is converted from being a 5 per cent to a 12 per cent saver. Rostow made an increase in the rate of investment from 5 to 10 per cent an essential ingredient of his 'take-off' stage.
11. In terms of later studies, these will include non-constant returns, non-neutrality, aggregation biases, and intersectoral shifts of resources.
12. It is however argued by Atkinson and Stiglitz (1969) that technological change may not occur in the form of a complete shift of the production function, but is rather confined to certain points on the production function.
13. In the Cobb-Douglas case: $Y = A(t)K^b L^a = A(t)K^b \cdot L^a = K^b \cdot A(t)L^a$
14. Technical progress function in the context of vintage models has been discussed by Eltis (1973, Chapter 7).
15. See Solow (1959), Phelps (1966), Wickens (1970).
16. Berglas (1965) showed that the best fit occurs when the rate of embodied technical progress is 140 per cent per annum. Such a high rate is evidently implausible under any circumstances.
17. Solow (1962), Intriligator (1965).
18. You (1976).
19. See Denison (1964).
20. We have in fact performed some trial runs on our data based on Solow's (1959, 1962) methods of estimating the rate of embodied technical progress. However, the statistical fit has not been good, and implausible estimates are generated. In consequence, the results are not reported.
21. Durbin and Watson (1950, 1951). This discussion of the test here is limited to first-order positive autocorrelation which is the most frequently assumed in applied econometric research.
22. Some conclusive tests have been devised, but are invariably more complicated and costly in computations. See Henshaw (1966), Durbin (1970).
23. Durbin (1960).
24. This is always true unless there has been a rise in the average prices of capital goods (measured at constant prices) over time such that the amount of increase in price is exactly equal to the improvement in the efficiency of capital.
25. Some economists (notably Denison) have derived quality indices for labour, but invariably such indices are based on rather strong assumptions.
26. For a demonstration of this kind of possible error, see Moroney (1972, pp. 34–5).
27. For a proof, see Moroney (1972, p. 35).
28. Total manhours is the product of total number of workers and hours of

work per worker during a given period of time. In treating total manhours as a single variable, it is however implicitly assumed that the elasticities of production are the same with respect to the number of workers and hours of work. For further details and empirical tests, see Nadiri and Rosen (1969).

29. This assumption was made by Denison in his studies to enable him to construct labour quality indices. For a review of these types of assumptions, see Thirlwall (1969).

30. The value of non-residential and residential land can only be included in the capital stock estimates if we have relied on census valuations of property in making such estimates. But, even in this case the valuations are quite likely to be seriously understated insofar as they are based on historical book values, and since land appreciates through over.

31. See Denison (1967, p. 182).

32. It should be noted that even in the estimations of the Cobb-Douglas production function in which it has been divided through by the labour force, the estimations still yield estimates of the output elasticity of both labour and capital and thus enable us to study the contributions of capital and labour.

33. Of course, the results in this case will be less precise than the case where a continuous time-series for the entire period is available.

34. This is usually confined to the contribution of reallocating human resources from the agricultural to the non-agricultural sectors.

35. Denison (1962, 1967, 1974), Kendrick (1961, 1973), Solow (1957). Solow's later work is however more concerned with the estimation of production functions by econometric techniques.

36. See e.g. Williamson (1969, 1971), Lampman (1967), Correa (1970), Bruton (1967), and Psacharopoulos (1969).

37. Gaathon (1961).

38. See also Chen (1977a). There already exist a number of studies on the sources of growth in Japan. The findings of all of them are consistent with those of the Western developed countries, i.e. a large proportion of output growth (over 50 per cent) is explained by total factor productivity. See Ohkawa (1968), Kanamori (1972), and most recently Denison and Chung (1976).

39. For instance, Aukrust (1965) found that only 38 per cent of output growth was accounted for by the 'residual' in Japan for the period 1950–8.

40. Correa (1970); the nine Latin American countries are Argentina, Brazil, Chile, Columbia, Ecuador, Honduras, Mexico, Peru, and Venezuela.

41. Bruton (1967); the five countries are Argentina, Brazil, Chile, Columbia, and Mexico.

42. See Lampman (1967), Gaathon (1971), and Psacharopoulos (1969).

43. See Denison (1967); the nine Western countries are Belgium, Denmark, France, Germany, Italy, Netherlands, Norway, United Kingdom, and the United States.

44. Kaldor (1966), Denison (1967), Kindleberger (1967).

45. Johnson and Mellors (1961).

46. Ishikawa (1967).

47. Lewis (1954), Fei and Ranis (1964), Jorgenson (1961).

48. For example, given that the growth rates of capital and labour are 5 per cent

and 3 per cent respectively; when capital share is 0.5, the weighted sum of the growth rates of capital and labour is 4 per cent, and when capital share is 0.3 the weighted sum is 3.6 per cent.

49. Kindleberger (1967).
50. This has been done by Bodkin and Klein (1967).
51. Kmenta (1967).
52. In a study of the American manufacturing industries, Besen (1967) was unable to reject the Cobb-Douglas hypothesis in 19 out of 20 industries.
53. See Moroney (1970).
54. In setting a side equation assuming some optimisation behaviour of the firm, we have to assume the presence of a perfect factor market in which factors are paid their marginal products. This implies a constant returns to scale production function as the aggregation problem will arise if variable returns prevail. But, some studies have ignored this implication and proceed to estimate a variable returns to scale production function. These include Ferguson (1965), Katz (1969), Griliches and Ringstad (1971).
55. Nerlove (1958).
56. It should of course be noted that the qualifications and justifications discussed above in connection with the estimation of the Cobb-Douglas production function also apply to the estimation of the CES production function. Thus we must interpret the results here with the same degree of caution.
57. See Eckaus (1955), Griliches (1964), and Kelley, Williamson & Cheetham (1972).
58. The method used here is adopted from Brown (1966, Chapter 10).
59. See Nelson (1965).
60. There are many versions of the VES production function. The important contributions are: Liu and Hildebrand (1965), Sato and Hoffman (1968), Lu and Fletcher (1968), Revankar (1971), Lovell (1973).
61. See Nerlove (1967).

Chapter 5

1. For a detailed survey on endogenous technical progress, see Chen (1975).
2. Kaldor's technical progress function was revised in Kaldor and Mirrlees (1962). In the revised version, it was postulated that the proportionate growth rate of productivity on newly installed equipment is an increasing function (but at a decreasing rate) of the proportionate growth rate of gross investment per worker. Thus, it is a vintage model in which technical progress takes place only when it is embodied in new capital goods through investment. Using the growth rate of investment per worker instead of capital per worker as the factor affecting the growth rate of productivity, the revised model avoids the problems associated with the notion of a quantity of capital. This revised model is not used here as we are not dealing with vintage models of growth and technical progress.
3. See e.g. Asher (1956), Alchian (1959).
4. Under conditions of a steady growth of output, in the limit the learning effect (using cumulative output as an index of experience) is indistinguishable statistically from either the effect of exponential exogenous technical

progress or the effect of economies of scale. For a proof, see David (1970, p. 542).

5. In both Arrow's and Kaldor's models of growth, the equilibrium rate of technical progress (i.e. when in a steady state) is independent of investment activities despite the fact that both include an endogenous technical progress function dependent on investment. On the other hand, Eltis' formulation of the technical progress function makes the rate of technical progress dependent on investment in a steady state.

6. The ability to utilise the international backlog of technological progress in the fifties is often regarded as one of the major factors contributing to the rapid economic growth of Japan in the post-war period. See e.g. Ohkawa and Rosovsky (1973).

7. Capital goods here are defined as those under category seven of the Standard International Trade Classification of 1968.

8. The estimation of the CES production function with endogenous technical progress has also been performed. The conclusions that can be drawn from such results are similar to the Cobb-Douglas case and the CES results are therefore not reported and discussed.

9. Technical progress has been assumed to be Harrod-neutral in all the endogenous theories we have reviewed. This assumption is made simply because it is necessary for a steady state solution. As we are solely concerned with the technical progress function here, it is legitimate for us to assume that technical progress is Hicks-neutral.

10. The coefficients, β a, c, b, and m in the estimating equations (8) and (9), and (13) to (17) are of course different between equations. For simplicity, subscripts have been omitted.

11. The goodness-of-fit as revealed by the R^2 and the F-values.

12. Sheshinski (1967) in using cross-sectional and time-series data of several industries covering six countries (USA, UK, Canada, West Germany, Australia, and Norway) over the period 1950–60, found that cumulative gross investment is a more suitable index. The discrepancy between his and our finding is largely due to the fact that in the economies of our study the rate of growth of output can almost keep pace with that of investment while in the advanced economies the former as a rule lags behind the latter.

13. It has been said that the liberation in 1945 created a country in which no Koreans had held high-level government posts and few had held responsible positions in the government-education bureaucracy. 90 per cent had not even had an elementary school education. The mechanically operable economic infrastructure at the end of Japanese occupation was only a fraction of that in place five years earlier.

14. We obtained in the last chapter a negative capital coefficient for Japan in the estimation of the Cobb-Douglas production function for the manufacturing sector for the period 1955–70. We now realise that such an implausible result could very well be due to the mis-specification of the technical progress function. If we had specified the function along the lines of Eltis, we would have obtained a very sensible estimate of the capital coefficient.

15. This is probably due to multicollinearity arising from possible close correlation between M'/M and K/L.

Chapter 6

1. Such historical factors on the one hand reduced the importance of *entrepôt* trade and on the other hand enabled Hong Kong to increase its supply of capital, labour, and entrepreneurship without much cost and in a very short period of time. See Szczepanik (1958).

2. Exports and imports refer to exports and imports of goods only. In the cases of Hong Kong and Singapore where *entrepôt* trade has been important, exports and imports refer to retained imports and domestic exports. Manufacturing exports are those belonging to categories 3, 4, and 5 of the Standard International Trade Classification; capital goods imports to category seven of the Standard International Trade Classification.

3. Among the large volume of literature, see e.g. power, *et al.* (1971), Lin (1973), Brown (1973), Frank, Kim, and Westphal (1975), Westphal (1977).

4. See Hicks (1953), Johnson (1955).

5. The elasticity of labour supply is evidently an important factor affecting wage changes. But this was not considered in Beckerman's original model. The controversy between Beckerman (1963) and Balassa (1964) centred on this point.

6. This implies the Keynesian mechanism that money supply increases with increases in foreign reserves and hence the interest rate falls and investment rises.

7. See e.g. Ball (1962).

8. In the cases where a substantial proportion of imports is financed by capital inflow, export earnings and capital inflow are assumed to have performed the same function in financing imports. More about capital inflow will be discussed in the next chapter.

9. It can be seen that in equation (16) the saving rate, s, does not explicitly appear. In fact, in the present specification, the saving rate accommodates itself to the growth rate determined by equation (16). It changes over time as a function of X/Y. For a rigorous treatment, see Findlay (1972).

10. For example, Chenery and Bruno (1962), Chenery and Strout (1966), Chenery and Eckstein (1970).

11. For further discussion and some case studies, see Little, Scitovsky, and Scott (1970, Chapter 7).

12. For cross-section studies, see Emery (1967), Lubitz (1973), Michaely (1977). For time-series studies, see Maizels (1968, Chapter 1), Healey (1973).

13. Voivodas (1973).

14. Ideally, we should have a full, interactive model of economic growth for the economies under study that would encompass the real and financial factors that affect economic growth. This model could then be estimated and simulated to determine the relationship between the actual and simulated time path in income growth. It is not the intention of the present study to go as far as that, but it is an important area for further research.

15. See Nerlove (1958). This model has already been used in Chapter 4 when the ACMS method of estimating the CES production function is employed. It can be briefly explained as follows:

    Given that Y depends on X, there is a desired level of Y in period t, say Y_t^*, which depends on the value of X in period t, X_t, i.e.

    $$Y_t^* = a + b \, X_t + U_t \tag{i}$$

However Y_t^* is not normally observable. To replace it we can assume that the actually realised change in Y in any one period is only a fraction of the desired change. This gradual adjustment process may be expressed as:

$$Y_t - Y_{t-1} = \delta (Y_t^* - Y_{t-1}) + V_t \tag{ii}$$

where δ is the adjustment coefficient, $1/\delta$ gives the period required for the adjustment process to complete.

Substituting (i) into (ii), we obtain

$$Y_t - Y_{t-1} = \delta \left[(a + bX_t + U_t) - Y_{t-1} \right] + V_t$$

Rearranging, we have

$$Y_t = (\delta a) + (\delta b) X_t + (1 - \delta) Y_{t-1} + (V_t + \delta U_t) \tag{iii}$$

16. This is identical in mathematical form with the Koyck (1954) distributed lag model. But, it should be noted that the underlying behavioural assumptions are quite different. While the Nerlove method assumes a process of partial adjustment over time, the Koyck model assumed that the weights of the successive lagged variables decline continuously following the pattern of a geometric progression.

17. One of the serious drawbacks of other lag models (including the Koyck model which has identical equation form with the Nerlove model) is that the new error term is autocorrelated and that the lagged dependent variable is not independent of the new error term and consequently OLS estimation is biased.

18. The two-stage least squares programme used does this automatically. The programme used is an Algol two-stage least squares regression package written by C. Gilbert (based on Fortran least squares routines written by D. Henry).

19. For an early discussion, see Rasmann's 1962 letter to *Econometrica*.

20. See Nerlove and Wallis (1966).

21. See Malinvaud (1970, Chapter 14).

22. Durbin (1970).

23. *Ibid.*

24. In the literature the empirical investment demand function has been related to such factors as expected or actual output, profits, cost of capital goods, and liquidity. The investment function here relates investment demand to the import of capital goods. This function can be regarded as a new addition to the long list of investment functions in existence. For a survey of empirical studies on investment functions, see Jorgenson (1971), Klein (1974).

25. See Ohkawa and Rosovsky (1973, Chapter 7).

26. For instance, the introduction of imported capital goods into the agricultural and traditional service sectors helps to speed up the process of resources reallocation.

Chapter 7
1. Pesmazoglu (1972), Papanek (1973).
2. Modigliani and Ando (1957), Ando and Modigliani (1963).
3. For example Houthakker (1965).
4. Parabolic functions in the form of $S/Y = a + b\dot{Y} + c(\dot{Y})^2$ and $S/Y = a + b(\dot{Y}/N) + c(\dot{Y}/N)^2$ are also tried, but in all cases, no better results are obtained.
5. Equation (17) in the system is underidentified but consistent estimates of equation (14) can be obtained by the two-stage least squares method with the use of equation (17). For a discussion of goodness-of-fit tests in two-stage least squares estimations, see Chapter 6.
6. The results for Singapore:

$$S/Y = 0.0838 + 0.360(\dot{Y}) \qquad \text{S.E.} = 0.0280 \qquad \text{D–W} = 1.95$$
$$(0.244)$$

$$S/Y = 0.0055 + 0.0591\,(Y/N) \qquad \text{S.E.} = 0.0206 \qquad \text{D–W} = 1.50$$
$$(0.0205)$$

The results for Taiwan:

$$S/Y = -0.194 + 4.100(\dot{Y}) \qquad \text{S.E.} = 0.0852 \qquad \text{D–W} = 1.14$$
$$(1.867)$$

$$S/Y = -0.060 + 0.0271\,(Y/N) \qquad \text{S.E.} = 0.0131 \qquad \text{D–W} = 1.13$$
$$(0.0017)$$

7. It is suspected by the author that in the case of Japan, the choice of I (investment) as the pre-determined variable might have been more appropriate. This is however not pursued here.
8. Note that we cannot estimate equation (20) by expressing the variables as a proportion of income because in so doing the explanatory variables will be perfectly correlated with each other.
9. In the case of Korea, it is only significant at the ten per cent level.
10. It is remarkable to note that many researchers proceed to estimate equation (23) despite the fact that they begin with the relation:

$$S = c + aY + bF \tag{i}$$

Dividing (i) through by Y gives:

$$S = a + c/Y + b(F/Y) \tag{ii}$$

Equation (ii) is clearly not the same as equation (23). Thus, if one specifies (i) one has to regress S/Y on both $1/Y$ and F/Y instead of on F/Y alone. Also, very seldom (if ever) is the reason for dividing through by Y given. This can in fact be explained on the ground that equation (22′) or (i) is subject to heteroscedasticity as it is likely that the error term of such equations is correlated with the level of domestic saving. Dividing through by Y has the effect of removing heteroscedasticity.
11. Equations (23a) and (25a) are not applied to Japan as F_g in this case is small such that a distinction between the two types of capital inflows is not warranted.

12. The findings here tend to be different from those of Papanek (1973) who by taking a cross-section of 85 countries found that official inflow has a greater and more significant effect on saving than other types of inflow.
13. Recent studies on linkage effects show that such effects are much greater for manufacturing industries such as textiles and metal and electrical products to which private capital inflow is most likely to be attracted, than social overheads such as services and utilities where official inflow will usually concentrate. See e.g. Yotopoulos and Nugent (1973).
14. The problem of simultaneous-equation bias in such studies has recently been raised by Gupta (1975), Over, Jr. (1975).

Chapter 8
1. For a survey of this issue, see Cline (1975). This article has however quickly become out-dated because of the recent proliferation of books and articles. Recent studies include Chenery *et. al.* (1974), Chenery and Syrquin (1975), Ahluwalia (1976a, 1976b), Robinson (1976a, 1976b), Lal (1976), Knight (1976), Beckerman (1977), and Cromwell (1977). In addition, there has been an increasing number of studies on individual countries. See e.g. CAMS (1975), Arndt (1975), Pang (1975), Rao and Ramakrishnan (1976), Renaud (1976), Adelman and Robinson (1978), Mizoguchi, Kim, and Chung (1976), Foxley (1976), and Lee (1977).
2. For an elaboration on what causes the resurgence of interest in distributional problems, see Lal (1976).
3. See e.g. Tobin and Nordhaus (1972). Sen (1976) has incorporated income distribution indicators into the growth of output for the purpose of arriving at a better measurement of national economic welfare.
4. A very good exposition of these points can be found in Ahluwalia (1976b) and Cromwell (1977).
5. See references cited in note 1.
6. See also Beckerman (1977).
7. A Lorenz curve is one which indicates the share of total income which is received by the bottom X per cent of income units. It has percentage of income units on the horizontal axis and percentage of total income on the vertical axis.
8. For criticism of the Gini coefficient as a measure of inequality and its comparison with other measures, see Atkinson (1970), Champernowne (1974).
9. The Gini coefficient of manufacturing is 0.36 against an overall average of 0.44.
10. See Taeuber (1958).
11. See Reder (1969). This tendency has been called the separation propensity.
12. See Kuznets (1963).
13. *Ibid.*
14. The sample included 971 rural and 799 urban households; one-person households were excluded. For criticisms on data derived from this and other sample surveys, see Choo (1975).
15. For the measurement of inequality based on statistical models of income distribution, see Aitchison and Brown (1957).
16. This method is first used by Morgan (1962).

17. For further discussions of these surveys, see Choo (1975), and Mizoguchi, Kim, and Chung (1976).
18. The purpose of the study was to devise policies to improve income distribution in developing countries. The results have been published in Chenery, *et. al.* (1974). For a comment on data source of the World Bank-Sussex study, see Choo (1975).
19. See Mizoguchi, Kim, and Chung (1976, p. 273), Renaud (1976, p. 20).
20. See Pang (1975, p. 16).
21. So far, only two publications exist: Pang (1975), and Rao and Ramakrishnan (1976).
22. As can be seen from Table 7.5, though the two estimates are based on the same source of data, the calculated Gini coefficients are different because the mean incomes of people in various income groups are derived with different assumptions.
23. See Rao and Ramakrishnan (1976, Table 10).
24. In the manufacturing sector, in 1962, the 54 largest firms (which had a capital of more than NT$100 million) together accounted for 72 per cent of the total capital in manufacturing. In 1969, 143 such firms accounted for 79 per cent of the total. See *Report on Industrial Survey in Taiwan*, 1962 and 1969, Taipei: Executive Yuen.
25. It is perhaps true that in Hong Kong such forces are even weaker.
26. In Taiwan, the government has a monopoly on chemical fertilisers.

Bibliography

Abramovitz, M. A., 'Resource and Output Trends in the United States Since 1870,' *American Economic Review* (May 1956).

Adelman, I. and C. T. Morris, *An Anatomy of Patterns of Income Distribution in Developing Nations*, Part III of Final Report Prepared for Agency for International Development (1971).

Adelman, I. and C. T. Morris, *Economic Growth and Social Equity in Developing Countries* (Stanford: Stanford University Press, 1973).

Adelman, I. and S. Robinson, *Income Distribution Policy in Developing Countries: a case study of Korea* (London: Oxford University Press, 1978).

Ady, P., 'Growth Models for Developing Countries,' in A. Cairncross and M. Puri (eds.), *Employment, Income Distribution and Development Strategy, Essays in Honour of H. W. Singer* (London: Macmillan, 1976).

Ahluwalia, M. S., 'Income Distribution and Development: Some Stylized Facts,' *American Economic Review* (May 1976). (1976a)

Ahluwalia, M. S., 'Inequality, Poverty and Development,' *Journal of Development Economics*, No. 3 (1976). (1976b)

Ahluwalia, M. S. and H. Chenery, 'The Economic Framework,' in H. Chenery, *et. al.*, *Redistribution with Growth* (London: Oxford University Press, 1974).

Aitchison, J. and J. A. C. Brown, *The Lognormal Distribution* (Cambridge: Cambridge University Press, 1957).

Alchian, A., 'Cost and Outputs,' in M. Abramovitz (ed.), *The Allocation of Economic Resources* (Stanford University Press, 1959).

Ando, A. and F. Modigliani, 'The Life Cycle Hypothesis of Saving: Aggregate Implications and Tests,' *American Economic Review* (May 1963).

Argy, V., 'Structural Inflation in Developing Countries,' *Oxford Economic Papers* (March 1970).

Arndt, H. W., 'Development and Equality: The Indonesian Case,' *World Development* (February/March 1975).

Arrow, K. J., *et. al.*, 'Capital-Labour Substitution and Economic Efficiency,' *Review of Economics and Statistics* (August 1961).

Arrow, K. J., 'The Economics of Learning By Doing,' *Review of Economic Studies* (June 1962).

Asher, A., *Cost Quantity Relationships in The Airframe Industry* (The Rank Corporation 1956).

Atkinson, A. B., 'On the Measurement of Inequality,' *Journal of Economic Theory*, No. 3 (1970).

Atkinson, A. B. and J. E. Stiglitz, 'A New View of Technological Change,' *Economic Journal* (September 1969).

Aukrust, O., 'Investment and Economic Growth,' *Productivity Measurement Review* (1959).

Aukrust, O., 'Factors of Economic Development,' *Productivity Measurement Review* (February 1965).

Bacha, E. L., 'Foreign Capital Inflow and the Output Growth Rate of the Recipient Country,' *Journal of Development Studies* (April/July 1974).

Balassa, B., 'Growth Strategies in Semi-industrial Countries,' *Quarterly Journal of Economics* (February 1970).

Balassa, B., 'Industrial Policies in Taiwan and Korea,' *Weltwirschaftliches Archiv*, No. 1 (1971).

Ball, R. J., 'Capital Imports and Economic Development: Paradoxy or Orthodoxy,' *KYKLOS*, No. 3 (1962).

Bardhan, P. K., 'More on Putty-Clay,' *International Economic Review* (February 1973).

Basmann, R. L., 'Letter to the Editor,' *Econometrica* (January 1962).

Becker, G. and B. Chiswick, 'Education and the Distribution of Earnings,' *American Economic Review* (June 1966).

Beckerman, W., 'Projecting Europe's Growth,' *Economic Journal* (December 1962).

Beckerman, W., *et. al.*, *The British Economy in 1975* (London: Cambridge University Press, 1965).

Beckerman, W., 'Some Reflections on Redistribution with Growth,' *World Development*, No. 8 (1977).

Berglas, E., 'Investment and Technological Change,' *Journal of Political Economy* (1965).

Besen, S., 'Elasticities of Substitution and Returns to Scale in United States Manufacturing: Some Additional Evidence,' *Southern Economic Journal* (October 1967).

Bicanie, R., 'The Threshold of Economic Growth,' *KYKLOS*, No. 1 (1962).

Blaug, M., *The Cambridge Revolution: Success or Failure* (London: Institute of Economic Affairs, 2nd Edition 1975).

Bliss, C. J., 'On Putty-Clay,' *Review of Economic Studies* (1968).

Bodkin, R. G. and L. Klein, 'Nonlinear Estimation of Aggregate Production Functions,' *Review of Economics and Statistics* (1967).

Bose, J., 'A Note on Foreign Capital and Domestic Savings,' *Economic Affairs*, No. 4 (1976)

Brown, G. T., *Korean Pricing Policies and Economic Development in the 1960's* (Baltimore: The Johns Hopkins University Press, 1973).

Brown, M., *On The Theory and Measurement of Technological Change* (London: Cambridge University Press, 1966).

Brown, M. (ed.), *The Theory and Empirical Analysis of Production* (New York: Columbia University Press, 1967).

Bruno, M., 'A Note on the Implications of an Empirical Relationship between Output per Unit of Labour, the Wage Rate, and the Capital-Labour Ratio,' Stanford University, Unpublished Working Paper (July 1962).

Bruton, H. J., 'Productivity Growth in Latin American,' *American Economic Review* (December 1967).

Cairncross, A., *Factors in Economic Development* (London: Allen and Unwin, 1962).

CAMS (COUNCIL FOR ASIAN MANPOWER STUDIES), *Income Distribution, Employment and Economic Development in Southeast and East Asia* (Tokyo: Japan Economic Research Centre, 1975).

Carre, J., P. Dubois and E. Malinvaud, *French Economic Growth* (London: Oxford University Press, 1976).

Chae, M. K., 'Income Size Distribution for Korea,' Paper Presented at the Working Group Seminar on Income Distribution (Manila, 1972).

Champernowne, D. G., 'A Comparison of Measures of Inequality of Income Distribution,' *Economic Journal* (December 1974).

Chen, E. K. Y., 'Endogenous Technical Progress: A Survey,' *Hong Kong Economic Papers* (June 1975).

Chen, E. K. Y., 'The Empirical Relevance of the Endogenous Technical Progress Function,' *KYKLOS*, No. 2 (1976). (1976a)

Chen, E. K. Y., 'The Role of Women in Economic Development: an Analysis with special reference to Hong Kong,' in F. Legaspi (ed.), *The Role of Women in Develpment*, Manila: Santo Tomas University Press (1976). (1976b)

Chen, E. K. Y., 'Factor Inputs, Total Factor Productivity and Economic Growth: the Asian Case,' *The Developing Economies* (June 1977). (1977a)

Chen, E. K. Y., 'Domestic Saving and Capital Inflow: the Asian Experience,' *Economia Internazionale* (February 1977). (1977b)

Chen, E. K. Y., 'Domestic Saving and Capital Inflow in Some Asian Countries: A Time-Series Study,' *Asian Survey* (July 1977). (1977c)

Chen, E. K. Y., 'Economies of Scale and Capital-Labour Substitution in Hong Kong Manufacturing,' *Hong Kong Economic Papers* (April 1977). (1977d)

Chen, E. K. Y., 'The Economic Setting,' in D. G. Lethbridge (ed.) *Business Environment in Hong Kong* (Hong Kong: Oxford University Press, 1978). (1978a)

Chen, E. K. Y., 'Export Expansion and Economic Growth in Some Asian Economies: A Simultaneous-Equation Model,' in R. C. O. Matthews (ed.), *Measurement, History and Factors of Economic Growth* (London: Macmillan, 1978). (1978b)

Chen, E. K. Y. and R. Hsia, 'Technological Change, Factor Substitution and Industrial Growth in Hong Kong,' *Giornale degli Economisti e Annali di Economia* (March/April 1978). (1978c)

Chenery, H. B., 'Patterns of Industrial Growth,' *American Economic Review* (1960).

Chenery, H. B., 'The Pattern of Japanese Growth: 1914–54,' *Econometrica* (January 1962).

Chenery, H. B. and M. Bruno, 'Development Alternatives in an Open Economy,' *Economic Journal* (March 1962).

Chenery, H. B. and A. M. Strout, 'Foreign Assistance and Economic Development,' *American Economic Review* (September 1966).

Chenery, H. B. and L. Taylor, 'Development Pattern: Among Countries and Over Time, *Review of Eonomics and Statistics* (November 1968).

Chenery, H. B. and J. Eckstein, 'Development Alternatives for Latin American,' *Journal of Political Economy* (July 1970).

Chenery, H., *et. al.*, *Redistribution with Growth* (London: Oxford University Press, 1974).

Chenery, H. and M. Syrquin, *Patterns of Development 1950–70* (London: Oxford University Press, 1975).

Choo, H. C., 'Some Sources of Relative Equity in Korean Income Distribution: a historical perspective,' in CAMS (1975).

Clague, C., 'Capital-Labour Substitution in Developing Countries,' *Econometrica* (1969).

Clark, C., *The Conditions of Economic Progress*, 3rd Edition (London: Macmillan, 1957).

Cline, W. R., 'Distribution and Development: A Survey of Literature,' *Journal of Development Economics*, Vol. 1, No. 4 (1974/75).

Cobb, C. W. and P. H. Douglas, 'A Theory of Production,' *American Economic Review* (March 1928).

Cohen, B. I., 'Relative Effects of Foreign Capital and Larger Exports on Economic Development,' *Review of Economics and Statistics* (May 1968).

Correa, H., 'Sources of Economic Growth in Latin America,' *Southern Economic Journal* (July 1970).

Cromwell, J., 'The Size Distribution of Income: an International Comparison,' *Review of Income and Wealth*, No. 4 (1977).

Crouch, R. L., 'Economic Development, Foreign Aid, and Neo-Classical Growth,' *Journal of Development Studies* (April 1973).

David, P. A., 'Learning By Doing and Tariff Protection,' *Journal of Economic History* (September 1970).

David, P. S. and van de Klundert, 'Biased Efficiency Growth and Capital-Labour Substitution in the U.S., 1899–1960,' *American Economic Review* (June 1965).

Denison, E. F., *The Sources of Economic Growth in the U.S. and the Alternatives before us* (New York: Committee for Economic Development, 1962).

Denison, E. F., 'The Unimportance of the Embodied Question,' *American Economic Review* (March 1964).

Denison, E. F., *Why Growth Rates Differ* (New York: Brookings Institution, 1967).

Denison, E. F., 'The Classification of Sources of Growth,' *The Review of Income and Wealth* (March 1972).

Denison, E. F. and W. K. Chung, *How Japan's Economy Grew So Fast* (New York: Brookings Institution, 1976).

DiMarco, L. E. (ed.), *International Economics and Development* (New York: Academic Press, 1972).

Domar, E. V., 'The Capital Coefficient in the U.S.,' in F. A. Lutz and D. C. Hague (eds.), *The Theory of Capital* (London: Macmillan, 1961).

Domar, E. V., 'On the Measurement of Technological Change,' *Economic Journal* (1961).

Durbin, J., 'Testing for Serial Correlation in Least-Squares Regressions When Some of Regressors are Lagged Dependent Variables,' *Econometrica* (May 1970).

Eckaus, R. S., 'The Factor Proportions Problem in Underdeveloped Areas,' *American Economic Review* (September 1955).

Eltis, W. A., 'Capital Accumulation and the Rate of Industrialization of Developing Countries,' *Economic Record* (1970).

Eltis, W. A., 'The Determination of Technical Progress,' *Economic Journal* (September 1971).

Eltis, W. A., *Growth and Distribution* (London: Macmillan, 1973).

Eltis, W. A., *et. al.* (eds.), *Induction, Growth and Trade* (London: Oxford University Press, 1970).

Emery, R. F., 'The Relation of Exports and Economic Growth,' *KYKLOS*, No. 2 (1967).

Fabricant, S., 'Perspective on Productivity Research,' *Review of Income and Wealth* (September 1974).

Fei, J. C. and G. Ranis, *Development of the Labour Surplus Economy: Theory and Policy* (Homewood: Irwin, 1964).

Felix, D., 'Structural Imbalance, Social Conflict and Inflation,' *Economic Development and Cultural Change* (January 1960).

Ferguson, C. E., 'Substitution, Technical Progress, and Returns to Scale,' *American Economic Review* (1965).

Ferguson, C. E., *The Neo-Classical Theory of Production and Distribution* (London: Cambridge University Press, 1969).

Findlay, R., 'Some Theoretical Notes on the Trade-Growth Nexus,' in G. Ranis (ed.), *The Gap Between the Rich and Poor* (London: Macmillan, 1972).

Fisher, A. G. B., 'Primary, Secondary, and Tertiary Production,' *Economic Record* (June 1939).

Fisher, F. M., 'The Existence of Aggregate Production Functions,' *Econometrica* (October 1969).

Foxley, A., *Income Distribution in Latin America* (Cambridge: Cambridge University Press, 1976).

Frank, C. R., *et. al.*, *Foreign Trade Regimes and Economic Development: South Korea* (New York: Columbia University Press, 1975).

Gaathon, A. L., *Capital Stock, Employment and Output in Israel, 1950– 59* (Jerusalem: Bank of Israel, 1961).

Gaathon, S., *Economic Productivity in Israel* (New York: Praeger, 1971).

Geiger, T. and F. M. Geiger, *Tales of Two City-States: The Development Progress of Hong Kong and Singapore* (Washington: National Planning Association, 1973).

Girgis, M., 'Aggregation and Mis-specification Biases in Estimates of Factor Elasticity of Substitution: The Case of Egypt,' *Weltwirtschaftliches Archiv*, No. 1 (1974).

Glassburner, B. and J. Riedel, 'Government in the Economy of Hong Kong,' *Economic Record* (March 1972).

Green, H. A. J., *Aggregation in Economic Analysis* (Princeton: Princeton University Press, 1964).

Gregory, P. and J. Griffin, 'Secular and Cross-Section Industrialization Patterns: Some Further Evidence on the Kuznets-Chenery Controversy,' *Review of Economics and Statistics* (August 1974).

Griffin, K. B., 'Foreign Capital, Domestic Savings and Economic Development,' *Bulletin of the Oxford University Institute of Economis and Statistics* (May 1970).

Griffin, K. and J. Enos, 'Foreign Assistance: Objectives and Consequences,' *Economic Development and Cultural Change* (1969–70).

Griliches, Z., 'Specification Bias in Estimates of Production Functions,' *Journal of Farm Economics* (February 1957).

Griliches, Z., 'Research Expenditures, Education, and the Aggregate Agricultural Production Function,' *American Economic Review* (December 1964).

Griliches, Z. and V. Ringstad, *Economics of Scale and the Form of the Production Function* (Amsterdam: North-Holland, 1971).

Gupta, K. L., 'Foreign Capital and Domestic Saving: A Test of Haavelmo's Hypothesis with Cross-Country Data: A Comment,' *Review of Economics and Statistics* (May 1970).

Gupta, K. L., 'Foreign Capital Inflows, Dependency Burden, and Saving Rates in Developing Countries: a simultaneous-equation Model,' *KYKLOS*, No. 2 (1975).

Haavelmo, T., 'Comment on W. Leontief's 'The Rates of Long-Term Economic Growth and Capital Transfers from Developed to Underdeveloped Areas', in Pontificae Academic Scientiarum Scrips Varia, *Study Week on the Econometric Approach to Development Planning* (Amsterdam: North-Holland, 1965).

Hahn, F. H. and R. C. O. Matthews, 'The Theory of Economic Growth: A Survey,' *Economic Journal* (December 1964).

Harberger, A. C., 'The Dynamics of Inflation in Chile,' in C. F. Christ (ed.), *Measurement in Economics* (Stanford: Stanford University Press, 1963).

Harrod, R., *Towards a Dynamic Economics* (London: Macmillan, 1947).

Hasan, P., *Korea. Problems and Issues in a Rapidly Growing Economy* (Baltimore: The Johns Hopkins University Press, 1976).

Healey, D., 'Foreign Capital and Exports in Economic Development,' *Economic Record* (September 1973).

Heertje, A., *Economics and Technical Change* (London: Weidenfeld and Nicolson, 1977).

Hicks, J. R. *The Theory of Wages* [London: Macmillan, 1932 (revised 1963)].

Hicks, J. R., 'An Inaugural Lecture: The Long-Run Dollar Problem,' *Oxford Economic Papers* (June 1953).

Hicks, J. R., *Capital and Growth* (London: Oxford University Press, 1965).

Ho, Y. M., 'Development with Surplus Population – the Case of Taiwan: A Critique of the Classical Two-Sector Model, a la Lewis,' *Economic Development and Cultural Change* (1971/72).

Hodges, D. J., 'A Note on Estimation of Cobb-Douglas and CES Production Function Models,' *Econometrica* (October 1969).

Hong, W., *Factor Supply and Factor Intensity of Trade in Korea* (Seoul: Korea Development Institute, 1976).

Hong, W. and A. O. Krueger, *Trade and Development in Korea* (Seoul: Korea Development Institute, 1975).

Houthakker, H. S., 'On Some Determinants of Saving in Developed and Underdeveloped Countries,' in E. A. G. Robinson (ed.), *Problems in Economic Development* (London: Macmillan, 1965).

Hsia, R. et. al., *The Structure and Growth of the Hong Kong Economy* (Wiesbaden: Otto Harrassowitz, 1975).

Intriligator, M. D., 'Embodied Technical Change and Produtivity in the United States, 1929–58,' *Review of Economics and Statistics* (February 1965).

Ishikawa, S., *Economic Development in Asian Perspective* (Kinokuniya, Tokyo, 1967).

Johansen, L., 'Substitution versus Fixed Production Coefficients in the Theory of Economic Growth: a Synthesis,' *Econometrica* (April, 1959).

Johnson, H. G., 'Economic Expansion and International Trade,' *The Manchester School* (May 1955).

Johnston, B. F. and J. W. Mellors, 'Agriculture in Economic Development,' *American Economic Review* (September 1961).

Jorgenson, D. W., and Z. Griliches, 'The Explanation of Productivity Change,' *Review of Economic Studies* (June 1967).

Kaldor, N., 'Alternative Theories of Distribution,' *Review of Economic Studies*, No. 2 (1955–56).

Kaldor, N., 'A Model of Economic Growth,' *Economic Journal* (December 1957).

Kaldor, N., *Causes of the Slow Rate of Economic Growth of the United Kingdom* (London: Cambridge University Press, 1966).

Kaldor, N., 'Productivity and Growth in Manufacturing Industry: A Reply,' *Economica* (November 1968).

Kaldor, N. and J. A. Mirrlees, 'A New Model of Economic Growth,' *Review of Economic Studies* (June 1962).

Kanamori, H., 'What Accounts for Japan's High Rate of Growth,' *Review of Income and Wealth* (June 1972).

Katz, J. M., *Production Functions, Foreign Investment and Growth* (Amsterdam: North-Holland, 1969).

Kelley, A. C., J. G. Williamson and R. J. Cheetham, *Dualisitic Economic Development: Theory and History* (Chicago: Chicago University Press, 1972).

Kendrick, J., *Productivity Trends in the United States* (New York: Princeton University Press, 1961).

Kendrick, J., *Post-War Productivity Trends in the United States* (New York: Columbia University Press, 1973).

Kennedy, C. and A. P. Thirlwall, 'Surveys in Applied Economics: Technical Progress,' *Economic Journal* (March 1972).

Kennedy, K. A., *Productivity and Industrial Growth* (London: Oxford University Press, 1971).

Khan, M. H., 'The Capital Coefficient in the Process of Economic Growth,' *Economia Internazionale* (1965).

Kim, Y. C. and G. C. Winston, 'The Optional Utilization of Capital Stock and the Level of Economic Development,' *Economica* (November 1974).

Kindleberger, C. P., *Foreign Trade and The National Economy* (New Haven: Yale University Press, 1962).

Kindleberger, C. P., *Europe's Postwar Growth: The Role of Labour Supply* (Cambridge: Harvard University Press, 1967).

Kmenta, J., 'On Estimation of the CES Production Function,' *International Economic Review* (June 1967).

Knight, J. B., 'Explaining Income Distribution in Less Developed Countries: A Framework and an Agenda,' *Bulletin of the Oxford University Institute of Economics and Statistics* (August 1976).

Kravis, I., 'International Differences in the Distribution of Income,' *Review of Economics and Statistics* (November 1960).

Kravis, I. B., *et. al.*, *A System of International Comparisons of Gross Product and Purchasing Power* (Baltimore: The Johns Hopkins University Press, 1975).

Kuo, W., 'Income Distribution by Size in Taiwan Area: Changes and Causes,' in CAMS (1975).

Kuznets, S., 'Economic Growth and Income Inequality,' *American Economic Review* (March 1955).

Kuznets, S., 'Quantitative Aspects of the Economic Growth of Nations: V,' *Economic Development and Cultural Change* (July 1960).

Kuznets, S., 'Quantitative Aspects of the Economic Growth of Nations:

VI,' *Economic Development and Cultural Change* (July 1961).

Kuznets, S., 'Quantitative Aspects of the Economic Growth of Nations: VIII. Distribution of Income by Size,' *Economic Development and Cultural Change* (January 1963).

Kuznets, S., *Modern Economic Growth: Rate, Structure and Spread* (New Haven: Yale University Press, 1966).

Kuznets, S., *Population, Capital, and Growth* (London: Heinemann, 1974).

Lal, D., 'Distribution and Development: A Review Article,' *World Development*, No. 9 (1976).

Lamfalussy, A., *The United Kingdom and the Six: An Essay on Economic Growth in Western Europe* (Homewood: Irwin, 1963).

Lampman, R. J., 'The Sources of Post-war Economic Growth in the Philippines,' *Philippine Economic Journal*, No. 2 (1967).

Lave, L. B., *Technological Change: Its Conception and Measurement* (Englewood Cliffs: Prentice-Hall, 1966).

Lee, E., 'Development and Income Distribution: A Case Study of Sri Lanka and Malaysia,' *World Development*, No. 4 (1977).

Lee, J. K., 'Exports and the Propensity to save in LDCs,' *Economic Journal* (June 1971).

Lee, S. A., 'The Singapore Economy and its Development Problems,' *Developing Economies* (December 1973).

Lee, S. Y., 'Some Basic Problems of Industrialization in Singapore,' *Journal of Developing Areas* (January 1973).

Leibenstein, H., 'ICOR and the Growth Rates in the Short-run,' *Review of Economics and Statistics* (February 1966).

Lewis, W. A., 'Economic Development with Unlimited Supplies of Labour,' *Manchester School of Economics and Social Studies* (May 1954).

Lewis, W. A., *The Theory of Economic Growth* (London: Allen and Unwin, 1955).

Lin, C. Y., 'Industrial Development and Changes in the Structure of Foreign Trade, the Experience of Taiwan 1946–66,' *IMF Staff Papers* (1968).

Lin, S. C. Y., *Industrialization in Taiwan, 1946–72* (New York: Praeger, 1973).

Little, I., T. Scitovsky and M. Scott, *Industry and Trade in Some Developing Countries: A Comparative Study* (London: Oxford University Press, 1970).

Liu, T. C. and G. H. Hildebrand, *Manufacturing Production Functions in the United States, 1957* (Ithaca: Cornell University Press, 1965).

Lovell, C. A. K., 'Estimation and Prediction with CES and VES Production Functions,' *International Economic Review* (June 1973).

Lu, Y. C. and L. B. Fletcher, 'A Generalization of the CES Production Function,' *Review of Economics and Statistics* (1968).

Lubitz, R., 'Export-led Growth in Industrial Economies,' *KYKLOS*, No. 2 (1973).

Maddison, A., *Economic Progress and Policy in Developing Countries* (London: Allen and Unwin, 1970).

Maizels A., *Exports and Economic Growth of Developing Countries* (London: Cambridge University Press, 1968).

Marschak, J. and W. H. Andrews, 'Random Simultaneous Equations and the Theory of Production,' *Econometrica* (July 1944).

Massell, B. F., 'Capital Formation and Technological Change in United States Manufacturing,' *Review of Economics and Statistics* (May 1960).

Matthews, R. C. O., 'The New View of Investment: Comment,' *Quarterly Journal of Economics* (February 1964).

Matthews, R. C. O., 'Some Aspects of Postwar Growth in the British Economy in Relation to Historical Experience,' *Transactions of the Manchester Statistical Society* (1964/65).

Mayor, T. H., 'The Decline in the U.S. Capital-Output Ratio,' *Economic Development and Cultural Change* (July 1968).

Meadover, Jr., A., 'An Example of the Simultaneous-equation Problem: A Note on 'Foreign Assistance: Objectives and Consequences',' *Economic Development and Cultural Change* (July 1975).

Michaely, M., 'Exports and Growth: An Empirical Investigation,' *Journal of Development Economics* (March 1977).

Mikesell, R. F. and J. E. Zinser, 'The Nature of the Savings Function in Developing Countries: A Survey of the Theoretical and Empirical Literature,' *Journal of Economic Literature* (September 1973).

Mizoguchi, T., D. H. Kim and Y. I. Chung, 'Overtime Changes of the Size Distribution of Household Income in Korea: 1963–71,' *The Developing Economies* (September 1976).

Mizon, G. E., 'The Estimation of Non-Linear Econometric Equations: an Application to the Specification and Estimation of an Aggregate Putty-Clay Relation for the U.K.,' *Review of Economic Studies* (June 1974).

Modigliani, F., 'The Life Cycle Hypothesis of Saving and Intercountry Differences in the Saving Ratio,' in W. A. Eltis, *et. al.*, (eds.), *Induction, Growth and Trade* (London: Oxford University Press, 1970).

Modigliani, F. and A. Ando, 'Tests of the Life Cycle Hypothesis of Saving,' *B.O.U.I.E.S.*, (May 1957).

Morgan, J., 'The Anatomy of Income Distribution,' *Review of Economics and Statistics* (August 1962).

Morgan, T., 'Distribution of Income in Ceylon, Puerto Rico, the U.S., and the U.K.,' *Economic Journal* (December 1953).

Moroney, J. R., *The Structure of Production in American Manufacturing* (Chapel Hill: the University of North Carolina Press, 1972).

Nadiri, M. I., 'Some Approaches to the Theory and Measurement of Total Factor Productivity: A Survey,' *Journal of Economic Literature* (December 1970).

Nadiri, M. I. and S. Rosen, 'Interrelated Factor Demand Function,' *American Economic Review* (September 1969).

Nelson, R. R., 'Aggregate Production Functions and Medium Range Growth Projections,' *American Economic Review* (September 1964).

Nelson, R. R., 'The CES Production Function and Economic Growth Projections,' *Review of Economics and Statistics* (May 1965).

Nerlove, M., *Distribution Lags and Demand Analysis* (Washington: Government Printing Office, 1958).

Nerlove, M., 'Recent Empirical Studies of the CES and related Production Functions,' in M. Brown (ed.), *The Theory and Empirical Analysis of Production* (New York: Columbia University Press, 1967).

Nerlove, M., and K. F. Wallis, 'Use of the Durbin-Watson Statistic in Inappropriate Situations,' *Econometrica* (January 1966).

Nittamo, O., 'The Development of Productivity in Finnish Industry,' *Productivity Measurement Review* (1958).

O'Herliby, C. St. J., 'Capital-Labour Substitution and the Developing Countries: A problem of measurement,' *Bulletin of Oxford University Institute of Economics and Statistics* (August 1972).

Ohkawa, K., 'Production and Distribution of Japanese Economy for 1905–63,' *Keizai Kenkyu* (April 1968, in Japanese).

Ohkawa, K. and H. Rosovsky, *Japanese Economic Growth* (London: Oxford University Press, 1973).

Oshima, H. T., 'A Note on Income Distribution in Developed and Underdeveloped Countries,' *Economic Journal* (March 1956).

Oshima, H. T., 'Income Inequality and Economic Growth: the Postwar Experience of Asian Countries,' *Malayan Economic Review* (October 1970).

Paauw, D. S. and J. C. H. Fei, *The Transition in Open Dualistic Economies* (New Haven: Yale University Press, 1973).

Pang, E. F., 'Growth, Inequality and Race in Singapore,' *International Labour Review* (January 1975).

Papanek, G. F., 'The Effect of Aid and Other Resources Transfers on Savings and Growth in LDC's,' *Economic Journal* (September 1972).

Papanek, G. F., 'Aid, Foreign Private Investment, Saving and Growth in LDC's,' *Journal of Political Economy*, No. 1 (1973).

Patel, S. G., 'A Note on the ICOR and Rates of Economic Growth in the Developing Countries,' *KYKLOS*, No. 1 (1968).

Patrick, H. and H. Rosovsky (eds.), *Asia's New Giant: How the Japanese Economy Works* (Washington: the Brookings Institution, 1976).

Paukert, F., 'Income Distribution at Different Levels of Economic Development: a survey of evidence,' *International Labour Review*, No. 3 (1973).

Pesmazoglu, J., 'Growth, Investment and Saving Ratios: Some Long and Medium Term associations by groups of countries,' *Bulletin of the Oxford University Institute of Economics and Statistics* (November 1972).

Phelps, E. S., 'The New View of Investment: A Neo-Classical Analysis,' *Quarterly Journal of Economics* (November 1962).

Phelps, E. S., 'Factor-Price-Frontier Estimation of a 'Vintage' Model of the Post-War United States Nonfarm Business Sector,' *Review of Economics and Statistics* (1966).

Phelps-Brown, E. H. and B. Weber, 'Accumulation, Productivity and Distribution in the British Economy, 1870–1938,' *Economic Journal* (1953).

Power, J. H., G. P. Sicat and M. H. Hsing, *The Philippines and Taiwan* (London: Oxford University Press, 1971).

Psacharopoulos, G., *The Anatomy of a Rate of Growth* (Economic Research Centre, University of Hawaii, March 1969).

Rahman, Md. A., 'Foreign Capital and Domestic Saving: A Test of Haavelmo's Hypothesis with Cross-Country Data,' *Review of Economies and Statistics* (February 1968).

Rao, V. V. Bhanoji and M. K. Ramakrishnan, 'Economic Growth, Structural Change and Income Inequality: Singapore, 1966–1975,' *Malayan Economic Review* (October 1976).

Reddaway, W. B. and A. D. Smith, 'Progress in British Manufacturing Industries in the Period 1948–54,' *Economic Journal* (March 1960).

Reder, M. W., 'A Partial Survey of the Theory of Income Size

Distribution,' in L. Soltow (ed.), *Six Papers on the Size Distribution of Wealth and Income* (New York: National Bureau of Economic Research, 1969).

Renaud, B., 'Economic Growth and Income Inequality in Korea,' World Bank Staff Working Paper No. 240 (February 1976).

Revankar, N. S., 'Capital-Labour Substitution, Technological Change and Economic Growth: the U. S. Experience, 1929–53,' *Metroeconomica* (1971).

Riedel, J., *The Industrialization of Hong Kong* (Tubingen: J. C. B. Mohr, 1974).

Robinson, S., 'Toward an Adequate Long-run Model of Income Distribution and Economic Development,' *American Economic Review* (May 1976). (1976a)

Robinson, S., 'A Note on the U Hypothesis Relating Income Inequality and Economic Development,' *American Economic Review* (June 1976). (1976b)

Rostow, W. W., *The Stages of Economic Growth* (London: Cambridge University Press, 1960).

Sato, K., 'International Variations in the ICOR,' *Economic Development and Cultural Change* (July 1971).

Sato, K., *Production Functions and Aggregation* (Amsterdam: North Holland 1975).

Sato, R. and R. F. Hoffman, 'Production Functions with Variable Elasticity of Factor Substitution: Some Analysis and Testing,' *Review of Economics and Statistics* (1968).

Scott, M. F. G., 'Economic Growth and Balance of Payments,' in N. Kaldor (ed.), *Conflicts in Economic Policy* (Oxford: Basil Blackwell, 1971).

Sen, A. K., 'Real National Income,' *Review of Economic Studies* (January 1976).

Sheshinski, E., 'Testing of the Learning By Doing Hypothesis,' *Review of Economics and Statistics* (November 1967).

Solow, R. M., 'Technical Change and the Aggregate Production Function,' *Review of Economics and Statistics* (August 1957).

Solow, R. M., 'Investment and Technical Progress,' in K. J. Arrow *et. al.*, (eds.), *Mathematical Methods in the Social Sciences* (Stanford: Stanford University Press, 1959).

Solow, R. M., 'Technical Progress, Capital Formation, and Economic Growth,' *American Economic Review* (May 1962).

Solow, R. M., *Capital Theory and the Rate of Return* (Amsterdam: North Holland, 1963).

Soltow, L., 'Long-Run Changes in British Income Inequality,' *Economic History Review* (April 1968).

Soltow, L., 'Evidence of Income Inequality in the United States,' *Journal of Economic History* (June 1969).

Sommers, P. M. and D. B. Suits, 'A Cross-Section Model of Economic Growth,' *Review of Economics and Statistics* (May 1971).

Stern, R. M., *Foreign Trade and Economic Growth in Italy* (New York: Praeger, 1967).

Stoneman, C., 'Foreign Capital and Economic Growth,' *World Development* (January 1975).

Streeten, P. P. (ed.), *Unfashionable Economics* (London: Weldenfeld and Nicolson, 1970).

Suckling, J., 'Foreign Investment and Domestic Savings in the Republic of South Africa, 1957–1972,' *South African Journal of Economics* (September 1976).

Svennilson, I., 'Economic Growth and Technical Progress,' in OECD, *The Residual Factor and Economic Growth* (Paris, 1964).

Szczepanik, E., *The Economic Growth of Hong Kong* (London: Oxford University Press, 1958).

Taeuber, I. B., *The Population of Japan* (Princeton: Princeton University Press, 1958).

Temin, P., 'A Time-Series Test of Patterns of Industrial Growth,' *Economic Development and Cultural Change* (1967).

Thirlwall, A. P., 'Denison on Why Growth Rates Differ,' *Banca Nationale del Lavoro* (July 1969).

Thirlwall, A. P., *Inflation, Saving and Growth in Developing Economies* (London: Macmillan, 1974).

Thirlwall, A. P. and C. Barton, 'Inflation and Growth: the International Evidence,' *Banca Nazionale del Lavoro Quarterly Review* (September 1971).

Thirlwall, A. P., *Growth and Development* (London: Macmillan, 1972).

Tobin, J. and W. Nordhause, 'Is Growth Obsolete?' in National Bureau of Economic Research, *Economic Research: Retrospect and Prospect* Vol. V., Economic Growth (New York: Columbia University Press, 1972).

Treadgold, M. L., 'Inflation, Real Wages, and the Rate of Saving in the Philippines,' *Developing Economies* (September 1970).

Vanek, J. and A. Studenmuud, 'Towards a Better Understanding of the ICOR,' *Quarterly Journal of Economics* (August 1968).

Voivodas, C. S., 'Exports, Foreign Capital Inflow and Economic

Growth,' *Journal of International Economics*, No. 3 (1973).

Voivodas, C., 'Exports, Foreign Capital Inflow, and South Korean Growth,' *Economic Development and Cultural Change* (April 1974).

Voivodas, C. S., 'The Effect of Foreign Exchange Instability on Growth,' *Review of Economics and Statistics* (August 1974).

Wallich, H. C., 'Money and Growth: A Country Cross-section Analysis,' *Journal of Money, Credit, and Banking* (May 1969).

Weisskopf, T., 'The Impact of Foreign Capital Inflows on Domestic Saving in Underdeveloped Countries,' *Journal of International Economics* (February 1972).

Westphal, L. E., 'Research on Appropriate Technology,' Paper presented at the Conference on Technology, Employment and Development, Malaysia (January 1973).

Westphal, L. E., 'Korea's Experience with Export-led Industrial Development,' World Bank Staff Working Paper No. 249 (February 1977).

Wickens, M. R., 'Estimation of the Vintage Cobb-Douglas Production Function for the U. S., 1900–60,' *Review of Economics and Statistics* (May 1970).

Williamson, J. G., 'Personal Saving in Developing Nations: An Intertemporal Cross Section From Asia,' *Economic Record* (June 1968).

Williamson, J. G., 'Dimensions of Philippine Postwar Economics Progress,' *Quarterly Journal of Economics* (February 1969).

Williamson, J. G., 'Production Functions, Technological Change and the Developing Economies: A Review Article,' *Malayan Economic Review* (1969).

Williamson, J. G., 'Relative Price Changes, Adjustment Dynamics, and Productivity Growth: the Case of Philippine Manufacturing,' *Economic Development and Cultural Change* (July 1971).

Wright, T. P., 'Factors Affecting the Cost of Airplanes,' *Journal of the Aero-nautical Sciences*, No. 3 (1936).

Yeung, P., 'Exports, Re-exports and Economic Growth: the Case of Hong Kong,' *Malayan Economic Review* (April 1972).

Yotopoulos, P. A. and J. B. Nugent, 'A Balanced-Growth Version of the Linkage Hypothesis; A Text,' *Quarterly Journal of Economics* (May 1973).

You, J. K., 'Embodied and Disembodied Technical Progress in the U. S., 1929–1968,' *Review of Economics and Statistics* (February 1976).

You, P. S. and C. Y. Lim, *The Singapore Economy* (Singapore: Eastern Universities Press, 1971).

Zarembka, P., *Toward a Theory of Economic Development* (San Francisco: Holden-Day, 1972).

Zellner, A., J. Kmenta and J. Dreze, 'Specification and Estimation of Cobb-Douglas Production Function Models,' *Econometrica* (October 1966).

Index